BRITISH SHIPPING LAWS—VOLUME 6

General Editor

SIR BUSHBY HEWSON

Sometime one of Her Majesty's Judges of the Probate, Divorce and Admiralty Division of the High Court of Justice

Editor

RAOUL COLINVAUX

of Gray's Inn, Barrister-at-Law

FORMS AND PRECEDENTS

AUSTRALIA
The Law Book Company Ltd.
Sydney : Melbourne : Brisbane

CANADA AND U.S.A.
The Carswell Company Ltd.
Agincourt, Ontario

INDIA
N. M. Tripathi Private Ltd.
Bombay

ISRAEL
Steimatzky's Agency Ltd.
Jerusalem : Tel Aviv : Haifa

MALAYSIA : SINGAPORE : BRUNEI
Malayan Law Journal (Pte.) Ltd.
Singapore

NEW ZEALAND
Sweet & Maxwell (N.Z.) Ltd.
Wellington

PAKISTAN
Pakistan Law House
Karachi

Other Volumes in British Shipping Laws Series

Vol. 1. Admiralty Practice (*McGuffie, Fugeman and Gray*)

Vols. 2–3. Carriage by Sea (*Carver*, ed. Colinvaux)

Vol. 4. Collisions at Sea (*Marsden*, ed. McGuffie)

Vol. 5. CIF and FOB Contracts (*Sassoon*)

Vol. 7. Law of General Average and the York-Antwerp Rules (*Lowndes and Rudolf*, ed. Donaldson, Ellis and Staughton)

Vol. 8. International Conventions (*Singh*)

Vols. 9–10. Marine Insurance (*Arnould*, ed. Lord Chorley and Bailhache)

Vol. 11. Merchant Shipping Acts (*Temperley*, ed. Porges and Thomas)

Vol. 13. Ship-Owners (*Singh and Colinvaux*)

BRITISH SHIPPING LAWS—VOLUME 6

FORMS AND PRECEDENTS

By

RAOUL COLINVAUX
of Gray's Inn, Barrister-at-Law

DAVID STEEL
of Inner Temple, Barrister-at-Law

and

VINCENT E. RICKS
of the Admiralty Court

LONDON

STEVENS & SONS

1973

Published in 1973 by
Stevens & Sons Limited of
11 New Fetter Lane London
and printed in Great Britain by
The Eastern Press Limited of
London and Reading

SBN 420 43770 3

PREFACE

" Set it down to thyself as well to create good precedents as to follow them." Sir Francis Bacon, Att.-Gen. 1613

The *creation* of good precedents has been the major, but not the only, object of this book. The Admiralty parts, for instance, are intended not only to assist practitioners and officials in England, but all those in scores of Commonwealth States who, with a growing shipping interest, have adopted English Admiralty practice without the know-how necessary to apply it. In this respect this volume forms a supplement to *Admiralty Practice* (*British Shipping Laws*, Vol. 1).

All Admiralty pleadings, and pleadings of the Commercial Court, have been specially drafted for this volume by Admiralty counsel and counsel of the Commercial Bar, after perusal of dusty remains in Chambers of cases they and their forbears had produced for pending actions sometimes years before. Profiting from past mistakes, and the freshness of disciplined youth, these pleaders have devised document after document in true Baconian spirit!

The first chapter, on Model Bills of Lading, was solely devised as *precedents* which the mercantile world has been waiting for (or already using from B.S.L. Vol. 13, in modified form). The reliable draftsmanship, abbreviation in size, and ease in use is so obvious a need both to international trade generally, and to traders, shipowners, banks, insurers, and every clerk employed by any of them, that further comment is unnecessary. We emphasise much international consultation on the size and format of bills of lading and local work such as that done on the SITPRO committee (§ 1a). As to general conditions necessary, see §§ 1 and 5.

The Model Passenger Ticket (Chap. 2) follows in the footsteps of the Short Form Model Bill of Lading; see § 41. It naturally has relevance to all concerned with family holidays by sea, and it is hoped that it will be demanded of shipping lines by all reputable travel agents.

Charterparties caused the authors more difficulty. We were supplied after years of research, mainly by the Documentary Committee of the Chamber of Shipping of the United Kingdom, with a mass of charterparties in approved forms. As negotiated in practice, on the Baltic or some similar Exchange, each becomes a mass of typed clauses to meet the individual case upon, but mostly almost

C.S.—*a**

completely overriding, the approved form (see §§ 53, 54, 55), chosen or available (see §§ 51, 52). Our conclusion was inescapable: it was pointless to draft a model charterparty as a precedent in the Baconian sense. Special charters, for very limited purposes, such as a Yacht Charter Agreement (§ 106) are a different matter; this, however, is merely exhibited, not as a precedent, but because it is in general use.

However, we could and did do something. Many clauses in approved forms are referred to by name in typed clause, and therein incorporated, without merchant, broker or shipowner seeming to have any idea of the scope and possibly disastrous consequences of their wording as applied to the individual charter in question. The Centrocon Arbitration Clause stands at the apex of this international commercial folly. (See §§ 96, 97, for its history and effect.) Alternative clauses, in approved forms, are set out in *toto* thereafter. On such grounds most clauses commonly incorporated by name in typed charters, but often inaccessible, are set out in full in Chapter 3.

For these reasons, an enormous proportion of the material perused has been discarded in preparing this slim volume. Nothing has been printed which is contained in other volumes of *British Shipping Laws*.

With a view to ensuring that this volume formed an efficient reference book, the authors decided that the index should be wholly drafted by them personally. It is the most utilitarian part of any book. What would *Whitaker* be worth without one!

Our deepest thanks go out to many professional pleaders, to all maritime bodies in the City of London (including in particular Protection and Indemnity Clubs and the Chamber of Shipping) and to a myriad of other advisers (not least individual shipping companies) and others who have assisted us in years past. We can only pray that this book will now aid them as small recompense for their toil.

February 23, 1973

RAOUL COLINVAUX
DAVID STEEL
VINCENT E. RICKS

CONTENTS

TABLE OF CASES

TABLE OF STATUTES

TABLE OF PRECEDENTS

1. Model Liner Bills of Lading

1. The Boxes

2. Preambles

3. Conditions

2. Model Passenger Ticket

3. Charterparties

1. Approved Forms

2. Charterparty Clauses

3. Form of Agreement for Charter of Yacht

4. Commercial Court: Carriage by Sea

4. COMMERCIAL COURT: CARRIAGE BY SEA—*continued*

5. COMMERCIAL COURT: MARINE INSURANCE

6. ADMIRALTY PLEADINGS

1. Statements of Claim

6. Admiralty Pleadings—*continued*

2. Defences

3. Further Pleadings

7. The Writ

1. Writ in Rem

7. The Writ—*continued*

2. Writ in Personam

3. Indorsement of Writ

7. The Writ—*continued*

8. Arrest

1. Warrant of Arrest

2. Affidavit to Lead Warrant of Arrest

3. Ancillary Forms

4. Release from Arrest

8. Arrest—*continued*

9. Interlocutory Proceedings

1. Preliminary Acts

2. Summonses and Notices

3. Limitation of Actions (Time)

9. Interlocutory Proceedings—*continued*

10. Judgment in Default

11. Reference to Registrar

12. Limitation of Liability

12. Limitation of Liability—*continued*

13. Appeal

14. Arbitration

1. Collision

2. Salvage

15. County Court

1. Commencement of Action

15. County Court—*continued*

PARA.

2. Arrest

3. Appearance

4. Bail

5. Pleadings and Preliminary Act

6. Appraisement

7. Judgment and Execution

15. County Court—*continued*

8. Reference to Registrar

Part One

CONTRACTS OF CARRIAGE BY SEA

CHAPTER 1

MODEL LINER BILLS OF LADING

Introduction

1 THE Model All-Purpose Bill of Lading, designed for liner use, was first published in *Shipowners* [B.S.L. 13, Chap. 9] in 1967. Since then it has been adopted by many lines around the maritime world as a basis for their liner bills of lading. By 1970, however, it was obvious that it needed radical amendment because of (i) the need for a short form model bill of lading, and (ii) the growth of containerisation trade.[1] The following forms (with other amendments) are designed to meet these needs.

Full consideration is given in *Shipowners* [B.S.L. 13, § § 696 to 722] of the need and effect of the original Model Bill.

Note on Model Short Form Bill

1a The difficulty that arose following the international standardisation of the size of bills of lading (A4 size paper; see § 3, *infra*) was that they were far too small to accommodate, in legible type, terms and conditions essential to international trade, which constantly become more complex (*e.g.* on account of the development of container trade). The usual answer to this problem has been the clumsy expedient of printing the Conditions of bill on its reverse side in print far too small to be readily legible.

The recommended answer to this problem is the Short Form Bill of Lading, which incorporates the Conditions, hitherto usually printed on the reverse side of the bill of lading, in a booklet freely available to all concerned.

In 1970 the SITPRO report appeared, a report by the Thorneycroft Committee on the Simplification for International Trade Procedures.

Its recommendations included this, regarding short form bills of lading and other documents:

> "4. The short form concept . . . should be adopted for the simple receipt-type transport documents and eventually extended to the bill of lading."

See paragraphs 5.35 to 5.39 of the Report for the need for adopting a short form bill of lading as opposed to those with a "mass and variety of small print on the reverse" (para. 5.35).

[1] See clauses 1A and 24A of Conditions, *infra*, § § 8 and 15.

1. The Boxes

Model Liner Bill of Lading

2 [*Front Page*]

	BILL OF LADING 1 ____________	B/L No.
SHIPPER	ALL PURPOSE	Reference No.
CONSIGNEE (if "Order state Notify Party")	[*Insert here name of Company or Line, in print*]	
NOTIFY PARTY (ONLY if not stated above; otherwise leave blank)	Managers: Brokers: Agents:	[*Print as appropriate*]

* LOCAL VESSEL	* FROM (Local Port of Loading)
OCEAN VESSEL	PORT OF LOADING
PORT OF DISCHARGE	* FINAL DESTINATION (if on-carriage)
† FREIGHT PAYABLE AT	NUMBER OF ORIGINAL Bs/L

PARTICULARS DECLARED BY SHIPPER

MARKS AND NUMBERS	NUMBER AND KIND OF PACKAGES: DESCRIPTION OF GOODS	GROSS WEIGHT—KILOS	MEASUREMENT

NUMBER OF PACKAGES (in words)

[*Insert Free Disposal clauses*] [1a]	PLACE AND DATE OF ISSUE:
	[*Signature*] AS AGENTS

* Applicable only when document used *inter alia* as a contract for forwarding to the Port of Loading and/or from the Port of Discharge.[2]

† Subject to clause 5 (1) of the Conditions.

1a For "Free Disposal clauses," see Preambles: § 4, *infra*, for long form bills; § 6, *infra*, for short form bills.

2 The words used in *Simpler Export Documents* (S.E.D.), App. 8B (see § 3, *infra*), are: "Applicable only when document used as Through Bill of Lading." This is inapplicable to the Model Bill which is designed as a contract for forwarding apart from the main ocean voyage, which alone is a contract of carriage. See § 8 *et seq.*, *infra*.

Note on Model Liner Bill of Lading (Boxes)

3 This precedent (§ 2, *supra*) is based on the document entitled "Bill of Lading" set out in Appendix 8B to *Simpler Export Documents* issued in 1965 by the Board of Trade.

The boxes are the only part of the bill of lading which must be filled up by hand or in type (or left blank).[3]

The United Nations Economic Commission for Europe (ECE) set up a Working Party in 1961 to explore ways of standardising and simplifying export documents, and it designed the "ECE" layout. The International Chamber of Shipping [4] in consultation with the International Chamber of Commerce then agreed on a suitable size for such documents (international A4 size paper—11·69 by 8·27 inches), which was adopted by the Working Party.

Meanwhile, in 1962, the Board of Trade set up the JLCD (Joint Liaison Committee on Documents used in the International Carriage of Goods).

The JLCD produced a paper in 1965 issued by the Board of Trade, "Simpler Export Documents" (referred to as S.E.D.). Their short form of bill of lading (on A4 size paper) forms Appendix 8B to the paper. But the JLCD failed to draft in full the bottom part of S.E.D. Appendix 8B which they termed "Free Disposal."

2. Preambles

Long Form Bill of Lading: Preamble

4 SHIPPED in apparent good order and condition, unless otherwise stated herein, on board the above Ocean Vessel (or on board the above Local Vessel, if named above, for forwarding subject to clause 30 on the reverse side of this Bill of Lading) the goods or packages said to contain goods, hereinafter called "the Goods," specified above for carriage from the above named Port of Loading (or other port or place determined by the Carrier under the said clause 30) by the above Ocean Vessel (or vessel substituted under the said clause 30) on a voyage as described and agreed by clauses 7 to 12 and 19 of this Bill of Lading and discharge, such carriage and discharge being always subject to the exceptions, limitations, conditions and liberties hereinafter agreed, in like order and condition at the Port of Discharge named above or such other port or place as is provided in the clauses hereinbefore referred to, or so near thereunto as she may safely get, always afloat, where the Carrier's responsibilities and liabilities shall in all cases and all circumstances whatsoever finally cease, for delivery unto the abovementioned Consignee or to his or their assigns.

If the Final Destination is named above the Goods shall be forwarded in accordance with clause 31 on the reverse side of this Bill of Lading subject to the exceptions, limitations, conditions, and

[3] As to how the boxes should be filled in, see *Shipowners* [B.S.L. 13, §§ 707 to 710].
[4] See *Shipowners* [B.S.L. 13, § 345 *et seq.*].

liberties therein or otherwise hereinafter agreed for delivery unto the abovementioned Consignee or to his or their assigns.

This bill of lading is referred to in the Conditions on the reverse side hereof (which are incorporated in this bill of lading) as " the Bill of Lading."

[In accepting this Bill of Lading any local customs or privileges to the contrary notwithstanding the Shipper, Consignee and Owner of the Goods and the Holder of this Bill of Lading agree to be bound by all the stipulations, exceptions and conditions stated herein whether written, printed, stamped or incorporated on the front or reverse side hereof, as fully as if they were all signed by such Shipper, Consignee, Owner or Holder.] [5]

If the Ocean Vessel is not owned by or chartered by demise to the Company or Line by whom this Bill of Lading is issued (as may be the case notwithstanding anything that appears to the contrary) this Bill of Lading shall take effect only as a contract of carriage with the Owner or demise Charterer as the case may be as principal made through the agency of the said Company or Line who act solely as agents and shall be under no personal liability whatsoever in respect thereof.[6]

Agents signing this Bill of Lading on behalf of the said Company or Line have only the limited authority at common law of a vessel's master signing a Bill of Lading.

IN WITNESS WHEREOF the above stated number of Bills of Lading all of this tenor and date have been signed one of which being accomplished, the others to stand void.

Note on Preamble to Long Form Bill of Lading (*amended 1971*) [7-8]

5 The draft in § 3, *supra*, is based upon the preamble to the original Model All-Purpose Bill of Lading (see *Shipowners* [B.S.L. 13], 1967, § 724). It is now abbreviated and designed to fit neatly in legible type into the Free Disposal part of the S.E.D. form of bill of lading (see § 2, *supra*) by removal of the freight clauses into the Conditions on the reverse side of the bill of lading.

Model Short Form Bill of Lading: Preamble

6 SHIPPED in apparent good order and condition, unless otherwise stated hereon, on board the Ocean Vessel (or on board the Local Vessel, if named above, for forwarding subject to clause 30 of the Company's Conditions) the Goods described, marked and numbered as above (contents, quality, value, weight, measurement, quantity, number,

5 This paragraph may be omitted: it has no legal effect, but some shipowners like it.

6 For the " demise clause ": see Carver [B.S.L. 2, § 418].

7, 8 See *Shipowners* [B.S.L. 13, § 719].

gauge, specification, brand and countermarks unknown) for carriage from the Port of Loading (or other port or place determined by the Carrier under the said clause 30) by the Ocean Vessel (or vessel substituted under the said clause 30) on a voyage as described and agreed by clauses 7 to 12 and 19 of the Company's Conditions and discharge, such carriage and discharge being always subject to the exceptions, limitations, conditions and liberties agreed in the Company's Conditions, in like good order and condition at the Port of Discharge or such other port or place as is provided in the clauses hereinbefore referred to, for delivery unto the Consignee or to his or their assigns.

7 If the Final Destination is named hereon the Goods shall be forwarded in accordance with clause 31 of the Company's Conditions, subject to the exceptions, limitations, conditions and liberties therein, or otherwise agreed for delivery unto the Consignee or to his or their assigns.

The Company's Conditions are the Bill of Lading Conditions of the Company (a copy of which can be inspected, or supplied on request to the office of the Company or of any of its principal Agents). This Bill of Lading is referred to in the said Conditions (incorporated herein) as " the Bill of Lading." [9]

If the Ocean Vessel is not owned by or chartered by demise to the Company (otherwise referred to as " the Carrier ") this Bill of Lading shall take effect only as a receipt by and contract of carriage with the owner or demise charterer (herein and in the Company's Conditions referred to in that event as " the Carrier ") as principal made through the agency of the Company who then act solely as agents and shall be under no personal liability whatever in respect thereof.

Agents signing this Bill of Lading on behalf of the Company have only the limited authority at common law of a vessel's master signing a bill of lading.

In witness whereof the number of original Bills of Lading stated above all of the tenor and date has been signed, one of which being accomplished the others to stand void.

3. Conditions [10]

1. *Clause paramount*

8 Where the port of shipment is in territory where legislation giving

[9] This paragraph should be printed in red or heavy type.

[10] These are now drafted so as to be applicable to both long form and short form bills of lading, having reference to their respective preambles.

Clauses 1 to 29 regulate the terms upon which the goods are to be *carried*, as opposed to being forwarded under clause 30 or 31.

compulsory effect to the International Convention relating to Bills of Lading of August 25, 1924, is in force, the contract evidenced by the Bill of Lading shall, subject to clauses 30 and 31 hereunder, have effect subject to such legislation for the period beginning with whichever of the following operations is agreed to be first performed by the Carrier namely loading, handling, stowing or carrying the Goods on the vessel until the completion of whichever of the following operations is agreed to be last performed by the Carrier, namely carrying the Goods on, or discharging them from the vessel, and if and to the extent that any provision of the Bill of Lading (including these Conditions) is repugnant to or inconsistent with the said legislation, such provision shall be null and void in relation to that period, but no further.

Whether or not the contract evidenced by the Bill of Lading is so subject to such legislation the Carrier shall at all times when performing that contract be entitled to the benefit of all privileges, rights and immunities contained in the Schedule to the Carriage of Goods by Sea Act 1924.

1A. *Containerisation clause*

If the cargo is stated by the Shipper to be Container cargo the following special conditions shall apply:

(i) The Carrier shall be entitled to stow any Container on deck or under deck at his option, without notice to the Shipper or anyone else.

(ii) All such cargo, notwithstanding clause 1 above, shall be carried on terms set out in the International Convention for the Unification of Certain Rules of Law Relating to Bills of Lading, signed at Brussels on August 25, 1924, and hereinafter referred to as "the Hague Rules," subject to paragraph (iii) hereof.

(iii) Notwithstanding Article 1 (*c*) of the Hague Rules the said Rules shall apply to the carriage of any Container whether stowed on or under deck.

(iv) It is agreed by the Carrier and every Shipper, Consignee and Owner of any Container or goods contained therein shipped under the Bill of Lading that the Carrier, Shipper, Consignee and Owner of any Container or such goods shall be entitled to general average contribution, notwithstanding that such Container or goods was/were stowed on deck, in the event of jettison of such Container or goods, or any other general average loss to which the Carrier, Shipper, Consignee and/or Owner of such Container or goods would have been entitled had such Container or goods been stowed under deck.

2. *Exemptions and immunities of all servants and agents of the Carrier* [11]

9 It is hereby expressly agreed that no servant or agent of the Carrier (including every independent contractor from time to time employed by the Carrier) shall in any circumstances whatsoever be under any liability whatsoever to the Shipper, Consignee, Owner of the Goods or Holder of the Bill of Lading for any loss, damage or delay or otherwise of whatsoever kind arising or resulting directly or indirectly from any act, neglect or default on his part while acting in the course of or in connection with his employment and, but without prejudice to the generality of the foregoing provisions in this clause, every exemption, limitation, condition and liberty herein contained and every right, exemption from liability, defence and immunity of whatsoever nature applicable to the Carrier or to which the Carrier is entitled hereunder shall also be available and shall extend to protect every such servant or agent of the Carrier acting as aforesaid and for the purpose of all the foregoing provisions of this clause the Carrier is or shall be deemed to be acting as agent or trustee on behalf of and for the benefit of all persons who are or might be his servants or agents from time to time (including independent contractors as aforesaid) and all such persons shall to this extent be or be deemed to be parties to the contract evidenced by the Bill of Lading.

The Carrier shall be entitled to be paid by the Shipper, Consignee, Owner of the Goods or Holder of the Bill of Lading (who shall be jointly and severally liable to the Carrier therefor) on demand any sum recovered or recoverable by either such Shipper, Consignee, Owner, Holder or any other from such servant or agent of the Carrier for any such loss, damage, delay or otherwise.

3. *Reservation of all Carrier's rights and privileges*

Nothing herein contained shall prevent the Carrier from claiming in the courts of any country the benefit of, or derogate in any way from, any statutory protection or exemption from or limitation of liability afforded to the Carrier or to the vessel by the laws of that or of any other country.

4. *Carrier's exemption clause*

Subject to clause 1 hereof the Carrier shall not be responsible for loss or damage to or in connection with the Goods of any kind whatsoever (including deterioration, delay or loss of market) however

[11] This clause is a species of the genus of *Adler* v. *Dickson* clause, so called because it was intended to circumvent the decision in *Adler* v. *Dickson* (*The Himalaya*) [1955] 1 Q.B. 158 (see Carver [B.S.L. 3, §§ 1481, 1487]). As to this variant, see *Shipowners* [B.S.L. 13, § 713]. *Cf.* Himalaya Clauses (not recommended), § 66, *infra*; Model Passenger Ticket, *infra*, § 40, clause 21 (b) and (c).

caused (whether by unseaworthiness or unfitness of the vessel or of any other vessel, tender, lighter or craft or of any other mode of conveyance whatsoever or by faults, errors or negligence, or otherwise howsoever).

In particular and without prejudice to the generality of the foregoing[12]:

A. The Carrier shall be under no such responsibility: (i) at any time prior to the loading of the Goods on to and subsequent to the discharge of the Goods or part thereof from the vessel when but for the provisions of this clause such goods would be the responsibility of the Carrier and (ii) in the case of live animals or of cargo which in the Bill of Lading is stated as being carried on deck and is so carried (none of which is subject to the legislation referred to in clause 1 hereof) at any time when, but for the provisions of this clause such goods would be the responsibility of the Carrier.

B. Unless the Bill of Lading is subject to such legislation as is referred to in clause 1 hereof the Carrier shall not be liable for loss of or damage to or in connection with the Goods or part thereof of any kind whatsoever (including deterioration, delay or loss of market) arising or resulting from: unseaworthiness (whether or not due diligence shall have been exercised by the Carrier, his servants or agents or others to make the vessel seaworthy); Act, neglect or default of the Master, mariner, pilot or the servants or agents of the Carrier in the navigation or in the management of the vessel or in the care of the cargo; fire; perils, dangers and accidents of the sea or other navigable waters; act of God; act of War; act of public enemies; arrest or restraint of princes, rulers or people, or seizure under legal process; quarantine restrictions; act or omission of the Shipper, Consignee, Owner of the Goods, or Holder of the Bill of Lading, his agents or representatives; strikes or lock-outs or stoppage or restraint of labour from whatever cause, whether partial or general; riots and civil commotions; saving or attempting to save life or property at sea; wastage in bulk or weight or any other loss or damage arising from inherent defect, quality, or vice of the Goods; insufficiency of packing; insufficiency or inadequacy of marks; latent defects: any other cause whatsoever, whether or not of a like kind to those above mentioned, and including negligence on the part of the Carrier, his servants, agents or others.

5. (i) *Freight*

10 Full freight hereunder shall be due and payable at the port or place where the Bill of Lading is issued by the Shipper in cash without deduction on receipt of the Goods or part thereof by the Carrier

[12] This part of the clause (A and B) is already covered by the opening paragraph of the clause but explains the meaning thereof to those unlearned in the law.

for shipment even if stated in the Bill of Lading to be payable elsewhere and shall be deemed to have been fully earned upon such receipt of such goods. All charges due hereunder together with freight (if not paid at the aforesaid port or place) shall be due from and payable on demand by the Carrier, by the Shipper, Consignee, Owner of the Goods or Holder of the Bill of Lading (who shall be jointly and severally liable to the Carrier therefor) at such port or place as the Carrier may require, vessel or cargo lost or not lost from any cause whatsoever.

The freight stated herein to be paid or payable has been calculated and based upon the particulars of the Goods furnished by the Shipper to the Carrier; the Carrier shall be entitled at any time to open and to re-classify or re-weigh or re-measure or re-value any goods, and freight shall be paid on the proper classification or the excess weight or measurement or value (if any) as the case may be so ascertained. The expenses of and incidental to re-classifying or re-weighing or re-measuring or re-valuing shall be borne by the Carrier if the classification or weight or measurement or value as furnished by the Shipper is found to be correct, but otherwise such expenses shall be considered as freight and shall be borne and paid by the Shipper, Consignee or Owner of the Goods. The Shipper shall, if required by the Carrier so to do, furnish forthwith on demand to the Carrier the invoice or a true copy thereof relating to the Goods.

5. (ii) *Acknowledgment of weight, quality, marks, etc.*

Where, in the case of goods shipped in bulk, the weight stated herein is a weight ascertained or accepted by a third party other than the Carrier or the Shipper, no acknowledgment is made as to quantity, weight or quality. Where the number of packages or pieces is stated in the Bill of Lading no acknowledgment is made as to quantity, weight or quality. The Carrier is responsible only for leading marks provided that the goods have been correctly marked with those leading marks before shipment and that those correct leading marks are stamped in letters at least two inches high and in such manner as should ordinarily remain legible until the end of the voyage. No acknowledgment is made as to the contents of cases, packages, barrels or containers. Value unknown unless it shall have been declared by the Shipper before shipment and inserted in the Bill of Lading. The Carrier, his servants and agents shall not under any circumstances whatever be under any liability for insufficient packing or inaccuracies, obliteration or absence of marks, numbers, address or description, nor for delivery to drop marks, or quality marks, or countermarks, or numbers. If on the arrival of the vessel at the Port of Discharge or at such other port or place as is referred to in clauses 8, 9, 10, 11 and/or 12 of these Conditions any of the Goods cannot be identified by reason of insufficiency of marks, obliteration of marks or no marks then in any such case the Shipper, Consignee, Owner of the Goods or Holder of the Bill of Lading shall accept as due delivery of the Goods under the Bill of Lading any bales or packages which may be on board the vessel and be tendered them by the Carrier or his agents notwithstanding that such bales or packages do not bear the marks and description stated to be declared by the Shipper in the Bill of Lading. If any bagged or baled goods are landed slack or torn the Shipper, Consignee, Owner of the Goods and/or Holder of the Bill of Lading shall accept such proportion of the sweepings as may be allotted by the Carrier or his agents as due delivery of the Goods under the Bill of Lading.

6. *No acknowledgment as to accuracy*

Unless the Bill of Lading is subject to such legislation as is referred to in the first paragraph of clause 1 hereof, and notwithstanding clause 5 hereof, no acknowledgment whatever is made by the Carrier as to the accuracy of any of the particulars stated to be declared by the Shipper in the Bill of Lading.

7. *Voyage*

The vessel may at any time whatsoever whether before or after shipment or before or after proceeding towards or calling at the port of discharge proceed by any route whatsoever in the Carrier's or Master's absolute discretion (whether or not such route is the nearest or most direct or customary or advertised route between the ports of shipment or discharge) and (but without prejudice to the foregoing) may tow or be towed, sail with or without pilot and/or tugs, adjust speed and course for suitable arrival in ports, sail at reduced speed for any purpose whatsoever, tip or list vessel for inspection and/or repairs and proceed under sail and adjust navigational instruments and engage in trial trips of any description (including speed, engine and all other tests whatsoever) whether loaded or unloaded, and whether during such trial trips the vessel be manned or navigated either wholly or partially by the Carrier's Master, officers, servants or agents or the Master, officers, servants or agents of any other person, and carry live animals and every description of cargo on deck, and further may carry contraband, explosives, munitions or warlike stores or dangerous cargo of every kind to any extent and may sail armed and unarmed and may proceed to or stay at any port or place whatsoever (although in a contrary direction to or out of or beyond the customary or intended or advertised route to the port of discharge once or more often in any order backwards or forwards) for loading or discharging mails and/or cargo and/or stores and/or fuel (whether intended to be used or carried on this or any other voyage of the vessel or any other vessel or for storage or sale) embarking or disembarking passengers, pilots, officers, engineers or crew, towing or assisting vessels in all situations, saving life or property or for inspection of or repairs to the vessel or any part thereof, dry-docking with or without the Goods on board, bunkering, for the convenience or entertainment of passengers or for the convenience of exigencies of the mail service (whether the foregoing purposes or any of them be for this or any other voyage) or for any other purposes whatsoever and may otherwise sail, proceed or stay in any manner or for any purposes whatsoever (even if making in substance another voyage or other voyages) and all such routes, ports, places, sailings and actions shall be deemed to be included within the contractual and intended voyage and any departure in pursuance of the liberties hereby conferred shall not be deemed a deviation in law; the liberties hereby conferred shall not be considered as restricted by any words in the Bill of Lading, whether written or printed or by any circumstances attending or preceding the shipment of the Goods or by the nature of the Goods or construed by reference to whether any departure pursuant to such liberties would or would not frustrate the object of the Bill of Lading, any custom or rule of law notwithstanding and notwithstanding unseaworthiness or unfitness of the vessel at the commencement or at any stage of the voyage.

8. *Transhipment, etc.*

11 The Carrier his servants or agents may at any time and for any purpose whatsoever discharge the Goods or any part thereof from the vessel whether before or after sailing from the Port of Loading and land or store either on shore or afloat and/or re-ship on the vessel or tranship or forward the same (even though they have not been shipped on the Ocean Vessel named in the Bill of Lading) by another vessel or other vessels whether prior or subsequent in sailing to the vessel and whether sailing from the port of reception of the Goods or from any other port and whether belonging to the Carrier or to any other persons or by land or air or other transport. The Goods shall at all times during and after such discharge, while being so landed or in store or awaiting or during re-shipment transhipment or forwarding to another vessel be at the sole risk of the Shipper, Consignee, Owner of the Goods or Holder of the Bill of Lading for all purposes whatsoever, but after receipt into the custody of the vessel or other means of transport by which they are to be on-carried, the Carrier shall be entitled to the benefit of all the exceptions, limitations, conditions and liberties of that vessel's bill of lading or of the contract of carriage relating to such on-carriage in addition to the benefit of all the exceptions, limitations, conditions and liberties of the Bill of Lading. In the event of any conflict between any of the foregoing exceptions, limitations, conditions and liberties, the Carrier shall be entitled to the benefit of those most favourable to him.

In the event of there being no immediate opportunity for transhipping the Goods from the port where the Goods are discharged for transhipment, the Carrier his servants or agents shall be at liberty to enter and land the Goods, or to put them into craft or store, at the sole risk and expense of the Shipper, Consignee, Owner of the Goods or Holder of the Bill of Lading for all purposes whatsoever.

Nothing herein contained shall oblige the Carrier to tranship or forward the Goods by any mode or method or conveyance by which goods of the quantity or description or type of the Goods are not usually transhipped or forwarded or shall entitle the Shipper, Consignee, Owner of the Goods, or Holder of the Bill of Lading to any return of freight or free them or any of them from their obligations to pay the full freight due and payable hereunder. Nothing herein contained shall limit or affect the rights and liberties of the Carrier under clauses 7, 9, 10, 11 and 12 hereof.

9. *Carrier's liberties in the event of strikes, delay, etc.*

In the case of war, hostilities, warlike or naval operations or demonstrations, blockade or interdict of any port, civil strife, piracies, civil commotions, strikes, lockouts or stoppage of labour, quarantine, ice or closure by ice, any breach of the warranty hereinafter contained that the goods are and shall be lawful merchandise or the happening of any other matter or event whatsoever whether any of the foregoing are actual or threatened and whether taking place at or near the Port of Discharge or elsewhere in the course of the voyage and whether or not existing or anticipated before commencement of the voyage, which matters or events, or any of them in the judgment of the Master or Carrier may result in damage or delay (however long or short) to or loss of the vessel or the cargo or any part thereof or make it unsafe or imprudent for any reason to proceed on or continue the voyage or enter or discharge or continue to discharge cargo at the Port of Discharge, or give rise to delay (however long or short) or difficulty in reaching, remaining at, discharging or continuing to discharge at or leaving the Port of Discharge, the Carrier or Master may without notice to the Shipper, Consignee, Owner of the Goods, Holder of the Bill of Lading or any other person discharge the Goods or any part thereof at the Port of Loading or proceed to or stay at and discharge the goods at any other port or place whatsoever in any manner whatsoever as the Carrier or Master may elect, and when goods are so discharged from the vessel such goods shall be at the sole risk and expense of the Shipper, Consignee, Owner of the Goods and/or Holder of the Bill of Lading and the Carrier shall not be liable for any loss of or damage to or in connection with such goods of any kind whatsoever (including deterioration, delay or loss of market) howsoever caused and such discharge shall constitute complete delivery and performance under the contract evidenced by the Bill of Lading, full bill of lading freight and charges shall be deemed earned (and if not paid shall be promptly paid) and the Carrier shall be free from any further responsibility in respect of such goods and the Shipper, Consignee, Owner of the Goods and/or Holder of the Bill of Lading shall bear and pay all charges and expenses incurred in consequence of such discharge, the Carrier, Master and Agents acting solely as agents of the Shipper, Consignee, Owner of the Goods and/or Holder of the Bill of Lading after such goods have been so discharged.

10. *Carrier's liberties in event of war, etc.*

12 When and so long as a state of war (including civil war) exists rendering the voyage unsafe or impracticable or the vessel or her cargo in danger of capture or detention or delay and/or so long as any control over the use or movements of the vessel is exercised by any government or other authorities, and/or the insulated or other space on the vessel is requisitioned or controlled, the Carrier and/or his agents and/or the Master may (if such state of war, control or requisition makes it in his or their absolute discretion reasonable so to do) at any time before or after the commencement of the voyage cancel this engagement or alter or vary or depart from the proposed or advertised or agreed or customary route and/or delay or detain the vessel at or off any port or place and/or tranship the cargo at any port or ports, place or places without being liable for any loss or damage whatsoever directly or indirectly sustained by the Shipper, Consignee, Owner of the Goods or Holder of the Bill of Lading. The vessel in addition to any liberties expressed or implied herein, shall have liberty to comply with any orders or directions as to departure, arrival, routes, ports of call, stoppages, transhipment, discharge or destination, or otherwise howsoever given by any government or any department thereof or by any local authority or any person acting or perporting to act with the authority of any government or of any department thereof or of any local authority, or by any committee or person having under the terms of the war risks insurance on the vessel the right to give such orders or directions, and if by reason of, and in compliance with, any such orders or directions anything is done or is not done, the same shall not be deemed a deviation.

11. *Carrier's further liberties*

The Carrier in addition to any liberties expressed or implied herein shall, in the event of the imminence or existence of war, hostilities or warlike operations between any nations, cessation or prohibition or restriction of intercourse, commercial or otherwise, between nations, or of rebellion or civil war, sanctions imposed or measures taken by or against any government in consequence of, or connected with, any of the above matters, have the rights and liberties as set out in the preceding clauses.

12. *Everything to form part of contract voyage*

Anything done or not done by reason of, or in compliance with, the last five preceding clauses hereof or clause 19 shall be done or not done as part of and in fulfilment of the contractual and intended voyage, and in fulfilment of all the Carrier's obligations hereunder and in the case of discharge, jettison, landing, destination or rendering innocuous of the Goods or part thereof in pursuance of any of the liberties accorded by clauses 8, 9, 10, 11 and 19 hereof, the Carrier shall cease to be under any obligation to forward such goods to the Port of Discharge or Final Destination of the Goods named in the Bill of Lading, and all the remedies and rights of the Carrier his servants or agents shall have effect accordingly; and nothing so done or not done shall be a deviation, and the Shipper, Consignee, Owner of the Goods and/or Holder of the Bill of Lading shall pay the full freight if not prepaid, and if prepaid the Carrier shall be entitled to retain the same.

13. *Warranted lawful merchandise*

The Shipper warrants the Goods lawful merchandise at the Port of Loading, throughout the voyage and at the Port of Discharge or such other port or place as is referred to in clauses 8, 9, 10, 11 and/or 12 hereof.

14. *Port, customs, consular and other regulations*

13 All stamps, duties, fines, penalties and charges imposed by any government or authority (local or otherwise) on goods or on the vessel by reason of having such goods on board shall be for account of the Goods. The Shipper, Consignee, Owner of the Goods or Holder of the Bill of Lading shall comply with the regulations and requirements of the port, customs and other authorities, and shall bear and pay all duties, taxes, fines, imposts, expenses, loss or damage, of whatever nature incurred or suffered by reason of any breach thereof, or by reason of the illegal, incorrect or insufficient marking, numbering or

addressing of packages or description of their contents, and hereby indemnify the Carrier and his agents and the Master and the owners of the other cargo on board against all claims, demands, losses and expenses in respect thereof. In the event of the Goods not complying with the port, customs or other regulations at the Port of Discharge, or of any of the aforesaid matters arising, the Carrier shall be at liberty to bring back, or re-ship, such goods to the port of shipment or Port of Loading at the sole risk and expense of the Shipper, Consignee, Owner of the Goods and/or Holder of the Bill of Lading. Bills of lading must be made out in accordance with the prescriptions and regulations of port, customs or consular authorities. Consular, board of health or other certificates required to accompany the Goods or part thereof are to be procured by Shipper and any detention, charges or penalties occurring to steamer or cargo owing to the want of such certificates are to be borne by the Shipper, Consignee, Owner of the Goods and/or Holder of the Bill of Lading.

15. *Undertaking to customs*

The Carrier or his agents may, in respect of dutiable goods transhipped at the Port of Discharge, give such undertaking as the customs authorities at that port require with respect to dealing with such goods at the port where duty is payable, and all charges involved or liabilities incurred shall be borne by the Shipper, Consignee, Owner of the Goods, and/or Holder of the Bill of Lading.

16. *Discharge and delivery*

Notwithstanding any custom of the port to the contrary, the Goods are to be received by the Shipper, Consignee, Owner of the Goods and/or Holder of the Bill of Lading immediately on discharge from the vessel, and the vessel may commence discharging immediately on arrival without notice to the consignee or any other, and discharge continuously, irrespective of weather, by day and by night, Sundays and holidays included, any custom of the port to the contrary notwithstanding, on to quay, or into shed, warehouse, depot, hulk, lighter or any other premises, vehicle, vessel or craft as the Carrier or his agents may determine. Delivery overside to consignee's lighters is at the vessel's option, and if the Master or Carrier so elects, the Shipper, Consignee, Owner of the Goods and/or Holder of the Bill of Lading shall provide and pay for sufficient lighters and men to receive the Goods as fast as the vessel can deliver any custom of the port to the contrary notwithstanding. Whether the vessel's tackles or shore cranes or other means be employed in the course of delivery on to quay or otherwise, the Carrier shall not be responsible for any loss or damage to or in connection with any of the Goods, other goods or lighters, or for death of or injury to any of the men employed directly or indirectly by the Shipper, Consignee, Owner of the Goods and/or Holder of the Bill of Lading, or any other men whomsoever, after discharge of any of the Goods from the vessel, when such goods shall be at the sole risk and expense of the Shipper, Consignee, Owner of the Goods and/or Holder of the Bill of Lading, and the Shipper, Consignee, Owner of the Goods and/or Holder of the Bill of Lading shall jointly and severally indemnify the Carrier, his servants and agents against claims (including the cost of investigation and defending any such claim) which may be made against him or them or any of them in respect of any such loss, damage, death or injury. The collector or other proper officer of the port is hereby authorized to grant a general order for discharging immediately after the entry of the vessel.

17. [13] *Carrier's rights if bill of lading not produced*

14 If the Bill of Lading be not produced to the Carrier his servants or agents upon arrival of the vessel the Carrier his servants or agents may forthwith deliver the Goods to the Consignee or Notify party whose name or Notifying Address is named in the Bill of Lading without thereby incurring any liability to the Shipper, Consignee, Owner of the Goods and/or Holder of the Bill of Lading.

18. *Landing charges*

The Goods may in all cases be landed by the vessel, and the landing charges shall be payable by the Shipper, Consignee, Owner of the Goods and/or Holder of the Bill of Lading against delivery. Lighterage, if any, at Port of Discharge to be paid by the Shipper, Consignee, Owner of the Goods and/or Holder of the Bill of Lading, any custom or alleged custom of the port to the contrary notwithstanding.

19. *Dangerous and perishable goods*

Without prejudice to all other rights and liberties of the Carrier hereunder, the Carrier his servants and agents shall be at liberty in their absolute discretion to jettison, land, destroy or render innocuous any goods of an inflammable, explosive or dangerous nature or

[13] This clause is new but necessary. Modern export procedures frequently result in goods arriving at port of discharge before the bill of lading. Either (i) the consignee must wait (for goods often perishable), and probably the ship must be delayed, or (ii), as usually happens, the ship must indemnify the shipper's bank. (As to whether such an indemnity is legal, see *Hellenic Lines* v. *Chemoleum Corp.* [1972] 1 Lloyd's Rep. 350 (U.S. New York Supreme Ct.).) (ii) is unjust and uncommercial: the bank *should* know the shipper's credit; the carrier cannot.

declared or considered to be hazardous or prohibited goods by civil or military authority (whether or not the Carrier, his servants or agents shall have consented to the shipment thereof with knowledge of their nature and character) and any goods which shall in the course of carriage hereunder perish or become decomposed or which might become a danger to the vessel or her cargo. The Shipper, Consignee, Owner of such goods and/or Holder of the Bill of Lading shall bear and pay all charges and expenses incurred in or in consequence of such jettison, landing, destruction or rendering innocuous.

20. *Damaged packages, etc.*

The Shipper, Consignee, Owner of the Goods and/or Holder of the Bill of Lading shall bear and pay the cost of all mending, bailing and cooperage of and repairs to or replacement of packages, boxes, crates, wrappers, bags or barrels resulting from insufficiency of packing or from excepted perils.

21. *Stowage*

The Goods or part thereof may be stowed in poop, forecastle, deckhouse, shelter deck, passenger space, or any covered space commonly used in the trade for the carriage of such goods and when so stowed shall be deemed for all purposes to be stowed under deck.

22. *Shortages, etc.*

In the event of shortage of goods for any consignee, unclaimed goods of like kind and quality shall at the Carrier's option be deemed to constitute a part of the Goods and be accepted by such consignee as good delivery under the Bill of Lading. Where bulk goods or goods without marks or goods with the same or similar marks are shipped to more than one consignee the Shipper, Consignee, Owner of the Goods and/or Holder of the Bill of Lading shall jointly and severally bear any expense or loss in dividing the goods or parcels into pro rata quantities and any deficiency shall fall upon them in such proportion as the Carrier, his servants or agents shall decide.

23. *Valuable cargo*

Neither the Carrier nor the vessel shall be responsible for valuable cargo, such as specie, bullion, precious stones, bonds or other negotiable documents, until such goods are delivered to and receipted for by the Master or the officer on duty personally.

24. *Valuation*

(a) Whenever the value of the Goods is less than £100 sterling

(United Kingdom) per package or unit, their value in the calculation and adjustment of claims for which the Carrier may be liable shall for the purpose of avoiding uncertainties and difficulties in fixing value be deemed to be the invoice value, plus freight and insurance if paid, irrespective of whether any other value is greater or less.

(b) In case of any loss or damage to or in connection with goods exceeding in actual value £100 sterling (United Kingdom) per package, or in case of goods not shipped in packages, per unit, the value of the Goods shall be deemed to be £100 sterling, per package or per unit, on which basis the freight is adjusted and the Carrier's liability, if any, shall be determined on the basis of a value of £100 sterling, per package or per unit, or pro rata in case of partial loss or damage, unless the nature of the Goods and a valuation higher than £100 sterling shall have been declared in writing by the shipper upon delivery to the Carrier and inserted in the Bill of Lading and extra freight paid and in such case if the actual value of the Goods per package or per unit shall exceed such declared value, the value shall nevertheless be deemed to be the declared value and the Carrier's liability, if any, shall not exceed the declared value, and any partial loss or damage shall be adjusted pro rata on the basis of such declared value. In no event shall the Carrier be liable for more than the amount of damage actually sustained, and shall be entitled to deduct the amount of customs duties whether paid or unpaid from all claims for non-delivery whether partial or total.

24A. *Container cargo*

If the cargo is stated by the Shipper to be Container cargo, each Container (including the entire contents thereof) shall constitute one package for all purposes including limitation of the Carrier's liability.

25. *Refrigerator clause*

16 Specially cooled stowage is not to be furnished unless contracted for at an increased freight rate. Owners undertake, before loading refrigerated cargo in any insulated space, to obtain a certificate of a competent surveyor that such insulated space and the refrigerating machinery have been surveyed under working conditions and found in good condition and fit for the conveyance of refrigerated cargoes; said certificate to be obtained either at the first or at a later port of the vessel's voyage, whether or not refrigerated cargo is loaded at that port. It is hereby agreed that the existence of such certificate shall be deemed by all parties concerned conclusive evidence that the Carrier has exercised due diligence to make the said insulated space and refrigerating machinery seaworthy. The provisions of the clause

are in addition to the other provisions of the Bill of Lading (including these Conditions); and the Goods are subject to all of the other provisions of the Bill of Lading (including these Conditions).

26. *Emergency expenditure*

If the Carrier shall at any time incur any expenditure in restowing the Goods or in otherwise avoiding, remedying or ameliorating any accident to the Goods following any actual, threatened or anticipated casualty thereto for which the Carrier is not responsible by reason of any provision of the Bill of Lading (including these Conditions) and such expenditure is not admissible in general average or otherwise recoverable hereunder by the Carrier from the Shipper, Consignee, Owner of the Goods, or Holder of the Bill of Lading, the Shipper, Consignee, Owner of the Goods and Holder of the Bill of Lading shall nevertheless be jointly and severally liable to repay to the Carrier on demand all such expenditure so incurred by him.

27. *General average*

General Average shall be adjusted in London, or at such other port as may be selected by the Carrier, according to York-Antwerp Rules, 1950 (if in England supplemented by the practice of English Average Adjusters), save and except that no loss of or injury sustained by live animals, whether by jettison or otherwise, shall be recoverable. Adjustments shall be prepared at such port as shall be selected by the Carrier. If a salving vessel is owned or operated by the Carrier, salvage shall be paid for as fully as if the said salving vessel or vessels belonged to strangers. Such deposit as the Carrier or his agents may deem sufficient to cover the estimated contribution of the Goods and any salvage and special charges thereon shall, if required, be made by the Shipper, Consignee, Owner of the Goods and/or Holder of the Bill of Lading to the Carrier before delivery; provided that where applicable the following clause shall apply:

" New Jason Clause. (a) In the event of accident, danger, damage or disaster before or after the commencement of the voyage, resulting from any cause whatsoever, due to negligence or not, for which, or for the consequence of which, the Carrier is not responsible, by statute, contract or otherwise, the Goods, Shippers, Consignees or Owners of the Goods shall contribute with the Carrier in general average to the payment of any sacrifices, losses or expenses of a general average nature that may be made or incurred and shall pay salvage and special charges incurred in respect of the Goods.

(b) If a salving vessel is owned or operated by the Carrier, salvage shall be paid for as fully as if the said salving vessel or vessels belonged to strangers. Such deposit as the Carrier or his Agents may deem sufficient to cover the estimated contribution of the Goods and any salvage and special charges thereon shall, if required, be made by the Goods, Shippers, Consignees or Owners of the Goods to the Carrier before delivery."

28. *Both to Blame Collision Clause*

17 If the vessel comes into collision with another vessel as a result of the negligence of the other vessel and any act, neglect or default of the Master, mariners, pilot or the servants of the Carrier in the navigation or in the management of the vessel, the owners of the goods carried hereunder will indemnify the Carrier against all loss or liability to the other or non-carrying vessel or her owners insofar as such loss or liability represents loss of or damage to or any claim whatsoever of the owners of the said goods, paid or payable by the other or non-carrying vessel or her owners to the owners of the said goods and set off, recouped or recovered by the other or non-carrying vessel or her owners as part of their claim against the carrying vessel or Carrier. The foregoing provisions shall also apply where the owners, operators, or those in charge of any ship or ships or objects other than, or in addition to, the colliding ships or objects are at fault in respect to a collision or contact.

29. *Lien*

The Carrier his servants or agents shall have a lien on the Goods or any part thereof and a right to sell such goods whether privately or by public auction for all freight (including additional freight payable as is herein stipulated) primage deadfreight, demurrage, detention charges, salvage, average of any kind whatsoever, stamps, duties, fines or penalties and for all other charges and expenses whatsoever, which are for account of the Goods or of the Shipper, Consignee, Owner of the Goods and/or Holder of the Bill of Lading under the Bill of Lading (including these Conditions), and for the costs and expenses of exercising such lien and of such sale and also for all previously unsatisfied debts whatsoever due to him by the Shipper, Consignee, Owner of the Goods and/or Holder of the Bill of Lading. The lien hereby accorded may be exercised by the Carrier, his servants or agents notwithstanding that he or they may have parted with possession of the Goods, and the Carrier, his servants or agents shall at all times stand authorised by the Shipper, Consignee, Owner of the Goods and Holder of the Bill of Lading to give all such notices to any person or persons for the time being in possession of the Goods as may be required for the purpose of giving effect to the provisions of this clause. Nothing in this clause shall prevent the Carrier from recovering from the Shipper, Consignee, Owner of the Goods and/or Holder of the Bill of Lading the difference between the amount due from them or any of them to him and the amount realised by the exercise of the rights given to the Carrier under this clause.

30. *Pre-Carriage. This clause is applicable only where Local Vessel is named in the Bill of Lading*

(a) Where the Local Vessel is named in the Bill of Lading the Carrier shall act only as agent of the Shipper, Consignee, Owner of the Goods, or Holder of the Bill of Lading in arranging for the forwarding of the Goods to the Port of Loading named in the Bill of Lading (or such other port or place wheresoever as the Carrier may in his discretion determine), and the Carrier shall be under no liability whatsoever as carrier, bailee or otherwise in connection with the Goods until the Goods are loaded upon the Ocean Vessel named in the Bill of Lading (or such other vessel owned by the Carrier or otherwise as the Carrier may in his discretion substitute for the named Ocean Vessel) save where the Goods are so forwarded by carriage on a vessel owned by the Carrier in which event the said carriage shall be subject to all exceptions, limitations, conditions and liberties contained in the Bill of Lading (including these Conditions).

(b) Notwithstanding that the Goods have been loaded upon the Local Vessel named in the Bill of Lading such forwarding of the Goods to the Port of Loading named in the Bill of Lading may be effected by any mode or modes of conveyance (whether by land, sea or air) under one or more bills of lading or other contract or contracts of carriage all subject to such exceptions, limitations, conditions and liberties (including liberty to discharge the Goods at a port or place other than the Port of Loading named in the Bill of Lading) as the Carrier his servants or agents may in his or their discretion determine or agree or have ageed to upon behalf of the Shipper, Consignee, Owner of the Goods or Holder of the Bill of Lading who shall be deemed to have notice thereof.

(c) Any carrier with whom any such arrangements or agreements are made shall, in addition to being entitled to the benefit of whatever exceptions, limitations, conditions and liberties may be so agreed upon be further entitled to the benefit of all the exceptions, limitations, conditions and liberties herein contained, and for the purpose of this sub-clause, but not otherwise, the Carrier is or shall be deemed to be acting as agent and/or trustee on behalf of and for the benefit of that carrier and that carrier shall to that extent but not otherwise be or be deemed to be a party to the contract contained in or evidenced by the Bill of Lading. In the event of any conflict between any of the foregoing exceptions, limitations, conditions and liberties, that carrier shall be entitled to the benefit of those most favourable to him.

(d) Without prejudice to the foregoing sub-clauses (a), (b) and (c) of this clause, where either no Ocean Vessel or no Port of Loading is named in the Bill of Lading the Carrier shall act only as agent as aforesaid for the forwarding of the Goods to the Final Destination or, if such port or place is not named in the Bill of Lading, to the named Port of Discharge or, if no such port or places are named in the Bill of Lading, to the Port of Loading, and the Carrier shall be entitled also to the benefit of clause 31 herein, and also to the benefit of all other exceptions, limitations, conditions and liberties herein.

31. *On-Carriage. This clause is applicable* (*subject to clause* 30 (*d*) *above*) *only where the Final Destination is named in the Bill of Lading*

18 (a) Where the Final Destination is named in the Bill of Lading the Carrier may discharge the Goods at the Port of Discharge or without notice at such other port or place wheresoever (including the Port of Loading) as the Carrier may in his discretion determine for forwarding to the Final Destination and Carrier's responsibility shall finally cease on discharge of the Goods from the Ocean Vessel (or vessel substituted under clause 30 hereof). Thereafter (provided always that the Carrier is not by reason of any other provision of the Bill of Lading (including these Conditions) relieved of his obligations to forward the Goods to the Final Destination) the Carrier shall act only as agent of the Shipper, Consignee, Owner of the Goods or Holder of the Bill of Lading in arranging for the forwarding of the Goods to the Final Destination and the Carrier shall be under no further or other responsibility whatever, save that where the Goods are on-carried on a vessel owned by the Carrier the Carrier's liability as carrier shall be governed by the exceptions, limitations, conditions and liberties of the Bill of Lading (including these Conditions). After discharge from the Ocean Vessel the Carrier may store the Goods at any place or in any manner and forward them by any mode or modes of conveyance under one or more bill or bills of lading or other contract or contracts of on-carriage all subject to such exceptions, limitations, conditions and liberties (including liberty to discharge the Goods at a port or place other than the Final Destination) as the Carrier his servants or agents may in his or their discretion determine or agree to upon behalf of the Shipper, Consignee, Owner of the Goods or Holder of the Bill of Lading, who shall be deemed to have notice thereof.

(b) The Shipper, Consignee, Owner of the Goods or Holder of the Bill of Lading shall, if required by the Carrier so to do, forthwith provide the Carrier with all documents which may be necessary in order to clear the goods at the Port of Discharge or to store and forward them to the Final Destination.

(c) Any on-carrier with whom any arrangements or agreements are made by the Carrier acting as aforesaid shall, in addition to being entitled to the benefit of whatever exceptions, limitations, conditions and liberties may be agreed upon between him and the Carrier acting as aforesaid, be further entitled to the benefit of all the exceptions, limitations, conditions and liberties herein contained (or in the Bill of Lading), and for the purpose of this sub-clause, but not otherwise, the Carrier is or shall be deemed to be acting as agent or trustee on behalf of and for the benefit of that on-carrier and that on-carrier shall to that extent but not otherwise be or be deemed to be a party to the contract contained in or evidenced by the Bill of Lading. In the event of any conflict between any of the foregoing exceptions, limitations, conditions and liberties, the on-carrier shall be entitled to the benefit of those most favourable to him.

32. *Jurisdiction*

The contract evidenced by the Bill of Lading shall be governed by English law and any disputes thereunder shall be determined in England according to English law to the exclusion of the jurisdiction of the courts of any other country.

[The next paragraph is 31]

CHAPTER 2

MODEL PASSENGER TICKET[1]

31 [*Front cover*][2]

"............................" LINE

PASSAGE TICKET

All passengers are advised to take out full insurance covering themselves and their luggage during the intended voyage.
[*printed prominently*]

Please read the regulations and conditions of the enclosed contract.
[*printed prominently*]

32 [*Inside front cover*]

By the contract contained in this ticket the Owners[3] of the Vessel named herein agree to carry the Passengers named herein on a voyage as described and agreed in clauses 10 to 19 herein from the Port of Embarkation named herein, and by accepting or using this ticket all Passengers named herein (or embarking on the Vessel named herein) agree on their own behalf and on behalf of each other to be bound by all the conditions, limitations, exceptions and liberties specified in this passage ticket in favour of the Owners their servants and agents parties to this contract.[4]

The Owners reserve the right to cancel any sailing or not dispatch the Vessel on the intended voyage for any reason whatsoever on giving notice to the Passenger of such cancellation and repaying any passage money paid.

1 See note on model passenger ticket, *infra*, § 41.
2 Front covers vary in size and format from Line to Line. The neat format (but not the words used) which Cunard used on Queen Elizabeth II is recommended; size, 8 inches by 3·5 inches.
3 *Cf.* demise clause in bills of lading, *supra*, § 4, note 6.
4 See Conditions 21 (b) and (c), *infra*, § 40.

33 [*Particulars with carbon copies*]

Provisions Regarding Fares and Baggage. [*Note : Since each Line has different provisions regarding fares, baggage rates, return fares, breaking journeys, etc., it is impossible in a model passenger ticket to draft either* (i) *model boxes or* (ii) *model conditions relevant to such matters.*]	NAMES OF PASSENGERS	ACCOMMODATION RESERVED
		VESSEL
		SAILING ON OR ABOUT
		PORT OF EMBARKATION
		PORT OF DISEMBARKATION
		"X" LINE PER ISSUED AT DATE

Regulations

[*Printed in bold or red type*]

34 1. (a) *Embarkation*

The Passenger shall comply with all government travel requirements, present all exit, entry and other documents required by the law, and arrive for embarkation by the time fixed by the Owners or, if no time is fixed, sufficiently in advance of scheduled departure to permit completion of government formalities and departure procedures.

(b) *Ship's Regulations*

Passengers must comply with any regulation which the Owners or Master, in their or his sole discretion, may at any time consider necessary for the general good order, comfort and safety of all on board.

2. *Baggage*

(a) All baggage should be packed in substantial suitcases or trunks, fastened securely with case locks and strapped or roped to give added protection against damage or pilferage. The Passenger must see that baggage is distinctly labelled with his name, ship, date of sailing and destination.

(b) Baggage of Passengers must only contain their clothing and similar personal effects and individual packages must not exceed 2 cwts. or measure more than 4 ft. in length.[5] Packages containing plate, objets d'art, furniture, including domestic refrigerators, cookers, radios, gramophones, etc., wines, spirits, etc., cannot be accepted as baggage. The Owners reserve the right to refuse such packages unless tendered as cargo and freight prepaid thereon. If accepted for shipment with baggage, they will not be included in the Passenger's free allowance of baggage and the appropriate excess charge will be levied on the total measurent of the packages concerned.

(c) Baggage in excess of the free allowance is chargeable at current rates. Details of the relevant allowances in respect of adult passengers and children may be obtained on application to the Owners' offices or agents or on board.

3. *Valuables*

Passengers may hand to the Purser or other appropriate officer for safe custody money, watches, jewellery, or other valuables, declaring the value and paying a percentage thereon.

[5] This is an example, not a model clause: each Line has its own requirements for " hand baggage," " personal effects," " cabin baggage," etc.

4. *Children*

Children under 12 years of age shall take meals only in the part of the ship (if any) set aside for that purpose and at such times as the Ship's regulations may prescribe.

35 5. *Medical care*

(a) The Ship's Surgeon is authorised to charge for medical attendance, including medicines at fixed rates.

(b) Passengers who by reason of illness or through any other cause require special or extra accommodation, or special or extra attention in the course of the voyage, and not originally provided for, will be charged accordingly for the same.

6. *Wines*

The fares include victualling, but not wines, spirits, beer, mineral waters or other liquors. These are available for purchase on board at fixed prices and Passengers are not permitted to take on board any of the above for use during the voyage whether for consumption in their own cabins or otherwise. Any account for purchase of liquors, or of any other extras, including medical attention, or for the carriage of extra baggage, must be settled in cash, before the Passenger concerned leaves the Ship, in any currency in general use on board at the time of payment.

7. *Berths*

No berth or cabin is to be occupied by a Passenger without application to the agent on shore, or to the Purser or other appropriate officer on board. A Passenger occupying a cabin of two or more berths on the departure of the Ship (unless he has paid an additional sum for its exclusive occupation) shall not object to the vacant berth or berths being subsequently filled.

8. *Delay in port*

If the Ship is delayed by any cause whatsoever which is beyond the control of the Owners, or if for whatever reason Passengers remain on board after the arrival of the Ship at their port of destination, the Owners shall be entitled to charge Passengers for their maintenance for every day of the delay, or during which the Passengers remain on board, as the case may be, the charges to be as appropriate for the class of accommodation provided.

[*End regulations in bold or red type*]

[*Further conditions in smaller black print*]

Conditions

36 9. (a) "*Passenger*" in these conditions includes each and every passenger named herein.[6]

(b) "*Owners*" in these conditions includes charterers by demise of the Vessel.[7]

10. *Voyage* [8]

The Vessel may at any time whatsoever whether before or after embarkation proceed by any route whatsoever in the Owners' or Master's absolute discretion (whether or not such route is the nearest or most direct or customary or advertised route between the ports of embarkation and disembarkation) and may tow or be towed sail with or without pilots and/or tugs adjust speed and course for suitable arrival in ports, sail at reduced speed for any purpose whatsoever, and carry live animals and every description of cargo on or below deck, including contraband, explosives, munitions or warlike stores or dangerous cargo of every kind and may sail armed or unarmed *and* may proceed to or stay at any port or place whatsoever (although in a contrary direction to or out of or beyond the customary or intended or advertised route to the port of disembarkation once or more often in any order backwards or forwards) *for* loading or discharging mails and/or cargo and/or stores and/or fuel (whether intended to be used or carried on this or any other voyage of the Vessel or any other vessel or for storage or sale) embarking or disembarking passengers, pilots, officers, engineers or crew, towing or assisting vessels in all situations, saving life or property or for inspection of or repairs to the vessel or any part thereof, bunkering, for the convenience or entertainment of passengers or for the convenience of exigencies of the mail service (whether the foregoing purposes or any of them be for this or any other voyage) or for any other purposes whatsoever and may otherwise sail, proceed or stay in any manner or for any purposes whatsoever (even if making in substance another voyage or other voyages).

[6] See "Names of Passengers," *supra*, § 33.

[7] See also Inside front cover, *supra*, § 32. The effect is equivalent to that of the "demise clause" in bills of lading: see Carver [B.S.L. 2, § 418], *supra*, § 4, Note 6.

[8] Compare these conditions 10 to 19 with Model Bill of Lading Conditions 7 to 12 and 19, §§ 10, 11, 12 and 14, *supra*.

11. *Substitution of Vessel*

The Owners are at liberty to substitute any vessel for the Vessel named herein at the Port of Embarkation named herein, whether owned by themselves or not, for the purpose of wholly or in part fulfilling this Contract.

37 12. *Transhipment*

The Owners may at any time or for any purpose, whether at the Port of Embarkation or any other port, require the Passenger to proceed by any other vessel, or by conveyance by land or air, to the Port of Disembarkation named herein. After so requiring the Passenger the Owners shall act only as agents of the Passenger in arranging for forwarding him and his luggage to the said Port of Disembarkation and the Owners shall be under no further or other responsibility whatever (unless the Passenger is carried on a vessel owned by the Owners in which event the Owners' liability as carrier shall be governed by the conditions, limitations, exceptions and liberties specified herein).

13. *Failure to land*

If for any reason whatsoever the Passenger is prevented from landing or fails to land at the Port of Disembarkation named herein the Owners may carry him forward or backward for landing at any other port in their sole discretion and charge additional passage money for such conveyance to the port of landing.

14. *Omission to call at port*

If, in the opinion of the Master, entry into the Port of Embarkation or Disembarkation may result in inconvenience, delay, damage or danger either to the Vessel or any passenger or passengers or cargo for any reason whatsoever (including without prejudice to the generality of the foregoing quarantine restrictions, epidemic, ice congestion and whether actual or threatened strikes), the Vessel may omit to call at the Port of Embarkation named herein, in which event this Contract shall be cancelled, or may omit to call at the Port of Disembarkation named herein and carry the Passenger forward or backward to any other port in the Owners' sole discretion and land him and his baggage there, whereupon the obligations of the Owners under this Contract shall be deemed to have been duly fulfilled and the passage money earned in full.

15. *Special orders*

(a) The Vessel shall have liberty to comply with any orders, directions, recommendations or warnings as to departure, arrival, routes, ports of call, stoppages, destinations, zones, waters, delivery, embarkation or disembarkation, or in any other wise whatsoever or howsoever given by the Government of the nation under whose flag the Vessel sails or any other government or local authority including any *de facto* government or local authority or by any person or body acting or purporting to act as or with the authority of any such government or authority or by any committee or person having under the terms of the war risks insurance on the Vessel the right to give any such orders, directions recommendations or warnings. If by reason of or in compliance with any such orders, directions, recommendations or warnings, anything is done or is not done such shall not be deemed a deviation.

(b) If by reason of or in compliance with any such orders, directions, recommendations or warnings the vessel does not proceed to or is diverted from the Port of Disembarkation originally designated or to which she may have been ordered pursuant to the contract contained in this ticket the Vessel may proceed to any safe port of disembarkation which the Master or Owners in his or their discretion may decide on and there disembark the Passenger and land his luggage. Such disembarkation and/or landing shall be deemed to be due fulfilment of the said contract and the Owners shall be entitled to passage money as if disembarkation and/or landing has been effected at the named Port of Disembarkation. All extra expenses involved in reaching and disembarking and/or landing at any such other Port of Disembarkation shall be paid by the Passenger.

38 16. *War*

If the vessel is requisitioned by Her Majesty's Government or if in the opinion of the Owners or the Master war hostilities or warlike operations or the imminence or existence thereof (whether Great Britain is a belligerent or not) interferes or is likely to interfere in any way with the due performance by them of the said obligations or renders it commercially impracticable for them to fulfil the same, the Owners shall be at liberty to suspend or cancel their obligations under this Contract.

17. *Sickness*

(a) If the Passenger for any reason whatsoever, including (but not limited to) sickness, disease, injury or infirmity, bodily or mental, reasonably appears to the Owners or to the vessel's Surgeon or agent to be:

(i) unfit to proceed, likely to endanger health or safety on board, or likely to impair reasonable comfort on board; or

(ii) likely to be refused permission to land at his port of destination; or

(iii) likely to render the Owners liable for his maintenance or support;

Then in such case, the Owners may at their option either:

(1) refuse to embark such Passenger;

(2) disembark him at any port, or

(3) transfer him from one berth to another;

and in case the Passenger is refused embarkation or is disembarked no part of his passage money shall be refunded and the Owners shall not be liable for any loss or expense occasioned to the Passenger thereby; provided however that the Owners shall with reasonable diligence endeavour to resell the space after it is made available and will pay over the sum realised from any such resale, less reasonable cost to the Owners occasioned by action as hereinabove provided and by efforts to resell the space.

(b) Any Passenger who embarks, or allows any other Passenger for whom he is responsible to embark, when he or such other Passenger is suffering from any sickness, disease, injury or infirmity, bodily or mental, or to his knowledge has been exposed to any infectious or contagious disease, or for any other reason is likely to impair the health, safety or reasonable comfort of other persons on board, or for any reason is refused permission to land at his port of destination, shall be responsible for any additional passage money if he and/or such other Passenger is retained, oncarried, or returned on board any vessel belonging to the Owners, and for any loss or expense incurred by the Owners or the Master, directly or indirectly in consequence of such sickness, disease, injury, infirmity, exposure or refusal of permission to land, unless in the case of sickness, disease, injury, infirmity or exposure the same has been declared in writing to the Owners, or the Master, before embarkation and the consent in writing of the Owners, or the Master, to such embarkation has been obtained.

39 18. *Dangerous Goods*

(a) The Passenger warrants that no goods brought aboard by him, whether in his luggage or otherwise, are prohibited by any government or are of a dangerous nature and will be held absolutely responsible for and will fully indemnify Owners against any detention of the Vessel and any penalties, fines, expenses, loss, damage or liability of whatsoever kind resulting from a breach of this warranty.

(b) The Owners their servants and agents shall be at liberty in their absolute discretion to jettison, land, destroy or render innocuous any such goods, and the Passenger shall bear and pay all charges and expenses incurred in or in consequence of such acts by or on behalf of the Owners.

19. *Everything to form part of contract voyage*

Anything done or not done by reason of, or in compliance with, Conditions 10 to 18 hereof shall be done or not done as part of or as the case may be in fulfilment of the contractual and intended voyage, and of all the Owners' obligations hereunder and in the case of transhipment or disembarkation or landing of the Passenger and/or his luggage or other goods in pursuance of any of the liberties accorded by Conditions 12 and 14 to 19 hereof, the Owners shall cease to be under any obligation to forward the Passenger or his luggage to the Port of Disembarkation named herein, and all the remedies and rights of the Owners their servants or agents shall have effect accordingly and nothing so done or not done shall be a deviation, and all the obligations of the Owners shall be deemed to have been duly fulfilled and the passage money earned in full.

20. *Lien*

The Owners shall have a lien on the Passenger's luggage and other goods for payment of wine account, surgeon's fees, passage money or baggage charges unpaid, or any other debts whatsoever due to the Owners.

40 21. *Exemption from Liability*

(a) The Owners shall not be responsible for the death or sickness of or injury to the Passenger or loss of or damage to or in connection with his luggage or other goods however caused (whether by unseaworthiness or unfitness of the Vessel or any other vessel or mode of conveyance or by faults, errors or negligence or otherwise howsoever).

(b)[9] No servant or agent of the Owners (including every independent contractor from time to time employed by the Owners) shall in any circumstances whatsoever be under any liability whatsoever to the Passenger for death, sickness, injury, loss, damage, delay or otherwise arising or resulting directly or indirectly from any act, neglect or default on the part of such servant or agent while acting in the course of or in connection with his employment and every condition, limitation, exception and liberty herein contained and every right, exemption from liability, defence and immunity of whatsoever

[9] See *supra*, § 9, note 11, as to the effect of (b) and (c). Himalaya Clause A (*infra*, § 66) *not* recommended in a *model* passenger ticket in this respect.

nature applicable to the Owners shall also be available and extend to protect every such servant or agent of the Owners acting as aforesaid and for all the purposes of all the foregoing provisions of this clause, the Owners are contracting with the Passenger as agents of and trustees for such servants and agents, who are parties to the contract contained in this passage ticket.[10]

(c) The Owners shall be entitled to be paid by the Passenger or his personal representatives on demand any sum recovered or recoverable by such Passenger or his personal representatives from such servant or agent of the Owners for any such death, sickness, injury, loss, delay, damage or otherwise.[10]

(d) All the foregoing exemptions from liability shall equally apply to any ancillary contract or service (including the sale of wines, spirits, beers, mineral waters or other liquids or medical care), made or provided during or in connection with the performance of the contract contained in this passage ticket.

(e) In the event of any sale or supply of any goods whatever including medicines, victuals, wines, and other liquids, to the Passenger, any express or implied condition, statement or warranty statutory or otherwise not stated herein, by which the Owners their servants or agents might otherwise be liable to the Passenger, is hereby excluded.

22. *Jurisdiction* [11]

The contract in this passage ticket shall be governed by English law and any disputes thereunder shall be determined in England according to English law to the exclusion of the jurisdiction of the courts of any other country.

41 *Note on Model Passenger Ticket*

This was finally drafted in 1968 after consultation with those concerned and has not previously been published. It is designed to be comparable with the model bill of lading (*supra*, Chapter 1).

The scheme of the ticket is based on the format used by reputable Lines. It is intended (i) to be fair and comprehensible to the passenger (and his insurer); and (ii) to give legal effect to immunities intended (but often ineffectually expressed) by the owners, such as the insertion of an effective *Adler* v. *Dickson* clause (clause 21 (b) and (c) of § 40, *supra*; see note to § 9, clause 2, *supra*).

The regulations (§ § 34 and 35, *supra*) are those which a passenger can be expected to read, as opposed to the conditions (§ 36 *et seq., supra*) which can be understood only by lawyers. Each company will no doubt wish to vary the regulations to its own requirements.

[The next paragraph is 51]

10 *Adler* v. *Dickson* clause: see § 9, clause 2, *supra*.

11 *Quaere* the effect of this clause abroad. See Carver [B.S.L. 2] § 279.

CHAPTER 3

CHARTERPARTIES

1. APPROVED FORMS

Introduction

51 CHARTERPARTY forms acceptable on the Baltic Exchange, City of London, are listed below. They are used almost invariably with a mass of typed deletions, amendments and additions, referring *inter alia* to selected clauses in other charterparty forms or otherwise in general use.[1]

Forms 1 to 56 (*infra*, § 53), including ancillary documents, have been approved by both:

(i) the Chamber of Shipping of the United Kingdom,[2] Documentary Committee (hereinafter referred to as " the Chamber ");

(ii) the Baltic and International Maritime Conference Documentary Committee (hereinafter referred to as " Baltic International "). The Baltic Exchange in London is herein referred to as " Baltic, London." [3]

Forms A to C (*infra*, § 54) may also be regarded as approved precedents.

Forms D and E (*infra*, § 55) are documents approved in the United States of America and used on Baltic, London, mainly as a basis for typed variations.

Note on Charterparties in General Use

52 It is to be noted that of the fifty-six documents listed in Part I of the Schedule of Approved Documents (*infra*, § 53) not one has been amended since 1950 save the following:

18. Polcon, amended 1965.
19. Nubaltwood, amended (with Polish terms) 1967.
22. Sovietwood, 1961.
40. Austwheat, amended 1967.
49. Gencon, new lay-out, 1966.

In other words, the drafting of printed forms of charterparties of any importance has been static since 1950, save for trade with members of the Union of Soviet Socialist Republics and their satellites.

But, it should be added, Baltic, London, have made up with typed clauses for the delay that has been shown in preparing new forms of charter (save when dealing with Communist States).

53 **Approved Documents 1969** [4]

Coal (including Coke and Patent Fuel)	*Code Name*
1 Welsh Coal Charter, 1896	

[1] See *infra*, § 56 *et seq.*
[2] See *Shipowners* [B.S.L. 13, §§ 329 *et seq.*].
[3] See *ibid.*, §§ 92 *et seq.*
[4] See § 51, *supra.*

2 Welsh Coal Charter, 1896 (Patent Fuel)
3 Welsh Coal Charter, 1896, For Monte Video, Buenos Ayres, etc.
4 Welsh Coal Charter, 1896, To the Danube, Rosario, Rivers Parana or Uruguay
5 East Coast Coal Charter-Party, 1922 ... ... MEDCON
6 East Coast Coal Charter-Party, 1896, To Monte Video, Buenos Ayres, etc.
7 East Coast Coal Charter-Party, 1896, To the Danube, Rosario, Rivers Parana and Uruguay
8 Scotch Coal Charter, 1896
9 Scotch Coal Charter, 1896, For Monte Video, Buenos Ayres, etc.
10 Scotch Coal Charter, 1896, To the Danube, Rosario, Rivers Parana or Uruguay
11 Coasting Coal Charter-Party, 1920 ... ... COASTCON
12 Coasting Coal Charter-Party, 1913 ... ... WELCON
13 The Baltic and White Sea Conference Coal Charter, 1921 ... ... BALTCON
14 Coasting Charter-Party, 1921, For Mersey District Ports ... ... MERSEYCON
15 Coasting Charter-Party, 1922 (Sailing Ship), For Mersey District Ports ... ... MERSAIL
16 Coasting Coal Charter-Party (Sailing Ship), 1923 ... ... COASTCON SAILER
17 The Baltic and International Maritime Conference Continental Coal Charter 1945 ... ... CONTCOAL
(For Coal and Coke from Danzig/Brest Range)
18 Baltic and International Maritime Conference Polish Coal Charter, 1950 (Amended 1965) ... ... POLCON

Wood (including Pitwood, Props and Pulpwood)

19 Baltic Wood Charter Party, 1964 ... ... NUBALTWOOD
20 Baltic Wood Charter Party, 1964 (Polish Terms) Agreed 1967 ... ... NUBALTWOOD (Polish Terms)
21 Baltic Wood Charter, 1926 (Adapted for Leningrad Trade 1933)
22 Soviet Wood Charter Party, 1961 ... ... SOVIETWOOD
23 Pitch Pine Charter, 1906 ... ... PIXPINUS
24 British North American (Atlantic) Wood Charter-Party, 1914 ... ... BENACON
25 Pitwood Charter (France to Bristol Channel Ports), 1924 ... ... PITWOODCON

26 The Baltic and International Maritime Conference Prop and Pulpwood Charter, 1937 ... PROPCON
27 The Baltic and International Maritime Conference Wood Charter, 1937 ... ... CONTWOOD
28 Baltic Pulp and Paper Charter (from Finland to United Kingdom and Continent) ... ... BALTPULP

Grain

29 Azoff Berth Contract, 1910 ... ... AZCON
30 Danube Berth Contract, 1911 ... ... DANCON
31 Sulina and Kustendje Berth Contract, 1911 ... ... SULCON
32 Bulgarian Berth Contract, 1911 ... ... BULCON
33 Black Sea Berth Contract, 1912 ... ... RUSSCON
34 Black Sea, etc., Berth Contract Bill of Lading, 1902
35 The 1890 Azoff Charter-Party
36 The 1890 Black Sea Charter-Party
37 The 1890 Danube Charter-Party
38 River Plate Charter-Party, 1914 (Homewards) ... CENTROCON
39 Australian Grain Charter, 1928 ... ... AUSTRAL
40 Australian Grain Charter, 1956 (Amended October, 1967) ... AUSTWHEAT

Rice, etc.

41 Saigon Charter-Party

Stone

42 Stone Charter-Party, 1920 ... ... PANSTONE

Ore

43 Mediterranean Ore Charter, 1921 ... ... MEDITORE
44 Mediterranean Ore Charter, 1922 ... ... NECORE

Cement

45 Cement Charter-Party, 1922 ... ... CEMENCO
46 Cement Charter-Party (Sailing Ship), 1923 ... CEMENCOSAIL

General

47 Baltic and White Sea Conference Uniform General Charter 4 pp ... ... GENCON
48 Baltic and White Sea Conference Uniform General Charter 2 pp ... ... „
49 Baltic and White Sea Conference Uniform General Charter Layout, 1966 ... ... „

50 General Home Trade Charter, 1928 ... ... BRITCONT
51 General Home Trade Bill of Lading, 1928 ... "

Time
52 The Baltic and International Maritime Conference Uniform Time-Charter 4 pp ... "
53 The Baltic and International Maritime Conference Uniform Time-Charter 2 pp ... BALTIME 1939
54 Time Charter ... ... TRANSTIME 1946
55 Coasting and Short Sea Daily Hire Charter Party, 1954 ... ... COASTHIRE

Fertilisers
56 Chamber of Shipping Fertilisers Charter, 1942 ... FERTICON

Adopted Charter Party Forms

54 *A. Genorecon*

General Ore Charterparty, 1962. Published by Baltic (International). Adopted by the Chamber. Issued, January 8, 1963.

B. Saigon

Saigon Charter-Party, April, 1938. Agreed between the Chamber and Syndicat des Exportateurs Français D'Indochine. Amended, January 1, 1950.

C. Synacomex

Continent Grain Charter Party. *Adopté Paris* 1957, amended 1960, by French bodies, adopted by the Chamber and Baltic International.

55 *United States Charter Party Forms*

D. Baltimore

Baltimore Berth Grain Charter Party, 1913.

E. N.Y. Time 1 and N.Y. Time 2

Time Charters, Government Form. Approved by the New York Produce Exchange, 1913; last amended, 1946.

2. Charterparty Clauses [5]

Exceptions [6]

56 Centrocon, clause 29: Exceptions

"The Steamer shall not be liable for loss or damage occasioned by

[5] For details of charterparties referred to by code names, see *supra*, § 53 to § 55.
[6] For the meaning and effect of the words used in these exceptions clauses, see *Carriage by Sea* [B.S.L. 2].

the Act of God, by Quarantine Restrictions, by Perils of the Sea, or other Waters, by Fire from any cause or wheresoever occurring, by Barratry of the Master or Crew, by Enemies, Pirates, or Thieves, by Arrest or Restraint of Princes, Rulers or People, by Riots, Strikes or Stoppages of Labour, by explosion, bursting of Boilers, Breakages of Shafts or any Latent Defects in Hull, Machinery, or Appurtenances, by Collision, Stranding or other Accidents arising in the Navigation of the Steamer, even when occasioned by the negligence, default or error of judgment of the Pilot, Master, Mariners or other Servants of the Shipowners or Persons for whom they may be responsible (not resulting, however, in any case from want of due diligence by the Owners of the Steamer, or by the Ship's Husband or Manager). But nothing herein contained shall exempt the Shipowners from liability for damage or loss to cargo occasioned by bad stowage, by improper or insufficient Dunnage, by absence of efficient ventilation, or by improper opening of Valves, Sluices, or Ports. The Owners shall not be liable for any delay in the commencement or prosecution of the Voyage due to a General Strike or Lock-out of Seamen or other persons necessary for the movement or navigation of the Vessel.

The Steamer shall have the liberty to call at any Port or Ports in any order, for the purpose of taking Bunker Coal or other Supplies, to sail without Pilots, to tow and be towed, to assist Vessels in distress and to deviate for the purpose of saving life or property."

57 Saigon, clause 10 : Negligence, etc.

" The Act of God, perils, dangers and accidents of the sea or other waters of what nature and kind soever, fire from any cause on land or on water, barratry of the master and crew, enemies, pirates and robbers, arrests and restraints of princes, rulers and people, explosions, bursting of boilers, breakage of shafts, or any latent defect in hull and/or machinery, strandings, collisions, and all other accidents of navigation, and all losses and damages caused thereby are excepted, even when occasioned by negligence, default or error in judgment of the Pilot, Master, Mariners, or other servants of the shipowners, but unless stranded, sunk, burnt, or in collision, nothing herein contained shall exempt the shipowner from liability to pay for damage to cargo occasioned by fuel stain, by bad stowage, by improper or insufficient dunnage, or absence of customary ventilation, or by improper opening of valves, sluices and ports, or by causes other than those above excepted, and all the above exceptions are conditional on the vessel being seaworthy when she sails on the voyage, but any latent defects in the hull and/or machinery shall not be considered unseaworthiness, provided the same do not result from want of due diligence of the owners or any of them, or by the ship's Husband or Manager." [7]

58 Gencon, clause 9: Owners' Responsibility Clause

"Owners are to be responsible for loss of or damage to the goods or for delay in delivery of the goods only in case the loss, damage or delay has been caused by the improper or negligent stowage of the goods (unless stowage performed by shippers or their stevedores or servants) or by personal [8] want of due diligence on the part of the Owners or their Manager to make the vessel in all respects seaworthy and to secure that she is properly manned, equipped and supplied or by the personal act or default of the Owners or their Manager.

And the Owners are responsible for no loss or damage or delay arising from any other cause whatsoever, even from the neglect or default of the Captain or crew or some other person employed by the Owners on board or ashore for whose acts they would, but for this clause, be responsible, or from unseaworthiness of the vessel on loading or commencement of the voyage or at any time whatsoever.

Damage caused by contact with or leakage, smell or evaporation from other goods or by the inflammable or explosive nature or insufficient package of other goods not to be considered as caused by improper or negligent stowage, even if in fact so caused."

59 Baltime,[9] clause 13: Responsibility and Exemption

"The Owners only to be responsible for delay in delivery of the Vessel or for delay during the currency of the Charter and for loss or damage to goods on board, if such delay or loss has been caused by want of due diligence on the part of the Owners or their Manager in making the Vessel seaworthy and fitted for the voyage or any other personal [10] act or omission or default of the Owners or their Manager.

[7] "Due diligence." See in this context *Carriage by Sea* [B.S.L. 2, §§ 257 *et seq.*]. That the shipowner, "Ship's Husband or Manager," has been *personally* diligent is not enough; due diligence must have been exercised by those employed to make the vessel seaworthy (*cf.* note 10 to § 59, *infra*).

[8] See note 10 to § 59, *supra*.

[9] See also Transtime.

[10] "Personal" in this context means what it says: the Owners are not liable under the clause simply on the ground of negligence by their servants or agents: see *The Brabant* [1967] 1 Q.B. 588 (McNair J.), distinguishing *The Muncaster Castle* (*Riverstone Meat* v. *Lancashire Shipping Co.*) [1961] A.C. 807; *Carriage by Sea*, 12th ed. [B.S.L. 2, § 259A]. *Cf.* note 7 to § 57, *supra*.

The Owners not to be responsible in any other case nor for damage or delay whatsoever and howsoever caused even if caused by the neglect or default of their servants. The Owners not to be liable for loss or damage arising or resulting from strikes, lock-outs or stoppage or restraint of labour (including the Master, Officers or Crew) whether partial or general.

The Charterers to be responsible for loss or damage caused to the Vessel or to the Owners by goods being loaded contrary to the terms of the Charter or by improper or careless bunkering or loading, stowing or discharging of goods or any other improper or negligent act on their part or that of their servants."

60 Nubaltwood,[11] clause 12: Exceptions

"The Owners shall not be liable for loss or damage arising or resulting from unseaworthiness unless caused by want of due diligence on the part of the Owners to make the Vessel seaworthy, and to secure that the Vessel be properly manned, equipped and supplied, and to make the holds and all other parts of the Vessel in which goods are carried fit and safe for their reception, carriage and preservation. The Owners shall not be responsible for loss or damage arising or resulting from: Act, neglect, or default of the Master, mariner, pilot, or the servants of the Owners in the navigation or in the management of the Vessel: Fire, unless caused by the actual fault or privity of the Owners: Perils, dangers and accidents of the sea or other navigable waters: Act of God: Act of war: Act of public enemies: Arrest or restraint of princes, rulers or people, or seizure under legal process: Quarantine restrictions: Act or omission of the Shippers or owners of the goods, their Agents or representatives: Strikes or lockouts or stoppage or restraint of labour from whatever cause, whether partial or general: Riots and civil commotions: Saving or attempting to save life or property at sea: Wastage in bulk or weight or any other loss or damage arising from inherent defect, quality, or vice of the goods: Insufficiency of packing: Insufficiency or inadequacy of marks: Latent defects not discoverable by due diligence: Any other cause arising without the actual fault or privity of the Owners, or without the fault or neglect of the Agents or servants of the Owners." [12]

[11] See also Baltwood.
[12] See note 7 to § 57, *supra*.

61 Polcon, clause 18: Act of God

"Throughout the Charter losses or damages whether in respect of goods carried or to be carried or in other respects arising or occasioned by the following causes shall be mutually excepted, *viz.*:

The Act of God, perils of the seas, fire on board, in hulk, craft, or on shore, barratry of the Master or crew, enemies, pirates, robbers, or thieves, arrests and restraints of princes, rulers and peoples, collisions and strandings, explosion, bursting of boilers, breakage of shafts, or any latent defect, even if existing at the beginning of the voyage in the hull, boilers, machinery, or appurtenances, negligence, default, or error of judgment of the pilot, Master or crew, or other servants of the Owners, in the management or navigation of the Vessel, unseaworthiness, provided that the Owners have exercised due diligence to make the Vessel seaworthy." [13]

62 Azoff,[14] clause 14

"The Act of God, Perils, Dangers and Accidents of the Sea or other Waters of what nature and kind soever; Fire from any cause on Land or on Water, Barratry of the Master and Crew, Enemies, Pirates and Robbers, Arrests and Restraints of Princes, Rulers and People, Explosion, Bursting of Boilers, Breakage of Shafts, or any Latent Defect in Hull and/or Machinery, Strandings, Collisions and all other Accidents of Navigation, and all Losses and Damages caused thereby are excepted, even when occasioned by negligence, default or error in judgment of the Pilot, Master, Mariners, or other Servants of the Shipowners, but, unless stranded, sunk, or burnt, nothing herein contained shall exempt the Shipowner from liability to pay for Damage to Cargo occasioned by bad stowage, by improper or insufficient Dunnage, or absence of customary Ventilation, or by improper opening of Valves, Sluices and Ports, or by causes other than those above excepted, and all the above exceptions are conditional on the Vessel being Seaworthy when she sails on the Voyage, but any Latent Defects in the Hull and/or Machinery shall not be considered unseaworthiness, provided the same do not result from want of due diligence of the Owners, or any of them, or by the Ship's Husband or Manager." [15]

63 Genorecon, clause 27: Exceptions clause

"Notwithstanding anything herein contained no absolute warranty

[13] See note 7 to § 57, *supra.*
[14] Approved documents 35, 36 and 37, *supra,* § 53.
[15] See note 7 to § 57, *supra.*

of seaworthiness is given or shall be implied. The Owners, in all matters arising under or affecting this contract, shall be entitled to the like rights and immunities as are contained in Article IV of the Hague Rules, dated Brussels, August 25, 1924, the term ' carrier ' in the said Article being taken to mean Owners."

64 Baltimore, clause 1

" It is also mutually agreed that the Carrier shall not be liable for loss or damage occasioned by causes beyond his control, by the perils of the seas or other waters, by fire from any cause wheresoever occurring, by barratry of the master or crew, by enemies, pirates or robbers, by arrest and restraint of Princes, rulers or people, by explosion, bursting of boilers, breakage of shafts or any latent defect in hull, machinery or appurtenances, by collisions, stranding or other accidents of navigation of whatsoever kind (even when occasioned by the negligence, default or error in judgment of the pilot, master, mariners, or other servants of the shipowner not resulting, however, in any case, from want of due diligence by the owners of the ship or any of them, or by the Ship's Husband or Manager)." [16]

65 P. and I. Clubs Oilbunkering Deviation Clause [17]

" The vessel in addition to all other liberties shall have liberty as part of the contract voyage and at any stage thereof to proceed to any port or ports whatsoever, whether such ports are on or off the direct and/or customary route or routes to the ports of loading or discharge named in this Charter and there take oil bunkers in any quantity in the discretion of Owners even to the full capacity of fuel tanks, deeptanks and any other compartment in which oil can be carried, whether such amount is or is not required for the chartered voyage."

66 " Himalaya " Clauses [18]

(A) *For inclusion in Passenger Tickets:*

" By accepting or receiving this ticket, each passenger agrees without prejudice to its other provisions and both on his or her behalf and on behalf of any person or child travelling with him or her or in his or her care that neither the Captain, Officers, Crew and other personnel of the vessel named in this ticket or of any vessel owned or in the service of the Company nor any person employed by the

[16] See note 7 to § 57, *supra*.
[17] Adopted in Baltimore.
[18] Approved by Baltic International. *Cf. supra*, § 9, clause 2, and see note thereto.

Company at any time before, during or after the contemplated voyage shall be liable in respect of anything he may negligently do or omit to do in the course of or in connection with his employment which shall cause loss, damage or injury (whether fatal or otherwise) to the person and/or property of such passenger, person or child as aforesaid. For the purpose of the agreement expressed in this clause, the Company shall be deemed to contract on behalf of and for the benefit of all persons who are or may be its servants or agents from time to time and all such persons shall to this extent be or be deemed to be parties to the Contract contained in or evidenced by this ticket."

"All limitations, exceptions and conditions herein contained as to the liability of the Carrier shall apply also to the liability, if any, of his agents, vessels, employees and other representatives, and also to the liability, if any, of the owners, vessels, agents, employees and other representatives of any substituted vessel."

(B) *For inclusion in Bills of Lading:*
Either

"It is hereby expressly agreed that no servant or agent of the carrier (including every independent contractor from time to time employed by the carrier) shall in any circumstances whatsoever be under any liability whatsoever to the Shipper, Consignee or Owner of the goods or to any holder of this Bill of Lading for any loss, damage or delay of whatsoever kind arising or resulting directly or indirectly from any act, neglect or default on his part while acting in the course of or in connection with his employment and, without prejudice to the generality of the foregoing provisions in this clause, every exemption, limitation, condition and liberty herein contained and every right, exemption from liability, defence and immunity of whatsoever nature applicable to the carrier or to which the carrier is entitled hereunder shall also be available and shall extend to protect every such servant or agent of the carrier acting as aforesaid and for the purpose of all the foregoing provisions of this clause the carrier is or shall be deemed to be acting as agent or trustee on behalf of and for the benefit of all persons who are or might be his servants or agents from time to time (including independent contractors as aforesaid) and all such persons shall to this extent be or be deemed to be parties to the contract in or evidenced by this Bill of Lading."
Or

"The terms of this Bill of Lading constitute the contract of carriage, which is between the shipper and the owner or demise charterer of the ship designated to carry the goods. It is understood and agreed that, other than said shipowner or demise charterer, no person, firm or corporation or other legal entity whatsoever (including the master, officers and crew of the vessel and all agents and independent contractors) is, or shall be deemed to be, liable with respect to the goods as carrier, bailee or otherwise howsoever in contract or in tort. If however, it shall be adjudged that any other than said shipowner or demise charterer is carrier or bailee of the goods or under any responsibility with respect thereto, all limitations of and exonerations from liability provided by law or by the terms hereof shall be available to such other."

"All limitations of liability and other provisions herein contained shall inure not only to the benefit of the Carrier, his agents, vessels, employees and other representatives but also to the benefit of any independent contractor performing services to the goods."

Signing bills of lading [19]

67 **Gencon, clause 9: Bills of Lading**

"The Captain to sign Bills of Lading at such rate of freight as presented without prejudice to this Charter-party, but should the freight by Bills of Lading amount to less than the total chartered freight the difference to be paid to the Captain in cash on signing Bills of Lading."

68 **Baltime,[20] clause 9: Master**

"The Master to prosecute all voyages with the utmost despatch and to render customary assistance with the Vessel's Crew. The Master to be under the orders of the Charterers as regards employment, agency, or other arrangements. The Charterers to indemnify the Owners against all consequences or liabilities arising from the Master, Officers or Agents signing Bills of Lading or other documents or otherwise complying with such orders, as well as from any irregularity in the Vessel's papers or for overcarrying goods. The Owners not to be responsible for shortage, mixture, marks, nor for number of pieces or packages, nor for damage to or claims on cargo caused by bad stowage or otherwise.

If the Charterers have reason to be dissatisfied with the conduct

[19] For meaning of these clauses, see *Carriage by Sea* [B.S.L. 2, §§ 426 *et seq.*].
[20] Transtime, clause 9 as in Baltime.

of the Master, Officers, or Engineers, the Owners, on receiving particulars of the complaint, promptly to investigate the matter, and, if necessary and practicable, to make a change in the appointments."

69 **Baltimore (as amended in type)**

"Captain to call at Charterers' or their Agents' Office, as requested, and sign Bills of Lading, as presented, without prejudice to this Charter Party."

70 **N.Y. Time 1, from clause 8**

"The Captain . . . is to sign Bills of Lading for cargo as presented, in conformity with Mate's or Tally Clerk's receipts."

71 **N.Y. Time 2 (added in type)**

"Captain also to sign Bills of Lading if requested to do so by the Charterers or their Agents, but this clause does not relieve Owners of responsibility for proper stowage and correct discharge of cargo."

Clause Paramount

72 **Baltic Conference Addendum 1946, Code Name: "Genvoy"**

"All bills of lading under this Charter shall contain the following clauses:

General paramount clause [21]

"This Bill of Lading shall have effect subject to the provisions of any legislation relating to the carriage of goods by sea which incorporates the rules relating to Bills of Lading contained in the international Convention, dated Brussels 25th August, 1924 and which is compulsorily applicable to the contract of carriage herein contained. Such legislation shall be deemed to be incorporated herein, but nothing herein contained shall be deemed a surrender by the Carrier of any of its rights or immunities or an increase of any of its responsibilities or liabilities thereunder. If any term of this Bill of Lading be repugnant to any extent to any legislation by this clause incorporated, such term shall be void to that extent but no further. Nothing in this Bill of Lading shall operate to limit or deprive the Carrier of any statutory protection or exemption from, or limitation of, liability."

[21] *Cf.* Clause in model bill of lading conditions, *supra*, § 8, clause 1.

Canadian clause paramount[22]

"All the terms, provisions and conditions of the Canadian Water Carriage of Goods Act 1936, and of the rules comprising the Schedule thereto, are, so far as applicable, to govern this contract contained in the Bills of Lading issued under this Charter Party and the shipowners are entitled to the benefit of all privileges, rights and immunities contained in such act and in the Schedule thereto as if the same were herein specifically set out. If anything herein contained be inconsistent with the said provisions, it shall to the extent of such inconsistency and no further be null and void."

War Clauses[23]

73 Gencon, general war clause

"If the nation under whose flag the vessel sails should be engaged in war and the safe navigation of the vessel should thereby be endangered either party to have the option of cancelling this contract, and if so cancelled, cargo already shipped shall be discharged either at the port of loading or, if the vessel has commenced the voyage, at the nearest safe place at the risk and expense of the Charterers or Cargo-Owners.

If owing to outbreak of hostilities the goods loaded or to be loaded under this contract or part of them become contraband of war whether absolute or conditional or liable to confiscation or detention according to international law or the proclamation of any of the belligerent powers each party to have the option of cancelling this contract as far as such goods are concerned, and contraband goods already loaded to be then discharged either at the port of loading, or if the voyage has already commenced, at the nearest safe place at the expense of the Cargo-Owners. Owners to have the right to fill up with other goods instead of the contraband.

Should any port where the vessel has to load under this Charter be blockaded the contract to be null and void with regard to the goods to be shipped at such port.

No Bills of Lading to be signed for any blockaded port, and if the port of destination be declared blockaded after Bills of Lading have been signed, Owners shall discharge the cargo either at the port of loading, against payment of the expenses of discharge, if the ship has not sailed thence, or, if sailed at any safe port on the way as ordered by Shippers or if no order is given at the nearest safe place against payment of full freight."

[22] Adopted in Baltimore in type.
[23] *Cf.* War clause in clause 10 of model bill of lading conditions, *supra*, § 8.

74 Baltime, clause 21 : War

"(A) The Vessel unless the consent of the Owners be first obtained not to be ordered nor continue to any place or on any voyage nor be used on any service which will bring her within a zone which is dangerous as the result of any actual or threatened act of war, war, hostilities, warlike operations, acts of piracy or of hostility or malicious damage against this or any other vessel or its cargo by any person, body or State whatsoever, revolution, civil war, civil commotion or the operation of international law, nor be exposed in any way to any risks or penalties whatsoever consequent upon the imposition of Sanctions, nor carry any goods that may in any way expose her to any risks of seizure, capture, penalties or any other interference of any kind whatsoever by the belligerent or fighting powers or parties or by any Government or Ruler.

(B) Should the Vessel approach or be brought or ordered within such zone, or be exposed in any way to the said risks, (1) the Owners to be entitled from time to time to insure their interests in the Vessel and/or hire against any of the risks likely to be involved thereby on such terms as they shall think fit, the Charterers to make a refund to the Owners of the premium on demand; and (2) notwithstanding the terms of clause 11 hire to be paid for all time lost including any loss owing to loss of or injury to the Master, Officers, or Crew or to the action of the Crew in refusing to proceed to such zone or to be exposed to such risks.

(C)[24] In the event of the wages of the Master, Officers and/or Crew or the cost of provisions and/or stores for deck and/or engine room and/or insurance premiums being increased by reason of or during the existence of any of the matters mentioned in section (A) the amount of any increase to be added to the hire and paid by the Charterers on production of the Owners' account therefor, such account being rendered monthly.

(D) The Vessel to have liberty to comply with any orders or directions as to departure, arrival, routes, ports of call, stoppages, destination, delivery or in any other wise whatsoever given by the Government of the nation under whose flag the Vessel sails or any other Government or any person (or body) acting or purporting to act with the authority of such Government or by any committee or person having under the terms of the war risks insurance on the Vessel the right to give any such orders or directions.

(E) In the event of the nation under whose flag the Vessel sails becoming involved in war, hostilities, warlike operations, revolution,

[24] Section C is optional and should be deleted unless agreed.

or civil commotion, both the Owners and the Charterers may cancel the Charter and, unless otherwise agreed, the Vessel to be re-delivered to the Owners at the port of destination or, if prevented through the provisions of section (A) from reaching or entering it, then at a near open and safe port at the Owners' option, after discharge of any cargo on board.

(F) If in compliance with the provisions of this clause anything is done or is not done, such not to be deemed a deviation."

75 Transtime, clause 21 : War

" The Vessel to have liberty to comply with any order or directions as to departure, arrival, routes, ports of call, stoppages, destination, delivery or in any other wise whatsoever given by the Government of the nation under whose flag the Vessel sails or any other Government or any person (or body) acting or purporting to act with the authority of such Government or by any committee or person having under the terms of the war risks insurance on the Vessel the right to give any such orders or directions.

In the event of the nation under whose flag the Vessel sails becoming involved in war, hostilities, warlike operations, revolution, or civil commotion, both the Owners and the Charterers may cancel the Charter and, unless otherwise agreed, the Vessel to be re-delivered to the Owners at the port of destination, after discharge of any cargo on board."

76 Genorecon, clause 32 :

War risks

" 1. The Master shall not be required or bound to sign Bills of Lading for any blockaded port or for any port which the Master or the Owners in his or their discretion consider dangerous or impossible to enter or reach.

2. (A) If any port of loading or of discharge named in this charterparty or to which the Vessel may properly be ordered pursuant to the terms of the Bills of Lading be blockaded, or

(B) if owing to any war, hostilities, warlike operations, civil war, civil commotions, revolutions, or the operation of international law (a) entry to any such port of loading or of discharge or the loading or discharge of cargo at any such port be considered by the Master or the Owners in his or their discretion dangerous or prohibited or (b) it be considered by the Master or the Owners in his or their discretion dangerous or impossible for the Vessel to reach any such port of loading or of discharge—the Charterers shall have the right to order

the Vessel or the cargo or such part of it as may be affected to be loaded or discharged at any other safe port of loading or of discharge within the range of loading or discharging ports respectively established under the provisions of the charterparty (provided such other port is not blockaded or that entry thereto or loading or discharge of cargo thereat is not in Master's or Owners' discretion dangerous or prohibited). If there is no range of loading ports agreed this charterparty to be considered cancelled for the voyage in question.
If part cargo has already been loaded and no range of loading ports being agreed, the Owners must proceed with same (freight payable on loaded quantity only) having liberty to complete with other cargo on the way for their own account.
If in respect of a port of discharge no orders be received from the Charterers within 48 hours after they or their Agents have received from the Owners a request for the nomination of a substitute port, the Owners shall then be at liberty to discharge the cargo at any safe port which they or the Master may in their or his discretion decide on (whether within the range of discharging ports established under the provisions of the charterparty or not) and such discharge shall be deemed to be due fulfilment of the contract or contracts of affreightment so far as cargo so discharged is concerned. In the event of the cargo being loaded or discharged at any such other port within the respective range of loading or discharging ports established under the provisions of the charterparty, the charterparty shall be read in respect of freight and all other conditions whatsoever as if the voyage performed were that originally designated. In the event, however, that the Vessel discharges the cargo at a port outside the range of discharging ports established under the provisions of the charterparty, freight shall be paid as for the voyage originally designated and all extra expenses involved in reaching the actual port of discharge and/or discharging the cargo thereat shall be paid by the Charterers or cargo owners. In this latter event the Owners shall have a lien on the cargo for all such extra expenses.

3. The Vessel shall have liberty to comply with any directions or recommendations as to departure, arrival, routes, ports of call, stoppages, destinations, zones, waters, delivery or in any otherwise whatsoever given by the government of the nation under whose flag the Vessel sails or any other government or local authority including any de facto government or local authority or by any person or body acting or purporting to act as or with the authority of any such government or authority or by any committee or person having under the terms of the war risks insurance on the Vessel the right to give any such directions or recommendations. If by reason of or

in compliance with any such directions or recommendations, anything is done or is not done such shall not be deemed a deviation.
If by reason of or in compliance with any such direction or recommendation the Vessel does not proceed to the port or ports of discharge originally designated or to which she may have been ordered pursuant to the terms of the Bills of Lading, the Vessel may proceed to any safe port of discharge which the Master or the Owners in his or their discretion may decide on and there discharge the cargo. Such discharge shall be deemed to be due fulfilment of the contract or contracts of affreightment and the Owners shall be entitled to freight as if discharge has been effected at the port or ports originally designated or to which the Vessel may have been ordered pursuant to the terms of the Bills of Lading. All extra expenses involved in reaching and discharging the cargo at any such other port of discharge shall be paid by the Charterers and/or cargo owners and the Owners shall have a lien on the cargo for freight and all such expenses.

Clause 33, 'War clause'

(a) In the event of war involving two or more of the following countries, namely

....

....

....

or the country of the flag of the Vessel, either party to have the right to cancel this charterparty.

(b) If a world war breaks out or a situation arises that is similar to a world war, either party shall have the right to cancel this charterparty."

Note: (a) and (b) are alternatives and the one not agreed upon is to be deleted.

77 **Chamber of Shipping war risks clause 1 and 2** [25]

" 1. No Bills of Lading to be signed for any blockaded port and if the port of discharge be declared blockaded after Bills of Lading have been signed, or if the port to which the ship has been ordered to discharge either on signing Bills of Lading or thereafter be one to which the ship is or shall be prohibited from going by the Government of the Nation under whose flag the ship sails or by any other Government, the Owner shall discharge the cargo at any other port covered by this Charter Party as ordered by the Charterers (provided such other port is not a blockaded or prohibited port as above

[25] Issued by the Chamber of Shipping of the United Kingdom.

mentioned) and shall be entitled to freight as if the ship had discharged at the port or ports of discharge to which she was originally ordered.

2. The ship shall have liberty to comply with any orders or directions as to departure, arrival, routes, ports of call, stoppages, destination, delivery or otherwise howsoever given by the Government of the Nation under whose flag the vessel sails or any department thereof, or by any other Government or any department thereof, or any person acting or purporting to act with the authority of such Government or of any department thereof, or by any committee or person having, under the terms of the War Risks Insurance on the ship, the right to give such orders or directions and if by reason of and in compliance with any such orders or directions anything is done or is not done, the same shall not be deemed a deviation, and delivery in accordance with such orders or directions shall be in fulfilment of the Contract voyage and the freight shall be payable accordingly."

78 **Nubaltwood, clause 14: War**

"(*a*) If the nation under whose flag the Vessel sails shall be at war, whereby the free navigation of the Vessel is endangered, or if prohibition of export or blockade prevent the loading or completion of cargo, this Charter shall be cancelled forthwith at the last outward port or at any subsequent period when the difficulty may arise.

(*b*) The Vessel shall have liberty to comply with any orders or directions as to departure, arrival, routes, ports of call, stoppages, destination or otherwise howsoever given by the Government of the nation under whose flag the Vessel sails or any department thereof, or any person acting or purporting to act with the authority of such Government or of any department thereof, or by any Committee or person having, under the terms of the War Risks Insurance on the Vessel, the right to give such orders or directions and if by reason of and in compliance with any such orders or directions anything is done or is not done, the same shall not be deemed a deviation and delivery in accordance with such orders or directions shall be a fulfilment of the contract voyage and the freight shall be payable accordingly."

Ferticon, clause 14: War

"(1) No Bills of Lading to be signed for any blockaded port and if the port of discharge be declared blockaded after Bills of Lading have been signed, or if the port to which the ship has been ordered to discharge either on signing Bills of Lading or thereafter be one to which the ship is or shall be prohibited from going by the Government of the Nation under whose flag the ship sails or the United Kingdom Government or by any other Government, the owner shall discharge the cargo at any other port covered by this charter party as ordered by the Charterers (provided such other port is not a blockaded or prohibited port as above mentioned) and shall be entitled to freight as if the ship had discharged at the port or ports of discharge to which she was originally ordered.

(2) The ship shall have liberty to comply with any orders or directions as to departure, arrival, routes, ports of call, stoppages, destination, delivery or otherwise howsoever given by the Government of the Nation under whose flag the vessel sails or the United Kingdom Government or any department thereof, or any person acting or purporting to act with the authority of such Government or of any department thereof, or by any committee or person having, under the terms of the War Risks Insurance on the ship, the right to give such orders or directions and if by reason of and in compliance with any such orders or directions anything is done or is not done, the same shall not be deemed a deviation, and delivery in accordance with such orders or directions shall be a fulfilment of the contract voyage and the freight shall be payable accordingly."

80 Austwheat, clause 26: War Risks Clauses

"(A) If the nation under whose flag the Vessel sails shall be at war whereby the free navigation of the Vessel is endangered, or in case of blockade of or prohibition of export from the loading port, this charter shall be null and void at the last outward port of delivery or at any subsequent period when the difficulty may arise, previous to cargo being shipped.

(B) No Bills of Lading to be signed for any blockaded port and if the port of discharge be declared blockaded after Bills of Lading have been signed, or if the port to which the ship has been ordered to discharge either on signing Bills of Lading or thereafter be one to which the ship is or shall be prohibited from going by the Government of the Nation under whose flag the ship sails or by any other Government, the Owner shall discharge the cargo at any other port covered by this Charterparty as ordered by the Charterers (Provided such other port is not a blockaded or prohibited port as above mentioned) and shall be entitled to freight as if the ship had discharged at the port or ports of discharge to which she was originally ordered.

(C) The ship shall have liberty to comply with any orders or directions as to departure, arrival, routes, ports of call, stoppages, destination, delivery or otherwise howsoever given by the Government of the Nation under whose flag the vessel sails or any department thereof, or by any other Government or any department thereof, or any person acting or purporting to act with the authority of such Government or of any department thereof, or by any committee or person having, under the terms of the War Risks Insurance on the ship, the right to give such orders or directions and if by reason of and in compliance with any such orders or directions anything is done or is not done, the same shall not be deemed a deviation, and delivery in accordance with such orders or directions shall be a fulfilment or the contract voyage and the freight shall be payable accordingly."

80a Saigon, clause 40: War Risks

"(1) No Bills of Lading to be signed for any blockaded port and if the port of discharge be declared blockaded after Bills of Lading have been signed, or if the port to which the ship has been ordered to discharge either on signing Bills of Lading or thereafter be one to which the ship is or shall be prohibited from going by the Government of the Nation under whose flag the ship sails or by any other Government, the owner shall discharge the cargo at any other port covered by this Charter-party as ordered by the Charterers (provided such other port is not a blockaded or prohibited port as above mentioned) and shall be entitled to freight as if the ship had discharged at the port or ports of discharge to which she was originally ordered.

(2) The ship shall have liberty to comply with any orders or directions as to departure, arrival, routes, ports of call, stoppages, destination, delivery or otherwise howsoever given by the Government of the Nation under whose flag the vessel sails or any department thereof, or any person acting or purporting to act with the authority of such Government or of any department thereof, or by any committee or person having, under the terms of the War Risks Insurance on the ship, the right to give such orders or directions and if by reason of and in compliance with any such orders or directions anything is done or is not done, the same shall not be deemed a deviation, and delivery in accordance with such orders or directions shall be a fulfilment of the contract voyage and the freight shall be payable accordingly."

81 N.Y. Time 1, war risks clause [26]

"(1) No Bills of Lading to be signed for any blockaded port and

[26] Baltimore, war risks clause is in similar terms to those of the N.Y. Time 1 clause.

if the port of discharge be declared blockaded after Bills of Lading have been signed, or if the port to which the ship has been ordered to discharge either on signing Bills of Lading or thereafter be one to which the ship is or shall be prohibited from going by the Government of the Nation under whose flag the ship sails or by any other Government, the owner shall discharge the cargo at any other port covered by this Charterparty as ordered by the Charterers (provided such other port is not a blockaded or prohibited port as above mentioned) and shall be entitled to freight as if the ship had discharged at the port or ports of discharge to which she was originally ordered.

(2) The ship shall have liberty to comply with any orders or directions as to departure, arrival, routes, ports of call, stoppages, destination, delivery or otherwise howsoever given by the Government of the Nation under whose flag the vessel sails or any department thereof, or by any other Government or any department thereof, or any person acting or purporting to act with the authority of such Government or of any department thereof, or by any committee or person having, under the terms of the War Risks Insurance on the ship, the right to give such orders or directions and if by reason of and in compliance with any such orders or directions anything is done or is not done, the same shall not be deemed a deviation, and delivery in accordance with such orders or directions shall be a fulfilment of the contract voyage and the freight shall be payable accordingly."

Strike Clauses

82 Baltic Conference Special Strike Clause 1936 [27]

" Notwithstanding any provisions in this charterparty to the contrary or by way of modification, if the vessel shall suffer any loss of time through being delayed in or prevented from (a) giving notice of readiness (b) reaching her place of loading or discharge or (c) loading or discharging her cargo, as the direct or indirect result of any strike (partial or otherwise), lockout, dispute with workmen, riot, civil commotion, military restraint, or other like matter, the charterers shall be liable therefor and shall pay damages to the owners in respect of it. Such damages, if not in the form of demurrage, shall be assessed on the basis of the rate payable for demurrage."

83 Baltic Conference Strike Clause (Suspension of Voyage), 1951

" In the event of a strike or lockout at the port of discharge which might in the opinion of the Master or Shipowners delay the Vessel

[27] As far as ordinary strike clauses are concerned owners are recommended to use the strike clauses contained in the Gencon, Propcon or Contwood Charters.

berthing or the discharge or delivery of the cargo, the Shipowners shall have the right to suspend the voyage, should such strike or lockout still exist when the Vessel is ready to proceed to or during the voyage to the loading port and to make an intermediate voyage or voyages until the strike or lockout has ended. Should the Shipowners elect to suspend the voyage, they shall give to the Charterers not less than 5 days' written notice of the date on which they expect the Vessel to be available at the loading port to perform the voyage under this Charter. The Charterers shall within 36 hours of receipt of this notice declare whether they desire to cancel the Charter or whether the Vessel is to be brought to the loading port and fulfil the Charter after the strike or lockout has ended and the Vessel has performed her intermediate voyage or voyages. From 2 p.m. on Saturday to 9 a.m. on Monday shall be excluded from the said period of 36 hours."

[The next paragraph is 85]

85 Propcon, clause 8: Strikes, etc.[28]

" (*a*) If the cargo cannot be loaded and/or discharged by reason of a strike or lock-out of any class of workmen essential to the loading and/or discharge of the cargo, or by reason of epidemics, the time for loading and/or discharging shall not count during the continuance of such strike or lock-out or epidemic—except as provided under (*e*)—(a strike or lock-out of the Shippers' and/or Consignees' men only shall not exonerate them from any demurrage for which they may be liable under the Charter if by the use of reasonable diligence they could have obtained other suitable labour), and in case of any delay by reason of the before-mentioned causes, no claim for damages shall be made by the Shippers, the Consignees of the cargo, the Owners of the Vessel, or by any other party under the Charter.

(*b*) If there exist or notice be given of a strike or lock-out interfering with the loading of the cargo at the loading port or ports when the Vessel be ready to proceed to the first loading port from her last port of call (whether a discharging port or not) the Owners shall, after the Vessel has waited three consecutive calendar days, have the option, which shall be declared by telegram to the Charterers, of sending the Vessel to the loading port or cancelling the Charter forthwith.

(*c*) If a strike or lock-out affecting the loading of the cargo exist at the loading port on the Vessel's arrival there or commence before

[28] Contwood, clause 9, is in similar terms.

any cargo has been loaded and continue for six consecutive calendar days from the time of the Vessel's arrival, the Charter shall be cancelled forthwith.

(*d*) If a strike or lock-out occur at the loading port after part cargo has been loaded, and continue for six consecutive calendar days, the Vessel may proceed with the cargo then aboard, having liberty to fill up for the Vessel's benefit at any other port or ports either for the same destination or for any other port or ports whether any of such ports be in the course of the chartered voyage or not, and the Owners shall advise the Charterers by telegram that the Vessel has left the port.

(*e*) If a strike or lock-out, likely to affect the discharge, exist or notice thereof has been given before or on the arrival of the Vessel at or off the discharging port or if a strike or lock-out affecting the discharge commence or notice thereof be given later, the Owners or Master may ask the Charterers or their Agents to declare within twelve business hours *either* that they agree to reckon the laydays as if there were no strike or lock-out, *or* that they order the Vessel to a safe adjacent port where she can safely discharge without risk of being detained by strike or lock-out. On delivery of the cargo at such port all conditions of the Charter and of the Bills of Lading shall apply and the Vessel shall receive the same freight as if discharged at the original port of destination, except that if the additional sailing distance exceed 100 nautical miles the freight on the cargo delivered at the substituted port shall be increased in proportion, and that the Charterers shall refund to the Owners any additional port charges and pilotages incurred."

86 Nubaltwood, clause 9: Strikes, etc.

"(*a*) If the cargo cannot be loaded and/or discharged by reason of a strike or lock-out of any class of workmen essential to the loading and/or discharge of the cargo, or by reason of epidemics, the time for loading and/or discharge shall not count during the continuance of such strike or lock-out or epidemic, and in case of any delay by reason of the before-mentioned causes, no claim for damages shall be made by the Shipper, the Consignees of the cargo, the Owners of the Vessel or by any other party under this Charter.

(*b*) If within seven days of the Vessel's expected readiness to load there is a strike or lock-out interfering with the loading of cargo at the loading port or ports and the Vessel is ready to proceed to the first loading port from her last outward port of discharge or from her bunkering port if in ballast the Owners shall, after the Vessel has waited three consecutive calendar days, have the option, which shall be declared by telegram to the Charterers, of sending the Vessel to the loading port or cancelling the Charter forthwith.

(*c*) If before any cargo has been loaded the Vessel be delayed at the loading port by a strike for six consecutive calendar days either the Owners or Charterers shall thereafter be entitled by notice in writing to cancel the Charter.

(*d*) If a strike or lock-out occurs at the loading port after part cargo has been loaded and continues for six consecutive calendar days, the Vessel may proceed with the cargo then on board, having liberty to fill up for the Vessel's benefit at any other port or ports either for the same destination or for any other port or ports whether any of such ports be in the course of the chartered voyage or not, and the Owners shall advise the Charterers by telegram that the Vessel has left the port. In case of leaving with part cargo the Vessel shall deliver such part cargo at its port of delivery or shall, without undue delay, forward it thereto and there deliver it in accordance with this Charter."

87 Gencon, general strike clause [29]

"Neither Charterers nor Owners shall be responsible for the consequences of any strikes or lock-outs preventing or delaying the fulfilment of any obligations under this contract.

If there is a strike or lock-out affecting the loading of the cargo, or any part of it, when vessel is ready to proceed from her last port or at any time during the voyage to the port or ports of loading or after her arrival there, Captain or Owners may ask Charterers to declare, that they agree to reckon the laydays as if there were no strike or lock-out. Unless Charterers have given such declaration in writing (by telegram, if necessary) within 24 hours, Owners shall have the option of cancelling this contract. If part cargo has already been loaded, Owners must proceed with same (freight payable on loaded quantity only), having liberty to complete with other cargo on the way for their own account.

If there is a strike or lock-out affecting the discharge of the cargo on or after vessel's arrival at or off port of discharge and same has not been settled within 48 hours, Receivers shall have the option of keeping vessel waiting until such strike or lock-out is at an end against paying half demurrage [30] after expiration of the time provided for discharging, or of ordering the vessel to a safe port where she can safely discharge without risk of being detained by strike or lock-out. Such orders to be given within 48 hours after Captain or Owners have given notice to Charterers of the strike or lock-out affecting the

[29] See also Britcont, clause 8; Genorecon, clause 35.
[30] See *The Onisilos* [1971] 2 Q.B. 500.

discharge. On delivery of the cargo at such port, all conditions of this Charterparty and of the Bill of Lading shall apply and vessel shall receive the same freight as if she had discharged at the original port of destination, except that if the distance of the substituted port exceeds 100 nautical miles, the freight on the cargo delivered at the substituted port to be increased in proportion."

88 Ferticon, clause 8: Strikes, etc.

"Neither the Charterers nor the Shipowners shall be responsible for the consequences of any strikes or lock-outs preventing or delaying the fulfilment of any obligations under this charter unless the Vessel is already on demurrage, in which case demurrage shall accrue notwithstanding such strikes or lock-out. A strike or lock-out of the Shipper's or Receiver's men shall not prevent demurrage accruing if by the use of reasonable diligence he could have obtained other suitable labour.

If there is a strike or lock-out which in the opinion of the Master or Shipowners may affect the loading of the cargo, or any part of it, when the Vessel is ready to proceed from her last port or at any time during the voyage to the port or ports of loading or after her arrival there, the Master or Shipowners may ask the Charterers to declare that they agree to reckon the laydays as if there were no strike or lock-out. Unless such declaration in writing (by telegram, if necessary) is received by the Shipowners within 24 hours (Sundays and holidays excepted) after Charterers receive the request the Shipowners shall have the option of cancelling this charter. If part cargo has already been loaded, the Vessel may proceed with same (freight payable on loaded quantity only) having liberty to complete with other cargo for the Shipowners' account at any port for any port or ports whether such ports are in the course of the chartered voyage or not.

In the event of a strike or lock-out at the port of discharge which might in the opinion of the Master or Shipowners delay the Vessel berthing or the discharge or delivery of the cargo, the Shipowners shall have the right to suspend the voyage should such strike still exist when the Vessel is ready at or off the loading port outside the radius of port dues and to make an intermediate coasting voyage or voyages until the strike or lock-out has ended. Should the Shipowners elect to suspend the voyage they shall give to the Charterers not less than 5 days' written notice of the date on which they expect the Vessel to be available at the loading port to perform the voyage under this charter. The Charterers shall within 36 hours of receipt of this notice declare whether they desire to cancel the charter or whether the Vessel is to be brought to the loading port and fulfil the charter. From 2 p.m. on Saturday to 9 a.m. on Monday shall be excluded from the said period of 36 hours."

89 Centrocon, strike clause (amended) [31]

"If the cargo cannot be loaded by reason of Riots, Civil Commotions or of a Strike or Lock-out of any class of workmen, essential to the loading of the cargo, or by reason of obstructions or stoppages beyond the control of the Charterers caused by Riots, Civil Commotions or a strike or Lock-out on the Railways, or in Docks or other loading places, or if the cargo cannot be discharged by reason of Riots, Civil Commotions, or of a Strike or Lock-out of any class of workmen essential to the discharge, the time for loading or discharging, as the case may be, shall not count during the continuance of such causes, provided that a strike or Lock-out of the Shippers' and/or Receivers' men shall not prevent demurrage accruing if by the use of reasonable diligence they could have obtained other suitable labour at rates current before the Strike or Lock-out. In case of any delay by reason of the before mentioned causes, no claim for damages or demurrage, shall be made by the Charterers, Receivers of the cargo, or Owners of the Steamer. For the purposes, however, of settling despatch rebate accounts, any time lost by the steamer through any of the above causes shall be counted as time used in loading or discharging as the case may be."

90 Centrocon, clause 30: Strikes [32]

"If the Cargo cannot be loaded by reason of Riots, Civil Commotions or of a Strike or Lock-out of any class of workmen essential to the loading of the Cargo, or by reason of obstructions or stoppages beyond the control of the Charterers on the Railways, or in the Docks, or other loading places, or if the Cargo cannot be discharged by reason of Riots, Civil Commotions, or of a Strike or Lock-out of any class of workmen essential to the discharge, the time for loading or discharging, as the case may be, shall not count during the continuance of such causes, provided that a Strike or Lock-out of the Shippers' and/or Receivers' men shall not prevent demurrage accruing if by the use of reasonable diligence they could have obtained other suitable labour at rates current before the Strike or Lock-out. In case of any delay by reason of the before-mentioned causes, no claim for damages or demurrage, shall be made by the Charterers,

[31] Baltimore, typed clause.
[32] Original Centrocon clause.

Receivers of the Cargo, or Owners of the Steamer. For the purpose, however, of settling despatch money accounts, any time lost by the Steamer through any of the above causes shall be counted as time used in loading."

Ice Clauses

91 Gencon, general ice clause

Port of loading

" (a) In the event of the loading port being inaccessible by reason of ice when vessel is ready to proceed from her last port or at any time during the voyage or on vessel's arrival or in case frost sets in after vessel's arrival, the Captain for fear of being frozen in is at liberty to leave without cargo, and this Charter shall be null and void.

(b) If during loading the Captain, for fear of vessel being frozen in, deems it advisable to leave, he has liberty to do so with what cargo he has on board and to proceed to any other port or ports with option of completing cargo for Owners' benefit for any port or ports including port of discharge. Any part cargo thus loaded under this Charter to be forwarded to destination at vessel's expense but against payment of freight, provided that no extra expenses be thereby caused to the Receivers, freight being paid on quantity delivered (in proportion if lumpsum), all other conditions as per Charter.

(c) In case of more than one loading port, and if one or more of the ports are closed by ice, the Captain or Owners to be at liberty either to load the part cargo at the open port and fill up elsewhere for their own account as under section (b) or to declare the Charter null and void unless Charterers agree to load full cargo at the open port.

(d) This Ice Clause not to apply in the Spring.

Port of discharge

(a) Should ice (except in the spring) prevent vessel from reaching port of discharge Receivers shall have the option of keeping vessel waiting until the re-opening of navigation and paying demurrage, or of ordering the vessel to a safe and immediately accessible port where she can safely discharge without risk of detention by ice. Such orders to be given within 48 hours after Captain or Owners have given notice to Charterers of the impossibility of reaching port of destination.

(b) If during discharging the Captain for fear of vessel being frozen in deems it advisable to leave, he has liberty to do so with what cargo he has on board and to proceed to the nearest accessible port where she can safely discharge.

(c) On delivery of the cargo at such port, all conditions of the Bill of Lading shall apply and vessel shall receive the same freight as if she had discharged at the original port of destination, except that if the distance of the substituted port exceeds 100 nautical miles, the freight on the cargo delivered at the substituted port to be increased in proportion."

92 Baltime, clause 15: Excluded Ports: Ice

"The Vessel not to be ordered to nor bound to enter: (a) any place where fever or epidemics are prevalent or to which the Master, Officers and Crew by law are not bound to follow the Vessel (b) any ice-bound place or any place where lights, lightships, marks and buoys are or are likely to be withdrawn by reason of ice on the Vessel's arrival or where there is risk that ordinarily the vessel will not be able on account of ice to reach the place or to get out after having completed loading or discharging. The Vessel not to be obliged to force ice. If on account of ice the Master considers it dangerous to remain at the loading or discharging place for fear of the Vessel being frozen in and/or damaged, he has liberty to sail to a convenient open place and await the Charterers' fresh instructions.

Unforeseen detention through any of above causes to be for the Charterers' account."

93 Nubaltwood, clause 8: Ice

"(*a*) Where the charter provides for one loading port only, if when the Vessel is ready to proceed from her last port of call (whether a discharging port or not) or at any time during the voyage to the loading port the Owners be informed by the Shippers whose name first appears in the margin of this Charter and the Owners' agents at port of loading that in their opinion the port is not accessible and/or the shipment of the goods is not practicable by reason of ice, the Charter shall be cancelled forthwith and the Owners shall advise the Charterers by telegram.

(*b*) Where the Charter provides for one loading port only, if upon Vessel's arrival off the port or so near thereunto as she can get, ice, in the opinion of the Master, prevents the Vessel reaching or entering the port of loading, the Charter shall be cancelled forthwith and the Owners shall advise the Charterers by telegram.

If after arrival, the Master, for fear of the Vessel being frozen in, deems it advisable to sail, he shall be at liberty to leave either without cargo, in which case the Charter shall be cancelled forthwith and the Master shall notify the Charterers by telegram accordingly, or with part cargo and to fill up for the Vessel's benefit at any port for any port or ports whether such ports be in the course of the chartered voyage or not; but in case of leaving with part cargo the Vessel shall deliver such part cargo at its port of delivery or shall, without undue delay, forward it thereto and there deliver it in accordance with this Charter.

(*c*) Where the Charter provides for more than one loading port, if, in the opinion of the Master, the first loading port be inaccessible, or, if after arrival at any loading port the Master, for fear of the Vessel being frozen in, deems it advisable to sail without cargo or with a part cargo, the Vessel shall proceed in rotation to the next loading port named in the Charter which in the opinion of the Master is accessible. On arrival at such loading port the Charterers shall declare forthwith in writing, to the Master or Owners' Agents at such port, either to cancel the Charter to the extent to which it is unfulfilled or to load a full and complete cargo at the loading ports named in the Charter which, in the opinion of the Master, are accessible, completing, if necessary, at any other safe open port on the same coast and in the same country. In the event of the Charterers declaring to cancel the Charter to the extent to which it is unfulfilled the Vessel shall nevertheless have the right to fill up for Vessel's benefit at any port for any port or ports, whether in the course of the Chartered voyage or not, but shall without undue delay deliver any part cargo which had previously been loaded under this Charter at its port of delivery or forward it thereto and there deliver it in accordance with this Charter. If all ports be in the opinion of the Master inaccessible the Charter shall forthwith be cancelled and the Owners shall advise the Charterers by telegram.

(*d*) Clauses 8 (*a*), (*b*) and (*c*) shall not apply in the Spring.

(*e*) The Charterers' liability to supply cargo and to load shall not commence earlier than 48 hours after the navigation of lighters between the Shipper's wharf and/or quay and the Vessel is unimpeded by ice."

94 Centrocon, clause 28

"Should the Steamer be ordered to a Port of Discharge on the Continent inaccessible by reason of Ice, the Master shall have the option of waiting until the port is again open, or of proceeding to the nearest safe open port or roadstead (telegraphing his arrival there to Consignees), where he shall receive fresh orders for an open and accessible Port of Discharge, in the United Kingdom or Continent as above, within 24 hours after arrival, or lay days to count. If so ordered, the Steamer shall receive the same freight as if she had discharged at the port to which she was originally ordered, but if ordered to a port more than 100 nautical miles distant from such open port or roadstead, the freight shall be increased by one shilling per English ton as above. In no case shall the Steamer be ordered from a Port of Call in the United Kingdom to an Ice-bound port."

Arbitration Clauses: Centrocon Arbitration Clause

95 **Centrocon, clause 39**

" All disputes from time to time arising out of this contract shall, unless the parties agree forthwith on a single Arbitrator, be referred to the final arbitrament of two Arbitrators carrying on business in London who shall be Members of the Baltic and engaged in the Shipping and/or Grain Trades, one to be appointed by each of the parties, with power to such Arbitrators to appoint an Umpire. Any claim must be made in writing and Claimant's Arbitrator appointed within three months of final discharge and where this provision is not complied with the claim shall be deemed to be waived and absolutely barred. No award shall be questioned or invalidated on the ground that any of the Arbitrators is not qualified as above, unless objection to his acting be taken before the award is made." [32a]

Note on Centrocon Arbitration Clause

96 Centrocon, 1914, was designed as a voyage charter from the Argentine to the United Kingdom or near by in Europe. In such circumstances, clause 39 made commercial sense. Claims might reasonably be made, and an arbitrator appointed, within three months of final discharge.

The clause has now been incorporated, usually in typed clauses, in innumerable charterparties providing for maritime arbitration in London, since many approved forms of charterparty contain no arbitration clause. The Centrocon clause, however, is often criticised.[33]

97 *Effect of Clause*

(1) The clause bars a claim [34] (whether by action or in arbitration), if the claim is not duly made in time, even though the cause of action giving rise to the claim had not come to the knowledge of the claimant until too late for him to comply with the clause.[35]

(2) The clause bars a claim unless within three months of final discharge (i) the designated arbitrator is asked whether he is willing to act in the

[32a] " Dispute " includes a claim for a general average contribution: *The Evje* [1972] 2 Lloyd's Rep. 129. Under a consecutive voyage charterparty, " final discharge " means final discharge under each voyage: *The Simonburn* [1972] 2 Lloyd's Rep. 355.

[33] See *e.g. per* Mr. R. A. H. Clyde, Maritime Arbitrator, *Shipowners* [B.S.L. 13, § 789]. See also Baltic and International Maritime Conference Annual Report, 1964–1965, pp. 82, 83; " *Centrocon* Arbitration Clause. Not to be used."

[34] Subject to claims in court on the ground of unseaworthiness or negligence: see (4), *infra*.

[35] *The Himmerland* [1965] 2 Lloyd's Rep. 353 (Mocatta J.).

particular matter; (ii) he consents so to act; and (iii) his name and appointment is communicated to the other side.[36]

(3) *Semble*, once the claim has properly been made in accordance with the clause, it matters not that the claimant later changes the grounds upon which he originally made the claim. He is not time-barred by so doing.[37]

(4) The clause does not bar a claim *at law* [38] against the shipowners on the ground of unseaworthiness (whether the obligation of seaworthiness is express or implied) [39]: see Carver, 12th ed. [B.S.L. 2, § § 129, 176]. The clause is not one of procedure only,[40] but is in effect an exceptions clause. Nor, *semble*, would the clause bar such a claim on the ground of negligence.[41]

(5) As to extension of time for undue hardship (Arbitration Act, 1950, s. 27) see *Russell on Arbitration*; *Liberian Shipping Corporation* v. *King* (*The Pegasus*).[42]

(6) However, in so far as the clause states that an arbitrator must be appointed by a claimant within three months of the final discharge of the goods, it is *void* if incorporated into a bill of lading to which the Hague Rules apply because it is in conflict with Article III, rule 6, of the Rules which provides a year for suit to be brought against the carrier or the ship.[42a]

Variations of Centrocon Arbitration Clause, Extending Time-barring Period

98 Nubaltwood, clause 30: twelve month clause

" Any dispute arising out of this Charter or any Bill of Lading issued hereunder shall be referred to arbitration in accordance with the provisions of the Arbitration Act 1950, or any statutory modification or re-enactment thereof for the time being in force except in cases where the Charterer or Receiver is resident or carries on business in Scotland, then such disputes shall be referred to arbitration in accordance with the provisions of the Scottish Arbitration Act 1894, or any statutory modification or re-enactment thereof for the time being in force and Arbitrators shall have power to assess and award damages. All arbitrations, except those to which the Scottish Arbitration Act applies, shall in default of agreement between the parties to the contrary, be held in London and arbitrations to which the Scottish Arbitration Act 1894 applies shall in default of agreement between the parties be held at . . . .

36 *Tradax Export* v. *Volkswagenwerk A.G.* [1970] 1 Q.B. 537 (C.A.).

37 See *Rendal* v. *Arcos*, Carver [B.S.L. 2, § 195]; *Panchaud Frères S.A.* v. *Etablissements General Grain Company* [1969] 2 Lloyd's Rep. 109, 126 (Roskill J.).

38 Though, if out of time, the claimant is barred from arbitrating on this ground: *Ford* v. *Compagnie Furness* [1922] 2 K.B. 797.

39 *Atlantic Shipping* v. *Dreyfus* [1922] 2 A.C. 250.

40 See *ibid.*, *per* Lord Dunedin and Lord Sumner.

41 Since both the undertakings of seaworthiness and due care are overriding obligations: see *Carriage by Sea* [B.S.L. 2, § 100].

42 [1967] 2 Q.B. 86 (C.A.). See also *Luis de Ridder* v. *Nivose Societa di Navigazione* (1935) 53 Ll.L.R. 21 (undue hardship allowed); *Bulgaris* v. *La Plata* (1947) 80 Ll.L.R. 455 (ditto); *Jajasan* v. *Compania etc. Geamar* [1953] 1 Lloyd's Rep. 499 (undue hardship disallowed); *Steamship Co. of 1912* v. *Anglo-American Grain* [1958] 2 Lloyd's Rep. 341 (allowed); *Sigalas* v. *Man Moham Singh* [1958] 2 Lloyd's Rep. 298 (disallowed).

42a *The Ion* [1971] 1 Lloyd's Rep. 541.

The dispute shall be referred to a sole arbitrator to be agreed between the parties or failing such agreement to two arbitrators one to be appointed by each of the parties with power to appoint an Umpire. The Arbitrators and Umpire shall be commercial men.[43]

All claims must be made in writing and the Claimant's Arbitrator must be appointed within twelve months of the date of final discharge or of the date when the goods should have been so discharged otherwise the claim shall be deemed waived and absolutely barred."

99 Austral, clause 36: six month clause

"Any dispute arising under this charter about events happening in Australia shall, unless the parties agree forthwith upon a single Arbitrator, be settled by arbitration at the capital city of the Australian State in which the Vessel loads, each party appointing an Arbitrator and the two Arbitrators in the event of disagreement appointing an Umpire whose decision shall be final and binding upon both parties hereto. For the purpose of enforcing any award this agreement may be made a Rule of Court.

Any dispute arising under this charter, other than provided for in the preceding clause shall be settled in accordance with the provisions of the Arbitration Act 1950 in London, each party appointing an Arbitrator, and the two Arbitrators in the event of disagreement appointing an Umpire whose decision shall be final and binding upon both parties hereto.

The Arbitrators and Umpire shall be commercial men.

Any claim must be made in writing and claimant's Arbitrator appointed within six months of the Vessel's arrival at final port of discharge, otherwise all claims shall be deemed to be waived."

100 Austwheat, clause 34: six month clause

"Any dispute arising under this charter or any Bill of Lading issued hereunder about events happening in Australia shall, unless the parties agree forthwith upon a single Arbitrator, be settled by arbitration at the capital city of the Australian State in which the Vessel loads, each party appointing an Arbitrator and the two Arbitrators in the event of disagreement appointing an Umpire whose decision shall be final and binding upon both parties hereto. For the purpose of enforcing any award this agreement may be made a Rule of Court.

Any dispute arising under this charter or any Bill of Lading issued hereunder other than provided for in the preceding clause shall be

[43] "Commercial men" does not include members of the Commercial Bar, *The Bede* [1967] 2 Lloyd's Rep. 261.

settled in accordance with the provisions of the Arbitration Act 1950 in London, each party appointing an Arbitrator, and the two Arbitrators in the event of disagreement appointing an Umpire whose decision shall be final and binding upon both parties hereto.

The Arbitrators and Umpire shall be commercial men normally engaged in the Shipping Industry.

Any claim must be made in writing and claimant's Arbitrator appointed within six months of the Vessel's arrival at final port of discharge, otherwise all claims shall be deemed to be waived."

101 Synacomex, six month clause

All charterparties made for fixtures made on or after January 1, 1967, shall incorporate the following clause:

> "Any dispute arising out of the present contract shall be referred to arbitration of 'Chambre Arbitrale Maritime,' 73 Boulevard Haussmann, Paris (8[e]). The decision rendered according to the rules of Chambre Arbitrale Maritime shall be final and binding upon both parties. The right of both parties to refer any dispute to arbitration ceases six months after date of completion of discharge or, in the case of nonperformance, six months after the cancelling date as *per* clause 8. Where this provision is not complied with, the claim shall be deemed to be waived and absolutely barred."

Arbitration Clauses without Time Bar

102 Baltime, clause 23

"Any dispute arising under the Charter to be referred to arbitration in London (or such other place as may be agreed) one Arbitrator to be nominated by the Owners and the other by the Charterers, and in case the Arbitrators shall not agree then to the decision of an Umpire to be appointed by them, the award of the Arbitrators or the Umpire to be final and binding upon both parties."

Baltime 1939: Permissible addition to clause 23 "Arbitration," issued 1954

"If either of the appointed arbitrators refuses to act, or is incapable of acting, or dies, the party who appointed him may appoint a new arbitrator in his place; if one party fails to appoint an arbitrator, either originally, or by way of substitution as aforesaid, for seven clear days after the other party, having appointed his arbitrator, has served the party making default with notice to make the appointment, the party who has appointed an arbitrator may appoint that arbitrator to act as sole arbitrator in the reference and his award shall be binding on both parties as if he had been appointed by consent."

103 Coastcon, clause 30

" Any dispute arising under the provisions of this Charter applying to a loading or discharging port in the United Kingdom (including clause 9) shall be referred to a single Arbitrator agreed by the parties, or, in default of such agreement, to two Arbitrators, one to be appointed by each party and in case the said two Arbitrators cannot agree then to an Umpire appointed by the two Arbitrators, the arbitration to be held in the United Kingdom, and the award to be binding upon both parties hereto under the provisions of the Arbitration Act."

104 Baltcon, clauses 24A and 24B

" 24A. Should any dispute arise under the provisions applying to the Loading Port in this Charter or in the Strike Rules, the same shall be referred to two Arbitrators, one to be appointed by each party, sitting in the country of the Loading Port, and in case the said Arbitrators cannot agree, then to an Umpire, sitting in the same country, to be elected by the Arbitrators."

" 24B. Any such dispute under the provisions applying to the Discharging Port shall be settled in like manner, the Arbitrators and Umpire sitting in the country of the Discharging Port."

Clauses 24A and 24B are *optional* and either or both of them to be deleted on signing Charter by the parties unless mutually agreed.

105 New York Arbitration Clause 1954

" That should any dispute arise between Owners and the Charterers, the matter in dispute shall be referred to three persons at New York, one to be appointed by each of the parties hereto, and the third by the two so chosen; their decision or that of any two of them, shall be final, and for the purpose of enforcing any award, this agreement may be made a rule of the Court. The Arbitrators shall have discretion to award the winning party its costs of the arbitration, including wholly or partly the fees and disbursements of its attorneys and/or agents."

106 3. FORM OF AGREEMENT FOR CHARTER OF YACHT

Yacht Charter Agreement

MEMORANDUM OF AGREEMENT made this .... 19..... between......... of .... (hereinafter called " the Owner ") AND .... of .... (hereinafter called " the Charterer ") being the Charter of the

Yacht ....
Number in the party to be not more than .... NAMES OF MEMBERS IN THE PARTY ....

.... WITNESSETH :—

1. *Term, Hire, Payments*

In consideration of the covenants hereinafter contained, the Owner agrees to let and the Charterer agrees to hire the above-mentioned Yacht
FROM .... 19..... TO .... 19 ..... Daily rate .... No. of days .... Total Fee .... Port of Embarkation .... Port of Debarkation .... A deposit of .... of the Charter Fee amounting to .... shall be paid on the signing of this Agreement and the balance thereof in advance payments as follows shall be paid .... on or before the commencement of the cruise.

2. *Delivery*

The Owner agrees to deliver the Yacht to the Charterer in full commission and in proper working order, outfitted as a Yacht of her size, type and accommodation, with full equipment, and fully furnished, including china, linen, glass and silverware; staunch and clean and in good condition throughout and ready for service; and agrees to allow demurrage pro rata to the Charterer for any delay in delivery.

But should it be impossible for the Owner to make delivery as stipulated through causes beyond his control and should such delivery be not made within .... days thereafter then this Agreement may be cancelled by the Charterer and any Charter money paid in advance shall be returned to him.

3. *Crew*

The Owner agrees to provide the Yacht with a proper crew and to pay their wages during the term of Charter. It is agreed that the Charterer shall determine the general movements, programme and destination of the yacht within the limits of this agreement, but it is understood that the Captain is in full command, and the Charterer agrees to depend upon the Captain for the safe navigation of the vessel, and to abide by his judgment as to sailing, weather, anchorage etc., at all times.

The Owner having exercised all reasonable care in the selection of the Captain and crew shall not be responsible for any injury suffered by the Charterer or his party either in person or property during the term of this Charter.

4. *Insurance*

The Owner agrees to keep the Yacht fully insured against Fire, Marine and collision risks, and with protection and Indemnity coverage, for the term of this Charter, the policy to be held by him as full protection for any and all loss or damage that may occur to, or by, the Yacht during the Charter period, and the Charterer shall thereby be relieved of any and all liability for such loss or damage; and in the case of any accident or disaster the Charterer shall give the Owner or his representative .... prompt notice of same.

But should the Owner fail to, or elect not to, carry such insurance he shall then assume the same responsibility as if the Yacht were so insured.

5. *Accident*

The Owner agrees that should the Yacht after delivery sustain breakdown of machinery or be disabled or damaged by fire, grounding, collision or other cause so as to prevent the use of the vessel by the Charterer for a period of not less than forty-eight consecutive hours at any time, the same not being brought about by any act or default of the Charterer, the Owner shall make a pro rata return of hire to the Charterer for such period in excess of the said forty-eight hours the Yacht shall be disabled or unfit for use.

Provided, however, that in case the Yacht be lost or said damage be so extensive that the Yacht cannot be or is not repaired within .... days, then the Charter price shall be abated pro rata and Charter money paid in advance shall be rebated pro rata from the time of such damage, and the Charterer shall have the right to terminate this Charter.

6. *Running Expenses*

The Charterer agrees to accept the Yacht delivered as hereinbefore provided, and to pay all running expenses during the term of this Charter, which will include pilotage and port charges, fuel, fresh water, deck, engine room and all other consumable stores, also the provisions and supplies for himself and his party, including food for the Captain and crew. The Charterer also agrees to pay for Cables and Telegrams which may be despatched by the Owner or the Agent in arranging the cruise, or which may be transmitted over the Yacht's Radio Telephone during the cruise.

The wages of the Captain and crew are paid by the Owner.

7. *Navigation Limits*

The Charterer agrees to restrict the cruising of the Yacht to the following waters:—

8. *Replacements*

The Charterer agrees to be responsible for, and to replace or make good any injury to the Yacht, her equipment or furnishings, caused personally by himself or any of his party, but not if caused by any of the crew, and if not collectable under the Owners Insurance.

The Charterer further agrees to leave all linen, napery, etc., re-laundered and in good condition, fair wear and tear excepted, upon expiration of the Charter term.

9. *Re-delivery*

The Charterer agrees to surrender the Yacht at the expiration of his Charter at .... free and clear of any indebtedness that may have been incurred for his account during the term of Charter, and in as good condition as when delivery was taken, fair wear and tear from ordinary use and any loss or damage that he shall not be liable to make good excepted.

Should the Charterer fail to make re-delivery of the Yacht as stipulated, unless due to causes beyond his control, he shall pay demurrage pro rata to the Owner for the time that such re-delivery is delayed.

10. *Restricted Use*

The Charterer agrees that the Yacht shall be employed exclusively as a pleasure vessel for the sole and proper use of the members of the party named above or individuals substituted for them and for their family, guests, servants, etc., during the term of this Charter, and shall not transport merchandise, or embark passengers for pay, or engage in any trade nor in any way violate the laws of Customs, Immigration, Harbour or Government regulations of any Government within the jurisdiction of which the Yacht may be at any time, and shall comply with the law in all other respects.

11. *Non-Assignment*

The Charterer agrees not to assign this agreement or sub-Charter the Yacht without the consent of the Owner in writing.

12. *Defaults*

It is mutually agreed that should any instalment or Charter money not be paid on the date designated, or within three days thereafter, the Owner shall have the right to resume possession of the Yacht and terminate the Charter, without prejudice to his rights in respect of any arrears of Charter money, or of any breach by the Charterer of the conditions herein contained.

13. *Brokerage*

This Charter and any extension thereof, or subsequent Charter between the parties thereto, shall be subject to the appropriate brokerage fee as agreed between the Owner and his principal Agent, and is payable by the Owner to

....

....

(a) Upon the signing of each Agreement and payment of the first instalments of hire.
(b) Upon payment of hire for extensions or any subsequent Charters.

14. *Additional Conditions* (if any)

It is further agreed by the parties hereto that:—

15. *Cancellations*

In the event of cancellation by the Charterer of this Charter-Party, the deposit shall not be returnable to the Charterer, but without prejudice to this condition the Agents shall use their best endeavours to arrange a fresh Charter-Party upon similar terms and for the same period as in this Charter-Party. If the Owner(s) or the Agent shall succeed in arranging a fresh Charter-Party in all respects as advantageous to the Owner(s) as this present Charter-Party the said deposit shall thereupon be repaid to the Charterers (less commission): but if the Owner(s) or the Agents shall not be able to arrange a fresh Charter-Party or shall be able to arrange a fresh Charter-Party but only on terms which are not in all respects as advantageous to the Owner(s) as the terms of this present Charter-Party the said deposit shall be repaid to the Charterer with a deduction therefrom by way of compensation to the Owner(s) less commission at the standard rate on the deduction only.

16. In the event of this agreement being executed on behalf of either party by an agent, the agent shall neither be entitled to sue nor be liable to be sued upon the contract.

17. Should the Owner and Charterer be unable to reconcile any differences that may arise with respect to this Agreement such dispute shall be referred to three arbitrators: one to be chosen by each of the aforesaid parties and the third by the two so chosen. The decision in writing signed by any two of said arbitrators shall be final and

binding upon both Owner and Charterer, the expense in connection with such arbitration to be equally divided between them.

To the true and faithful performance of the foregoing Agreement, the said parties hereto bind themselves, their heirs, executors, administrators and assigns, each to the other.

IN WITNESS WHEREOF the parties have hereunto set their hands the day and year first above written.

Signed by the CHARTERER ....

Signed on behalf of the OWNER ....

[The next paragraph is 120]

Part Two

PLEADINGS

CHAPTER 4

COMMERCIAL COURT[1]: CARRIAGE BY SEA

120 *Note.* Headings to these pleadings should be as in the action. The form in the case of ordinary actions in the Commercial Court is as follows:

In the High Court of Justice [*Writ no.*]
Queen's Bench Division
(Commercial List)
Between ... plaintiffs
and
... defendants

Claim for Damage to Cargo: Bill of Lading[2]

POINTS OF CLAIM

121 1. By five bills of lading Nos. 123–127 dated Sydney, January 18, 19—, the defendants acknowledged shipment on board their vessel the MACBETH of 10,000 cartons of instant tea in apparent good order and condition for carriage to and delivery at London to the order of the shippers.

2. The plaintiffs at all material times were owners of the said goods or alternatively indorsees of the said bills of lading to whom the property in the goods passed upon and by reason of the indorsement. Further or alternatively the plaintiffs presented the bills of lading to the defendants in London and the defendants thereupon delivered up the said goods to the plaintiffs.

3. In the premises the defendants were under a duty as carrier by sea for reward or alternatively expressly or impliedly contracted by the bills of lading to deliver the goods in like good order and condition as when shipped.

4. In breach of duty and/or contract the defendants delivered 3,000 cartons damaged by seawater, in that they were wet and/or damp and/or stained and/or otherwise damaged by water.

Particulars

Delivered wet and/or damp	:	1970 cartons
Stained	:	1015 cartons
Otherwise damaged	:	15 cartons

[1] For practice in Commercial Court, see *Shipowners* [B.S.L. 13, §§ 758 *et seq.*].
[2] *Cf.* Statements of claim for damage to cargo in Admiralty Court, *infra*, §§ 200, 201.

5. Further or alternatively the said damage was caused by the negligence of the defendants their servants or agents in breach of the defendants' duty as carriers and/or bailees for reward. The plaintiffs rely upon the fact that such damage occurred as sufficient evidence of negligence.

6. Further or alternatively, the contracts contained in or evidenced by the said bills of lading were subject to the (Australian) Sea-Carriage of Goods Act 1924. Article III, rule 1 of the Schedule attached to that Act provides that:

> " The carrier shall be bound before and at the beginning of the voyage to exercise due diligence to—
> (a) Make the ship seaworthy;
> (b) . . . .
> (c) Make the holds, . . ., and all other parts of the ship in which goods are carried, fit and safe for their reception, carriage and preservation."

7. In breach of contract and/or duty the defendants failed to make the ship seaworthy at the commencement of the said voyage and/or to make the holds fit for the reception, carriage and/or preservation of the said goods.

Particulars

[*Showing details of unseaworthiness and unfitness of the holds*]

8. Further or alternatively, Article III, rule 2 of the said Schedule provides that:

> " Subject to the provisions of Article IV the carrier shall properly and carefully load, handle, stow, carry, keep, care for and discharge the goods carried."

9. In breach of contract and/or duty the defendants, their servants or agents failed to take reasonable care in and about the stowage and carriage of the said goods.

Particulars

[*Setting out the facts relied upon*]

10. By reason of the defendants' said breaches of duty and/or contract and/or negligence the plaintiffs have suffered loss and damage.

Particulars

[*Showing details of the loss in value resulting from the damage pleaded*]

And the plaintiffs claim:

(i) £0,000, or alternatively, damages;

(ii) Interest.

Defence to Claim for Damage to Cargo: Bill of Lading

POINTS OF DEFENCE [3]

122 1. Save and except that no admission is made as to the alleged good order and condition of the goods, paragraph 1 of the Points of Claim is admitted.

2. No admissions are made regarding paragraphs 2 and 3 of the Points of Claim.

3. As to paragraph 4 of the Points of Claim, the alleged or any breaches of duty and/or contract are denied and no admission is made as to the condition of the goods.

4. Paragraph 5 of the Points of Claim is denied.

5. Clause 32 of the said bills of lading, to which the defendants will refer for their full terms and effect, provided as follows:

> "The contract evidenced by this bill of lading shall be governed by English law and any disputes shall be determined in England according to English law to the exclusion of the jurisdiction of the courts of any other country."

Further the said bills of lading did not expressly incorporate the Hague Rules scheduled to the (Australian) Sea-Carriage of Goods Act 1924. In the premises it is denied that the said bills of lading were subject to the said Act.

6. The said bills of lading further provided inter alia:

> "4. Carrier's exemption clause. The carrier shall not be responsible for loss or damage to or in connection with the goods of any kind whatsoever (including deterioration, delay or loss of market) however caused (whether by unseaworthiness or unfitness of the vessel or of any other vessel, tender, lighter or craft or of any other mode of conveyance whatsoever or by faults, errors or negligence, or otherwise howsoever).
>
> In particular and without prejudice to the generality of the foregoing:
>
> ....
>
> (b) The carrier shall not be liable for loss of or damage to or in connection with the goods or part thereof of any kind whatsoever (including deterioration, delay or loss of market) arising or resulting from: unseaworthiness (whether or not due diligence

[3] *Cf.* Defence to cargo claim in Admiralty Court, § 226, *infra.*

shall have been exercised by the carrier, his servants or agents or others to make the vessel seaworthy); act, neglect or default of the master, mariner, pilot or the servants or agents of the carrier in the navigation or in the management of the vessel or in the care of the cargo; . . . perils, dangers and accidents of the sea or other navigable waters; . . . act or omission of the shipper, consignee, owner of the goods, or holder of this bill of lading . . . wastage in bulk or weight or any other loss or damage arising from inherent defect, quality, or vice of the goods; insufficiency of packing . . . latent defects; any other cause whatsoever, whether or not of a like kind to those above mentioned, and including negligence on the part of the carrier, his servants, agents or others."

7. Further or alternatively if, which is denied, the said bills of lading were subject to the (Australian) Sea-Carriage of Goods Act 1924, the Schedule to the said Act further provides by Article IV, rules 1 and 2, as follows:

"1. Neither the carrier nor the ship shall be liable for loss or damage arising or resulting from unseaworthiness unless caused by want of due diligence on the part of the carrier to make the ship seaworthy. . . .

"2. Neither the carrier nor the ship shall be responsible for loss or damage arising or resulting from:

(a) Act, neglect, or default of the master, mariner, pilot, or the servants of the carrier in the navigation or in the management of the ship. . . .

(c) Perils, dangers and accidents of the sea or other navigable waters. . . .

(i) Act or omission of the shipper or owner of the goods, his agent or representative. . . .

(n) Insufficiency of packing. . . ."

8. Paragraph 7 of the Points of Claim is denied.

9. Further or alternatively, if, which is denied, the vessel was unseaworthy as alleged or at all, the defendants rely on clause 4 (b) of the bills of lading. Further or alternatively the defendants before and at the beginning of the voyage exercised due diligence to make the vessel seaworthy and the holds and all other parts of the ship safe for the reception, carriage and presentation of the goods.

Particulars

[*Setting out the facts relied upon*]

10. Further or alternatively, the alleged damage to the goods arose

or resulted from an act, neglect or default of a servant or servants of the carrier in the management of the ship.

Particulars

[*Showing details of the mismanagement relied upon*]

11. Further or alternatively, the alleged damage to the goods arose or resulted from perils of the sea.

Particulars

[*Setting out the facts relied upon*]

12. Further or alternatively, the alleged damage to the goods arose or resulted from an act and/or omission of the shipper and/or owner of the goods.

Particulars

[*Showing details of the act and omission*]

13. Further or alternatively, the alleged damage to the goods arose or resulted from insufficiency of packing.

Particulars

[*Showing details of the insufficiency of packing*]

14. In the premises and by reason of clause 4 (b) of the bills of lading and/or the provisions of the Schedule to the said Act relied upon, the defendants are not liable for the damage alleged or at all.

15. Paragraph 8 of the Points of Claim is admitted.

16. Save and except that the alleged loss and damage is not admitted paragraphs 9 and 10 of the Points of Claim are denied.

17. Further or alternatively, if, which is denied, the defendants, their servants or agents failed to take reasonable care in and about the stowage and carriage of the said goods, the defendants rely on clause 4 (b) of the bills of lading and, in the premises, are under no liability in respect of the loss and damage alleged.

Claim under a Voyage Charterparty (Gencon)

POINTS OF CLAIM

123 1. By a charterparty in the Gencon Form dated Brussels, April 5,

19—, it was agreed between the defendants as owners of the motor vessel CLEOPATRA and the plaintiffs as charterers that the vessel should proceed to Rotterdam and there load a full and complete cargo of 5,000 tons of powdered milk in bags for carriage to and delivery at Lagos, Nigeria.

2. The charterparty to which the plaintiffs will refer for its full terms and effect expressly provided as follows:

> Clause 2. "Owners are to be responsible for loss or damage to the goods . . . caused by the improper or negligent stowage of the goods . . . or by personal want of due diligence on the part of the owners or their manager to make the vessel in all respects seaworthy . . . or by the personal act or default of the owners or their manager."
>
> Clause 25. "Vessel to have clear and dry holds to charterers' satisfaction and to be suitable for loading and carriage of powdered milk."

3. The vessel duly loaded 5,000 tons of powdered milk in good order and condition at Rotterdam on April 7, 19— and proceeded to Lagos where she arrived on May 20, 19—.

4. The plaintiffs were at all material times the owners of the said cargo and the same was shipped by or on behalf of the plaintiffs.

5. In breach of their duties as carriers and/or bailees for reward, and/or in breach of the said charterparty, the defendants did not deliver the said cargo in the same good order and condition as when shipped but delivered it wetted and damaged by seawater and/or fresh water.

Particulars

[*Here set out the details of the damage to the cargo*]

6. In breach of clause 25 of the said charterparty, the vessel did not have clean and dry holds nor was it suitable for the loading and/or carriage of powdered milk.

Particulars

(i) At all material times, the heating pipes running between Nos. 2 and 3 holds were cracked in several places and leaked water. As a result the cargo was loaded into holds the floors of which contained pools of dirty water. In addition, during the course of the voyage, further leakage took place damaging other parts of the cargo.

(ii) The hatch covers were rusty and warped and insufficiently secure to withstand normal weather conditions. During the course of the voyage, the vessel encountered average weather conditions. Nevertheless, No. 1 hatch cover was destroyed and a large quantity of seawater shipped before temporary repairs could be effected. As a result, the whole quantity of cargo stowed in No. 1 hold was damaged by seawater and/or fragments of the said hatch cover.

7. Further or alternatively, the said damage was caused by the improper or negligent stowage of the goods, and/or by the personal want of due diligence on the part of the owners or their manager to make the vessel in all respects seaworthy, and/or by the personal act or default of the owners or their manager.

Particulars

(i) As the master well knew, Nos. 2 and 3 holds were unfit for the reception of a cargo of powdered milk in bags for the reasons set out in paragraph 6 hereof but he nevertheless instructed the stevedores to load cargo into those holds and No. 2 deep tank.

(ii) Before the commencement of the voyage, the master, orally informed the defendants of the condition of the aforesaid heating pipes and hatches. All the defects were visible to the naked eye. The master requested the defendants to inspect the said defects and/or authorise him to have the same repaired. The defendants refused to inspect the vessel nor would they authorise the master, nor take any steps at all, to remedy the said defects.

8. By reason of the defendants' said breach or breaches of duty as carriers and/or bailees for reward, the plaintiffs have suffered loss and damage amounting to £0,000.

Particulars

[*Here set out the plaintiffs computation of the amount of loss incurred*]

And the plaintiffs claim:

(i) £0,000, or alternatively, damages;

(ii) Interest.

Defence to Claim under a Voyage Charterparty (Gencon)

POINTS OF DEFENCE

124 1. Paragraphs 1 and 2 of the Points of Claim are admitted. The defendants will refer to the charterparty for its full terms and effect. It was further provided by clause 2 of the charterparty as follows:

> " And the owners are responsible for no loss or damage or delay arising from any other cause whatsoever, even from the neglect or default of the captain or crew or some other person employed by the owners on board or ashore for whose acts they would, but for this clause be responsible, or from unseaworthiness of the vessel on loading or commencement of the voyage or at any time whatsoever. . . ."

2. Paragraph 3 of the Points of Claim is admitted save as regards the alleged quantity of the powdered milk loaded, which is not admitted, and save as regards the allegation that the powdered milk was in good order and condition when shipped, which is denied. The powdered milk was loaded subject to protests by the master that it was wet and of poor quality and infested with fleas. It was loaded from open lorries which prior to the commencement of loading had stood unattended on the quayside for 3 to 4 days during heavy rainstorms.

3. No admission is made in respect of paragraph 4 of the Points of Claim.

4. It is admitted that X tons of the said cargo were delivered wetted. No admission is made as to whether or, if so, how much of, such wetting resulted from the penetration of seawater or freshwater. Save as aforesaid, paragraph 5 of the Points of Claim is denied.

5. It is admitted that No. 1 hatch cover was destroyed during the course of the voyage and that temporary repairs were effected. No admission is made as to the amount, if any, of seawater shipped through No. 1 hatch. Save as aforesaid, paragraph 6 of the Points of Claim is denied.

6. Further or alternatively, if, which is denied, the holds or other cargo spares were unfit as alleged or at all, upon the arrival of the vessel at Rotterdam, the holds and other cargo spaces were inspected and orally approved by representatives of the plaintiffs. In reliance on the said representatives' approval, the defendants proceeded to load and stow the cargo in the vessel's holds and other cargo spaces. In the premises, the plaintiffs are estopped from contending that the holds or other cargo spaces were unfit as alleged or at all, and/or have waived their right, if any (which is denied), to contend that the defendants were in breach of clause 25 of the charterparty.

7. Further or alternatively, the damage alleged was caused by the inherent vice of the cargo.

Particulars

(i) The bags in which the powdered milk was packed were rotted and torn, allowing part of the contents to escape.

(ii) The powdered milk was excessively moist and/or infested with fleas and/or of poor quality.

(iii) The defendants further rely on the facts and matters pleaded in paragraph 2 hereof.

8. Further or alternatively, if, which is not admitted, seawater was shipped into No. 1 hold when the No. 1 hatch cover was destroyed, the defendants will if necessary contend that the alleged damage was caused by perils of the seas, namely storms and heavy weather experienced during the voyage.

Particulars

[*Here detail the bad weather encountered by quotation from the vessel's logs and otherwise*]

9. Paragraph 7 of the Points of Claim is denied. The defendants repeat paragraph 6 of the Points of Defence.

10. Further or alternatively, the vessel underwent a special survey at Piraeus in 19—, when a full inspection and overhaul took place. She then performed one voyage (Argentine/United Arab Republic) carrying a cargo of maize in bulk in respect of which no claim was received and she was thereafter laid up at Port Said until March 19—. The defendants had no knowledge of the alleged defects or unfitness and no reason to believe that the vessel was defective or unfit to receive cargo either as alleged or at all. For the reasons set out in paragraph 8 hereof, the defendants will if necessary contend that all the alleged damage was caused by perils of the sea.

11. Further or alternatively, if, which is not admitted, the master was aware of the alleged condition of the said heating pipes and hatch covers, it is denied that he informed the defendants as alleged or at all. Neither the defendants nor their manager had any communication with the master whilst the vessel was at Rotterdam. If, which is not admitted, the master informed the defendants' agents in Rotterdam, Messrs. Jones & Company, of the alleged facts, the defendants were unaware of this and will contend that any action or inaction on the part of their agents did not amount to personal want of due diligence or personal act or default of the defendants or their manager, and, in the premises and by virtue of clause 2 of the charterparty, they are not liable as alleged or at all.

12. Paragraph 8 of the Points of Claim is denied.

Claim for Freight: Charterparty

POINTS OF CLAIM

125 1. By a charterparty dated London February 3, 19—, the plaintiffs agreed to charter to the defendants their motor vessel TIMON OF ATHENS to proceed to Genoa and there load a full and complete cargo of 8,000 long tons of grapes in trays for carriage to and delivery at Liverpool and/or Avonmouth in the defendants' option.

2. The charterparty further provided, *inter alia*, by clause 28:

> "The freight is to be paid on the nett weight shipped per long ton of 2,240 lbs. as follows: £2·50 (two pounds, fifty pence) in external sterling in London on arrival at the port of discharge. . . ."

3. In pursuance of the charterparty the said vessel duly loaded a cargo of 8,000 long tons of grapes in trays at Genoa and proceeded to Liverpool, where she arrived on March 4, 19—.

4. In the premises, the full freight due amounted to £20,000, and became payable by the defendants on March 4, 19—, but the defendants on March 4, 19— and thereafter have failed to pay the whole or any part thereof.

And the plaintiffs claim:

(i) £20,000, or alternatively, damages;

(ii) Interest.

Defence to Claim for Freight: Charterparty

POINTS OF DEFENCE

126 1. The defendants admit paragraphs 1 to 3 of the Points of Claim. They will refer to the charterparty for its full terms and effect.

2. Further, in pursuance of the option contained in clause 1 of the charterparty referred to in paragraph 1 of the Points of Claim, the defendants nominated both Liverpool and Avonmouth as ports of discharge. The vessel duly arrived at Liverpool on March 4, 19— and discharged 5,000 tons of the said grapes. She left Liverpool on March 9, 19— for Avonmouth. During the course of that voyage, she ran aground upon a reef off the north coast of Wales and was totally lost together with the remainder of her cargo.

3. It was an express term, upon the proper construction of the charterparty, or, alternatively, a term to be implied therein by operation of law, that, if more than one port of discharge were nominated, the freight payable on arrival at each port of discharge would be in respect only of that proportion of the cargo which was discharged at that port.

4. In the premises, the defendants are not liable to the plaintiffs for freight in respect of 3,000 out of the 8,000 tons of grapes shipped.

5. As to paragraph 4 of the Points of Claim it is denied that the full freight is or was due. The defendants are and have at all times been willing to pay to the plaintiffs freight in respect of 5,000 tons of grapes, amounting to £12,500.

Claim for Demurrage: Charterparty

POINTS OF CLAIM

127 1. By a charterparty dated Cairo September 20, 19—, the defendants chartered from the plaintiffs the motor vessel TROILUS to load a full and complete cargo of 4,000 tons of steel plates at Antwerp and to carry the same to "one safe berth, one or two safe ports in Egypt or Syria in charterers' option . . . and there deliver the cargo being paid freight."

2. The charterparty further provided, *inter alia,* by clause 6: that discharging time was to "commence at 2 p.m., if notice of readiness to discharge is given before noon, and at 8 p.m. next working day, if notice given during office hours after noon," and "Time lost in waiting for berth at or off the discharging port(s), whether in free pratique or not, to count as discharging time. . . ." It was provided by clause 7 that discharging port demurrage should be at the rate of £250 per day or pro rata for any part of a day. Clause 16 provided, *inter alia*:

> "Cargo to be . . . discharged at receivers' risk and expense at the rate of 800 tons per weather working day, Sundays and holidays excepted even if used. . . ."

3. Pursuant to the charterparty the vessel proceeded to Antwerp and loaded a cargo of 4,000 tons of steel plates. The defendants having duly nominated Port Said as the sole port of discharge, the vessel arrived off that port and anchored in the roads at 15.00 hours and tendered notice of readiness to discharge at 16.00 hours on December 29, 19—. The defendants failed to nominate a berth until January 10, 19—, on which date the vessel duly berthed having commenced shifting at 18.00 hours.

4. In the premises the time lost by the vessel in waiting for a berth was the period from 15.00 hours on December 29, 19—, to 18.00 hours on January 10, 19—, amounting to 12 days, 3 hours and the demurrage due to the plaintiffs is to be calculated on the basis that the said period counts as discharging time.

5. By reason of the premises, the defendants became liable to pay

demurrage in respect of the vessel's discharging at Port Said amounting to £3,750, as particularised in Schedule A hereto.

And the plaintiffs claim:

(i) £3,750, or alternatively damages;

(ii) Interest.

SCHEDULE A

(Under paragraph 5 of the Points of Claim)

Laytime Available at discharge (4,000 tons at 800 tons per day)	:	5 days
Vessel anchored Port Said roads	:	December 29, 19—, 15.00 hours
Vessel shifted to berth	:	January 10, 19—, 18.00 hours
Notice of readiness deemed to have been given and accepted	:	January 11, 19—, a.m.
Laytime deemed to commence	:	January 11, 19—, 14.00 hours
Time lost waiting for berth	:	December, 29, 19—, 15.00 hours to January 10, 19—, 18.00 hours, *viz.* 12 days, 3 hours.

			Time to Count		
			D	H	M
Thursday	11.1.19—	14.00–24.00	–	10	–
Friday	12.1.19—		1		
Saturday	13.1.19—		1		
Sunday	14.1.19—		–	–	–
Monday	15.1.19—		1	–	–
Tuesday	16.1.19—		1	–	–
Wednesday	17.1.19—	00.00–14.00		14	–
			5	–	–

	Time to Count		
	D	H	M
Vessel on demurrage as from 17.1.19—, 14.00 hours to 20.1.19—, 11.00	2	21	–
Add time lost waiting for berth	12	3	–
Total demurrage	15	–	–
at £250 per day,	£3,750		

Defence to Claim for Demurrage: Charterparty

POINTS OF DEFENCE

128 1. Paragraphs 1 and 2 of the Points of Claim are admitted. The defendants will refer to the charterparty for its full terms and effect.

2. Clause 6 of the charterparty further provided as follows:

> ". . . However, where delay is caused to vessel getting into berth after giving notice of readiness, for any reason over which the charterer has no control, such delay shall not count as used lay time. . . ."

The charterparty also provided, *inter alia*:

> " 19. General Exception Clause. . . . And neither the vessel, nor master or owner, nor the charterer, shall, unless otherwise in this charter expressly provided, be responsible for any loss or damage or delay or failure in performing hereunder, arising or resulting from: . . . perils of the seas; . . . restraint of princes, rulers or peoples. . . ."

3. Save and except that the defendants do not admit that they failed to nominate a berth until January 10, 19—, paragraph 3 of the Points of Claim is admitted. The defendants admit and aver that on December 29, 19— at about 15.00 hours local time the vessel arrived in the roads off Port Said and that she was unable to proceed to a berth in the port, which had been closed by order of the harbour master acting on the authority of the Government of the United Arab Republic owing to the conditions of wind and sea then prevailing. The vessel remained in the roads until 16.00 hours on January 10, 19— when the port was opened and she was able to proceed to No. 5 berth.

4. In the premises, the delay was caused not by the alleged or any failure of the defendants to nominate or procure a berth but by the vessel's inability to proceed to or lie at any berth in the said port and/or by the said conditions of wind and sea and/or by the said order of the harbour master. If, which is denied, there was a breach of clause 6 of the charterparty, the alleged loss and damage was not caused thereby. Further or alternatively, such loss and damage was caused as aforesaid by perils of the seas and/or by restraint of princes, rulers or peoples and by virtue of clause 19 of the charterparty, the defendants are not liable therefor.

5. Paragraph 4 of the Points of Claim is denied.

6. Paragraph 5 of the Points of Claim is denied. Further in respect of the claim for demurrage set out in Schedule A (under paragraph 5 of the Points of Claim) for the period January 17, 19— to January 20, 19—, the defendants rely on the custom of the port

that discharge was a joint operation. It was the duty of the plaintiffs to put the cargo on to the quay and of the defendants to remove it. At no time did the plaintiffs succeed in discharging the cargo on to the quay at the rate of 800 tons per weather working day. In the premises any delay in discharge was due to the fault of the plaintiffs and the defendants are not liable as alleged or at all.

Claim by Owners under a Time Charter

POINTS OF CLAIM

129 1. By a time charterparty in Baltime Form dated London, April 30, 19—, the plaintiffs chartered their motor vessel HAMLET to the defendants for a period of about 6 calendar months from the time of delivery at the Port of London, not before May 16, 19—, and upon terms therein set out.

2. During the period of the charterparty the vessel loaded, *inter alia*, consignments of oranges at Haifa for carriage to London. The defendants or their agents signed and issued bills of lading on behalf of the master, as follows:

Bill of Lading Number	Goods
13	2,000 crates
14	1,500 crates
17	2,100 crates

3. In the premises it was an express term of the charterparty (upon the true construction thereof) and/or a term implied by operation of law, that the defendants would indemnify the plaintiffs against all liabilities incurred by the plaintiffs under the said bills of lading and/or against all payments made in respect of such liabilities, if and to the extent that the plaintiffs would not have been liable in the circumstances under the terms of the charterparty.

4. Further or alternatively, it was a term of the charterparty implied by operation of law that the defendants and their agents would not sign or issue on behalf of the master or the plaintiffs bills of lading whose terms were less favourable as regards liability for loss of or damage to the goods carried thereunder than the terms of the charterparty.

5. Following discharge of the vessel at London, claims were made against the plaintiffs by the holders of the said bills of lading, alleging that goods shipped thereunder were delivered in a damaged condition as follows:

Particulars

B/L No.	Goods	Claim	Amount

[*Set out details*]

6. The plaintiffs were unable to dispute liability for the said claims under the bills of lading and on about December 1, 19—, they reasonably paid the sum of £7,900, in full and final settlement of the claims together with interest at 7 per cent. for the period from the date of discharge until the said date.

7. The damage consisted of deterioration and/or rotting of the oranges due to overripeness brought about as a result of the inadequate stowage of the cargo and the high temperatures at which the cargo was stowed.

Particulars

[*Give details of the inadequate storage and of the failure of the refrigerating machinery*]

8. The charterparty provides *inter alia* as follows:

"4. Whilst on hire the charterers to . . . arrange and pay for loading, trimming stowing . . . of cargoes.

9. . . . The owners not to be responsible for shortage, mixture, marks, nor for number of pieces or packages, nor for damage to or claims on cargo caused by bad stowage or otherwise. . . .

13. The owners only to be responsible . . . for loss or damage to goods on board if such loss . . . has been caused by want of due diligence on the part of the owners or their manager or their servants. . . .

The charterers to be responsible for loss or damage caused to the vessel or to the owners . . . by improper or careless loading, stowing or discharging of goods or any other improper or negligent act on their part or that of their servants."

9. In the premises the plaintiffs are not liable under the charterparty for the damage in respect of which claims were made under the bills of lading as aforesaid.

10. Wrongfully and in breach of the said express and/or implied term of the charterparty the defendants have failed and refused to indemnify the plaintiffs against the said payment or any part thereof.

11. Further or alternatively, the said bills of lading were signed and issued by or on behalf of the defendants as aforesaid in breach of the implied term of the charterparty set out in paragraph 4 hereof and the said sum is claimed as damages for the said breach.

And the plaintiffs claim:

(i) £7,900 or, alternatively, damages;

(ii) Interest.

130 **Defence to Claim under a Time Charter**

POINTS OF DEFENCE

1. The charterparty is admitted.

2. Save as aforesaid and that it is admitted that the defendants or their agents signed and issued bills of lading on behalf of the master paragraphs 1 to 5 of the Points of Claim are not admitted.

3. Save that the alleged inability of the plaintiffs to dispute liability for the claim under the bills of lading and the alleged reasonableness of their payment of £7,900 are denied, the defendants make no admission as to paragraph 6 of the Points of Claim.

4. Further or alternatively, the said bills of lading had effect and/or were expressly made subject to the provision of the Carriage of Goods by Sea Act 1924. The Schedule to that Act provides by Article IV, rule 2, as follows:

" 2. Neither the carrier nor the ship shall be responsible for loss or damage arising or resulting from:

. . . . . .

(i) act or omission of the shipper or owner of the goods, his agent or representative

. . . . . .

(m) . . . any . . . loss or damage arising from inherent defect, quality or vice of the goods . . .

(n) inefficiency of packing . . .

. . . . . .

(q) any other cause arising without the actual fault or privity of the carrier, or without the fault or neglect of the agents or servants of the carrier. . . ."

5. As to paragraph 7 of the Points of Claim, no admission is made as to the existence or nature of the alleged damage. It is denied that the same was brought about as alleged.

6. Further or alternatively, the alleged damage to the goods arose or resulted from the fact that when the goods were received by the plaintiffs, they were inadequately packed and/or boxed to withstand the normal incidents of carriage by sea for the said voyage.

Particulars

[*Here state the details of the inadequacies of packing*]

In the premises, and by reason of Article IV, rule 2 (i), and/or Article IV, rule 2 (n) of the said Schedule, the plaintiffs were not liable to the holders of the bills of lading therefor.

7. Further or alternatively, the alleged damage to the goods arose or resulted from the fact that when the goods were received by the plaintiffs, they were already damaged and/or affected by mould and/or fruit fly.

Particulars

[*Here state the details of the damage and the diseases*]

In the premises, the alleged damage arose or resulted from the inherent defect, quality or vice of the goods and, by virtue of Article IV, rule 2 (m) of the said schedule, the plaintiffs were not liable to the holders of the bills of lading therefor.

8. Further or alternatively, the plaintiffs, their servants or agents were guilty of no fault or negligence in the care and custody of the goods and, in the premises, by virtue of Article IV, rule 2 (q) of the said schedule, the plaintiffs were not liable to the holders of the bills of lading for the alleged loss or damage.

9. Paragraph 8 of the Points of Claim is admitted.

10. As to paragraph 9 of the Points of Claim, no admission is made as to the plaintiffs' liability under the charterparty. The defendants contend that the plaintiffs are not liable to the holders of the bills of lading as alleged or at all.

11. Save that it is admitted that the defendants have not paid the sum of £7,900, or any part thereof, to the plaintiffs, paragraphs 10 and 11 of the Points of Claim are denied.

Time Charter : Claim by Owners under an Off-hire Clause

POINTS OF CLAIM

131 1. By a time charterparty in the Baltime form, dated New York, March 3, 19—, the plaintiffs chartered their vessel the motor vessel MALVOLIO to the defendants for a period of 24 calendar months from the time the vessel was delivered and placed at the disposal of the defendants at the port of New York, not before June 6, 19—, and upon the terms therein set out.

2. The charterparty provided, *inter alia*, as follows:

Clause 11 (b). "In the event of the vessel being driven into port or to anchorage through stress of weather, trading to shallow harbours or to rivers or ports with bars, or suffering an accident to her chargo, any detention of the vessel and/or expenses resulting from such detention to be for the charterers' account even if such detention and/or expenses, or the cause by reason of which either is incurred, be due to, or be contributed by, the negligence of the owners' servants."

3. On September 9, 19— in accordance with the defendants' orders under the said charterparty, the vessel was navigating in the principal channel of the River Plate with a cargo of maize which she had loaded at Rosario. The vessel was bound for Buenos Aires in the River Plate to load further cargo for carriage to a port or ports in the United Kingdom.

4. At about 03.00 hours on September 9, 19—, the vessel grounded in the said river. She remained aground until about 07.00 hours on October 10, 19— when she was refloated and thereafter proceeded to Buenos Aires. The plaintiffs will if necessary contend that the said grounding was caused by negligent navigation on the part of the vessel's pilot and/or the fact that the buoys marking the principal channel were insufficiently and/or irregularly lit. At all material times pilotage in the River Plate was compulsory.

5. Rosario and/or Buenos Aires are, and were at all material times, ports with bars and were known so to be. In the premises, the grounding of the vessel and the consequent detention were due to the vessel trading to shallow harbours and/or to rivers and/or to rivers with bars and/or to ports with bars.

6. By reason of the said grounding, the vessel was damaged as a result of which the plaintiffs incurred expense as follows:

Particulars

(i) Repairs to the bottom of the vessel, which was damaged consequent upon the grounding, amounting to	£6,800
(ii) Further repairs necessary to restore the hull and machinery of the vessel to full working order, when the vessel arrived at Buenos Aires, amounting to	£2,100
	£8,900

7. Further or alternatively, the plaintiffs incurred expenses in connection with the grounding of the vessel as follows:

Particulars

(i) Expenses incurred in refloating the vessel, including the hiring of two tugs, for a total of 6 days in all, amounting to	£6,200

(ii) Expenses arising out of the additional bunkers used and additional overtime paid during the period when the vessel was aground, amounting to £1,004

£7,204

8. By reason of clause 11 (b) of the charterparty, the said expenses under paragraph 6 and 7 above, which were paid by the plaintiffs, were for the defendants' account, but, wrongfully and in breach of contract, the defendants have failed and refuse to indemnify the plaintiffs in respect of the said expenses or any part thereof.

And the plaintiff claims:

(i) Under paragraph 6: £8,900, or alternatively damages;
(ii) Under paragraph 7: £7,204, or alternatively damages;
(iii) Interest.

Time Charter: Defence to Claim under an Off-hire Clause

POINTS OF DEFENCE

132 1. Paragraphs 1 and 2 of the Points of Claim are admitted. The time charterparty, to which the defendants will refer as may be necessary for its full terms and effect, also contained the following provision:

> Clause 11 (a). "In the event of dry-docking or other necessary measures to maintain the efficiency of the vessel, deficiency of men or owners' stores, breakdown of machinery, damage to hull or other accident, either hindering or preventing the working of the vessel and continuing for more than twenty-four consecutive hours, no hire to be paid in respect of any time lost thereby, during the period in which the vessel is unable to perform the service immediately required. Any hire paid in advance to be adjusted accordingly."

2. Paragraph 3 of the Points of Claim is admitted.

3. Save that it is admitted that the vessel was aground between 03.00 hours on September 9, 19— and 07.00 hours on October 10, 19—, and thereafter proceeded to Buenos Aires, paragraph 4 of the Points of Claim is not admitted.

4. Paragraphs 5 to 7 of the Points of Claim are denied. If, which is denied, any of the expenses referred to in paragraphs 6 and 7 of the Points of Claim were incurred, the same did not result from any detention of the vessel within the meaning of clause 11 (b) of the said charterparty.

5. Further or alternatively, which is not admitted, if the vessel was damaged as alleged in paragraph 6 of the Points of Claim, such damage constituted fair wear and tear and the defendants are in no way liable in respect thereof.

6. Further or alternatively, the grounding of the vessel at or about 03.00 hours on September 9, 19—, constituted an accident hindering or preventing the working of the vessel and continuing for more than twenty-four consecutive hours, namely until the vessel was refloated at or about 07.00 hours on October 10, 19—. For the whole of that period the vessel was unable to perform the service immediately required, in that she was unable to proceed on her voyage, and the whole of such period accordingly represents time lost. In the premises and by virtue of clause 11 (a) of the said Charterparty, no hire was payable in respect of the said period. Further, on the true construction of the said charterparty, the defendants were under no obligation to make payment for bunkers consumed during, or overtime attributable to, the said period.

7. Further or alternatively, the defendants will contend that the grounding of the vessel as aforesaid was caused by the negligence of the pilot as set out in paragraph 4 of the Points of Claim, and not by any trading to rivers or ports with bars. In the premises, on the true construction of clause 11 (b) of the said charterparty, the vessel remained on hire and any detention resulting from such grounding was not for the defendants' account.

8. Further or alternatively, the defendants will contend that any detention arose from the failure on the part of the plaintiffs forthwith after such grounding to refloat and/or lighten the vessel.

9. Save that the defendants admit that they have not indemnified the plaintiffs in respect of the alleged expenses or at all, paragraph 8 of the Points of Claim is denied.

C.i.f. Contract: Claim by Sellers

POINTS OF CLAIM

133 1. By a contract in writing No. 1234 dated London, December 1, 19—, the plaintiffs agreed to sell and the defendants agreed to purchase 50 tons of Spanish pig iron, at a price of £1,000 per ton, c.i.f. Liverpool.

2. The contract, to which the plaintiffs will refer for its full terms and effect, provided, *inter alia*, "payment cash (before delivery if required) against documents or delivery order."

3. Pursuant to the said contract, the plaintiffs shipped the said

goods on board the motor vessel FALSTAFF and on February 28, 19—, the master of the said vessel signed bills of lading in respect thereof. On March 1, 19—, the plaintiffs despatched the bills of lading together with the relevant certificates of insurance and invoices to Jones' Bank, Hong Kong, to be tendered to the defendants in accordance with the said contract. Jones' Bank duly tendered the said documents to the defendants but the defendants, in breach of contract, have at all times failed to take up the said documents and/or to pay or arrange payment for the said goods or any part thereof.

4. In the premises, the plaintiffs claim for the price of goods sold and delivered to the order of the defendants, *viz.* 50 tons of Spanish pig iron at £1,000 per ton = £50,000.

And the plaintiffs claim:

(i) £50,000 or, alternatively damages;

(ii) Interest.

C.i.f. Contract: Defence and Counterclaim

POINTS OF DEFENCE AND COUNTERCLAIM

134 1. Paragraphs 1 and 2 of the Points of Claim are admitted. The defendants will refer to the contract for its full terms and effect.

2. It was an express term of the said contract that shipment of the said goods must be effected not later than February 28, 19—, and that bills of lading must be signed not later than that date.

3. Further or alternatively, it was an express or implied term and condition of the contract that true, accurate, and genuine bills of lading should be tendered by or on behalf of the plaintiffs.

4. Save that the defendants admit that documents, including those purporting to be bills of lading issued in accordance with the contract, were sent to Jones' Bank, Hong Kong, and that the Bank tendered the documents to the defendants which the defendants, as, in the circumstances hereinafter set out, they were fully entitled to do, have at all times refused to take up, paragraph 3 of the Points of Claim is denied.

5. The said bills of lading were neither true, nor accurate, nor genuine in that they were falsely and fraudulently dated February 28, 19—, whereas, in truth and in fact, the said goods were not shipped until March 5, 19—.

6. By reason of the premises, the bills of lading were a nullity and of no effect. Accordingly, there was a total failure of consideration under the said contract, and/or the plaintiffs were in breach of the said condition and the defendants are under no liability in respect of their failure to take up the shipping or at all.

7. Paragraph 4 of the Points of Claim is denied.

8. Further or alternatively, the defendants will rely on their Counterclaim herein by way of defence and/or set-off.

COUNTERCLAIM

9. The defendants repeat the premises.

10. The plaintiffs have, by reason of the premises, broken and repudiated the said contract by reason whereof the defendants have suffered loss and damage amounting to £950.

Particulars

Market price, spot, of Spanish pig iron, c.i.f. Liverpool £1,019 per ton, 50 tons at £1,019:	£50,950
Contract price, at £1,000 per ton:	£50,000
	£950

And the defendants counterclaim:

(i) Damages;

(ii) Interest.

C.i.f. Contract: Reply and Defence to Counterclaim

POINTS OF REPLY AND DEFENCE TO COUNTERCLAIM

135 1. The plaintiffs join issue with the defendants on their Points of Defence, save in so far as they consist of admissions and as appears herefrom.

2. By a telex dated March 1, 19—, the plaintiffs informed the defendants that the master of the vessel had inadvertently signed bills of lading in respect of the said goods, before the goods had been put on board and while they still remained on the dockside at Barcelona. The plaintiffs further informed the defendants that the shipping line had refused to cancel the said bills and/or to authorise the master to sign new bills in lieu thereof and that the goods could not be loaded during a strike of stevedores at Barcelona. The plaintiffs inquired whether, in the circumstances, the defendants would accept the bills dated February 28, 19—, as proper documents under the said contract. The defendants, by telex dated March 4, 19—, informed the plaintiffs that the said bills "may be in order pending our bank's acceptance."

3. In the premises, the defendants represented, and/or the plaintiffs reasonably understood them to represent, that the bills of lading dated February 28, 19—, would be acceptable documents under the contract, notwithstanding that the goods had been shipped at a later date and/or that the defendant would take up and pay for such documents. In reliance upon the said representation, the plaintiffs allowed the vessel to load the said goods and no longer insisted on receiving properly dated bills of lading from the master.

4. By reason of the premises, the said contract was varied in the terms of the said representation and/or the defendants waived their right, if any (which is not admitted), to reject the said documents and/or the defendants are estopped from relying on the inaccurate dating of the bills of lading and from insisting on the tender of accurately dated bills.

DEFENCE TO COUNTERCLAIM

5. The plaintiffs repeat the premises by reason whereof the plaintiffs are under no liability to the defendants as alleged in the Counterclaim in full.

F.o.b. Contract: Claim by Buyers

POINTS OF CLAIM

136 1. By a contract in writing dated New York, December 8, 19— the plaintiffs agreed to buy and the defendants to sell 1,000 cases of grapefruit in tins, at a price of $6 per case of 48 tins, f.o.b. San Francisco.

2. The contract was expressed to be governed by English law.

3. Further, it was an express or implied term and condition of the contract that the goods should correspond with their contract description, and/or it was an implied term that they should be of merchantable quality.

4. In accordance with the contract, the plaintiffs duly opened in favour of the defendants a confirmed and irrevocable letter of credit in the amount of $6,000, negotiable upon presentation of shipping documents in New York.

5. The defendants shipped from San Francisco on or about February 1, 19—, a consignment of grapefruit in tins and subsequently presented the relative shipping documents against, and received payment under, the said letter of credit. The consignment was discharged from the merchant ship FINLANDIA at Liverpool on or about March 7, 19—.

6. The said goods did not comply with the contractual description being shipped in 2,000 cases containing 24 tins, instead of in 1,000 cases containing 48 tins as specified by the contract.

7. Further or alternatively, the said tins were not of merchantable quality but were in a battered, dented and/or rusty condition.

8. In the premises, and/or by reason of section 13 and/or 14 (2) of the Sale of Goods Act 1893, the plaintiffs were entitled to reject the said goods, which they did by a telex message to the defendants, dated March 6, 19—. On or about March 10, 19—, the plaintiffs sold the consignment for the defendants' account.

9. By reason of the premises, the plaintiffs are entitled to recover the price paid to the defendants, less the proceeds of sale of the consignment for the defendants' account, and/or have suffered loss and damage in a like amount.

Particulars

Paid to the vendors pursuant to the contract	$6,000
(Converted at $2.40 to £1)	£2,500
Less: Nett proceeds of sale of the goods delivered in purported performance of the contract.	800
Nett loss	£1,700

And the plaintiffs claim:

(i) £1,700, or alternatively damages;

(ii) Interest.

F.o.b. Contract: Defence to Claim by Buyer

POINTS OF DEFENCE

137 1. Paragraphs 1 and 2 of the Points of Defence are admitted.

2. The defendants will refer to the said contract for its full terms and effect. It further provides as follows:

"All questions or disputes arising under this contract shall be referred to two arbitrators, one to be appointed by each party. In case such question or dispute arises respecting quality or condition, the buyer shall accept the goods and the arbitrators shall decide only the question of allowance (if any) to be made to the buyer. The arbitration shall be held in London and shall be claimed within 7 days of the arrival of the goods in London."

3. Paragraph 3 of the Points of Claim is not admitted.

4. Paragraphs 4 and 5 of the Points of Claim are admitted.

5. As to paragraph 6 of the Points of Claim, it is admitted and averred that the said goods were shipped in 2,000 cases of 24 tins each. By a letter dated January 22, 19—, the defendants requested the plaintiffs to agree to a variation of the original contract and accept delivery under the contract of cases containing either 24 or 48 tins at the defendants' option. The plaintiffs agreed to this by their letter of January 29, 19—. In the premises, the contract was varied so as to provide for delivery of cases containing either 24 or 48 tins. Further or alternatively, the plaintiffs waived their right to delivery of cases containing 48 tins. Further or alternatively, the plaintiffs by their letter of January 29, 19—, represented that they would not insist on delivery of cases containing 48 tins and the defendants relied on that representation by taking no further steps to acquire further cases of 48 tins to complete the said consignment and/or by shipping cases which contained 24 tins. In the premises, the plaintiffs are estopped from relying on their right to receive shipment of cases containing 48 tins.

6. Paragraph 7 of the Points of Claim is not admitted. The plaintiffs are put to strict proof of each and every allegation contained therein.

7. Further or alternatively, the said goods were shipped by the defendants in perfect order and condition. If, which is denied, the said tins arrived damaged as alleged or at all, the damage occurred during the course of the voyage San Francisco/Liverpool and, in the premises, since the property and the risk in the goods passed to the plaintiffs on shipment, the defendants are not in breach of contract as alleged or at all.

8. Further or alternatively, the goods arrived in Liverpool, on about March 2, 19—, as set out in paragraph 5 of the Points of Claim, and the dispute herein relates to the quality or condition thereof. The plaintiffs did not claim arbitration within 7 days of arrival as aforesaid or at any time prior to the issue of the writ in this action. In the premises, the claim herein is barred and cannot now be made.

9. Further or in the further alternative, upon the true construction of the contract and in the premises, an award is a condition precedent to the right of the plaintiffs to sue under the contract. The plaintiffs have neither sought nor obtained an award and accordingly have no right of action under the contract.

10. Paragraphs 8 and 9 of the Points of Claim are denied.

138 **General Average: Claim by Shipowners** [4]

POINTS OF CLAIM

1. The plaintiffs are, and at all materials times were, the owners of the motor vessel OTHELLO.

2. Pursuant to a charterparty dated, Venice, December 1, 19—, between the plaintiffs' managers, on their behalf, and H. Iago & Co. Ltd. of Venice, as charterers, the vessel loaded a full and complete cargo of 500 livestock at Venice for carriage to Nicosia.

3. The master acknowledged receipt of the said cargo by a bill of lading dated December 29, 19—. The defendants, at all material times, were the owners of the cargo and/or were indorsees and holders of the bill of lading which provided expressly that general average (if any) should be adjusted in London according to the York-Antwerp Rules 1950. Further or alternatively, the bill of lading expressly incorporated all the terms, conditions, clauses and exceptions contained in the charterparty which expressly provided that general average was to be settled in accordance with the said Rules.

4. The vessel sailed from Venice on December 29, 19—, with the said livestock on board. At about 09.00 on December 30, 19—, the main engine was stopped on account of a fall in oil pressure. On examination, the engine was found to be unserviceable due to a leak in an oil pipe and resulting seizing-up. At 18.00 on December 30, 19—, a gale was forecast and heavy seas were encountered. The vessel sent out a distress signal and subsequently was taken in tow by the motor vessel DESDEMONA to Brindisi, where she arrived on January 2, 19—, and her engine was repaired sufficiently to enable her to complete the voyage to Nicosia, where she discharged the said cargo.

5. In saving the vessel and cargo from common danger as aforesaid, the vessel incurred general average loss and expenditure including salvage charges totalling £7,600, of which £5,900 is attributable to cargo under the York-Antwerp Rules 1950. Particulars of the adjustment are set out in the statement of general average prepared by Messrs. Horatio & Co. Ltd. and dated September 1, 19—, a copy whereof was delivered to the defendants on or about September 2, 19—.

6. Further or alternatively, by a Lloyd's average bond, dated January 2, 19—, made after the arrival of the vessel at Nicosia, the defendants undertook to pay to the plaintiffs their proper proportion of salvage and/or general average and/or particular and/or other charges, in consideration whereof the cargo was released to them.

[4] *Cf.* Statement of claim in Admiralty Court, § 198, *infra.*

7. In the premises, the defendants are liable to contribute the sum of £5,900 in general average and/or as salvage charges, but wrongfully and in breach of contract they have failed and refuse to do so. And the plaintiffs claim:

(i) £5,900, or alternatively damages;

(ii) A declaration that they are entitled to general average contribution from the defendants in accordance with the said adjustment;

(iii) Interest.

139 General Average: Defence and Counterclaim

POINTS OF DEFENCE AND COUNTERCLAIM

POINTS OF DEFENCE

1. Paragraphs 1, 2, and 3 of the Points of Claim are admitted. The defendants will refer to the bill of lading dated Venice, December 29, 19—, as may be necessary for its full terms and effect.

2. It is admitted that on or about December 30, 19—, in the course of a voyage from Venice to Nicosia, the main engine of the vessel seized-up and the vessel was thereby disabled. It is further admitted that the vessel discharged the said cargo at Nicosia in the month of January, 19—. Save as aforesaid, no admission is made in respect of paragraph 4 of the Points of Claim.

3. It is admitted that the statement of general average, dated September 1, 19— was delivered to the defendants but no admissions are made as to the facts contained therein. Save as aforesaid, paragraph 5 of the Points of Claim is not admitted.

4. Paragraph 6 of the Points of Claim is admitted. It is admitted and averred that in breach of the contract contained in and/or evidenced by the bill of lading, the plaintiffs refused to deliver to the defendants the said cargo unless the defendants agreed to sign the Lloyd's average bond.

5. Save that it is admitted that the defendants have not paid the sum claimed or any part thereof, paragraph 7 of the Points of Claim is denied.

6. Further or alternatively, it was a term of the contract contained in and/or evidenced by the bill of lading implied by operation of law that the vessel was seaworthy for the voyage from Venice to Nicosia.

7. Further or in the further alternative, the bill of lading was expressly made subject to the Hague Rules. Article 3 (1) of the said Rules provides that the carrier shall be bound before and at the

beginning of the voyage to exercise due diligence to make the ship seaworthy. Article 4 (1) provides that, where loss or damage results from unseaworthiness, the burden of proving the exercise of due diligence is on the carrier.

8. In breach of contract, the vessel was not seaworthy at the beginning of the voyage from Venice to Nicosia, whereby the main engine was liable to and did seize up during the voyage.

Particulars

[*Showing details of unseaworthiness*]

9. The alleged general average sacrifice and expenditure, including salvage charges, were caused by the plaintiffs' said breach or breaches of contract. In the premises, and/or by virtue of Rule D of the York-Antwerp Rules 1950, the plaintiffs are not entitled to recover any contribution in general average. Further or alternatively, the defendants rely upon the matters hereinafter counterclaimed as a defence by way of set-off and/or by virtue of the Rule for the avoidance of circuity of action.

COUNTERCLAIM

10. The defendants repeat paragraphs 6 to 9 (inclusive) of the Points of Defence.

11. If, which is denied, the defendants are liable to pay the alleged or any contribution to the plaintiffs, the defendants counterclaim the like sum as damages for the breach or breaches of duty and/or contract hereinbefore set out.

And the defendants counterclaim damages.

[The next paragraph is 150]

CHAPTER 5

COMMERCIAL COURT: MARINE INSURANCE

Claim for Total Loss of Ship

POINTS OF CLAIM

150 1. The plaintiffs are and were at all material times the owners of the steamship SIEVE.

2. By a Lloyd's policy of marine insurance No. 10101, dated January 1, 19—, the plaintiffs caused the said vessel to be insured against the perils therein enumerated, including perils of the seas,[1] for a period of twelve months beginning on October 1, 19—. The plaintiffs were at all material times fully interested in the said policy [2] and will refer to the same for its full terms and effect.

3. On February 1, 19—, while insured as aforesaid, and in approximate position latitude 55° South, longitude 44° West, the said vessel encountered a storm of exceptional violence and sank.

4. In the premises, the said vessel became a total loss by perils of the seas.

5. The said policy was subscribed by the defendant (among others) in the sum of £2,000.

6. In the premises, the defendant is liable to pay the sum of £2,000 to the plaintiffs. But the defendant has failed and refused to pay the said sum or any sum to the plaintiffs.

And the plaintiffs claim £2,000, or alternatively damages.

Defence to Claim for Total Loss of Ship

POINTS OF DEFENCE

151 1. Paragraphs 1 and 2 of the Points of Claim are admitted.

2. Paragraphs 3 and 4 of the Points of Claim are denied. In particular, it is denied that the said vessel encountered a storm as alleged or at all. The vessel sank in a calm sea, with wind force 1.

[1] Particulars of perils of the seas are always necessary, *i.e.*, the precise nature of the casualty must be stated.

[2] Both an interest in the subject-matter insured (insurable interest) and an interest in the policy must be pleaded, except when the latter is self-evident, *i.e.*, the policy is in the assured's own name.

3. Further or alternatively, the defendant relies on section 39 (5) of the Marine Insurance Act 1906 and says that the vessel was, with the privity of the plaintiffs, sent to sea in an unseaworthy state and that the said alleged loss was due to such unseaworthiness.

Particulars

The vessel's shell plating was cracked and worn in way of Nos. 1 and 2 holds, with many rivets missing, and she was making water at the rate of about 2 foot per day. Her bilge pumps were inefficient owing to being choked with rust.

4. Further or alternatively, the defendant says that the said vessel was, with the knowledge and on the instructions of the plaintiffs, wilfully scuttled by her master and crew.

Particulars [3] [*giving details of the allegation*]

5. In the premises, the said alleged loss was not due to any peril insured against and the defendant is under no liability therefor.

6. The defendant admits the amount of his subscription to the said policy but denies that he is liable to pay the said or any sum to the plaintiffs.

[The next paragraph is 154]

Claim for Constructive Total Loss [4-5]

POINTS OF CLAIM

154 1. By a contract contained in or evidenced by a policy of marine insurance No. 12121 dated London, January 1, 19—, the defendants agreed to insure the plaintiffs in respect of their motor vessel BRUTUS valued at £500,000 for the period of twelve calendar months commencing noon February 1, 19—, against total, and/or constructive, and/or arranged, and/or compromised total loss.

2. The policy was further subject to the Institute War Clauses as attached as far as applicable, clause 1 whereof provides *inter alia* as follows:

"1. This policy covers:

(a) The risks excluded from the standard form of English marine policy by the clause: 'Warranted free of capture,

[3] See *Astrorlanis Compania Naviera S.A.* v. *Linard* [1972] 2 Q.B. 611 and *Palamisto General Enterprises S.A.* v. *Ocean Marine Ins. Ltd.* [1972] 2 Q.B. 625; *cf. Coulouras* v. *British General Insurance Companies* (1922) 11 Ll.L.R. 100.

[4-5] It is customary (but not, of course, necessary) in cases involving large sums or intricate calculations, to employ a firm of loss adjusters, a copy of whose statement is then normally delivered to the defendants by way of particulars.

seizure, arrest, restraint or detainment, and the consequences thereof or of any attempt thereat; also from the consequences of hostilities or warlike operations, whether there be a declaration of war or not; . . .'

(b) Loss of or damage to the interest hereby insured caused by:

(i) Hostilities, warlike operations, civil war, revolution, rebellion, insurrection or civil strife arising therefrom. . . ."

3. The plaintiffs at all material times were the owners of the said vessel and were and are fully interested in the said policy of insurance.

4. On about June 5, 19—, in the early hours of the morning, the vessel arrived at Port Suez en route to London from Auckland, New Zealand. On the same date, war broke out between Israel and the Arab States including Egypt. However, on June 6, 19—, at 6.45 a.m., an Egyptian pilot went on board the vessel and told the master that the Canal was in order. Accordingly, the vessel left Port Suez at 7.00 a.m. and proceeded towards the Canal. She reached the Bitter Lakes at about 11.00 a.m. and remained there until 7.00 p.m. when the master was informed that all navigation in the Canal was suspended. The Canal was thereupon closed to all traffic and has not since been reopened. The vessel was thereby imprisoned in the Canal and has not been able to leave. Repeated requests on behalf of the plaintiffs to the Egyptian and Israeli Governments that the Canal should be reopened and their vessel released, have been turned down. No agreement with regard to the clearing of the canal has been or is likely to be reached in the foreseeable future.

5. In the premises, the plaintiffs have been deprived of possession of their vessel by a peril insured against, namely war risks, and there is no likelihood that they will recover her within a reasonable time or at all.

6. Further or alternatively, during the course of her imprisonment in the Canal, the vessel has suffered loss and damage.

Particulars

(i) General depreciation and damage owing to condition of her imprisonment, inability to continue her voyage and inability to effect necessary maintenance and repairs.
(ii) Heavy marine growth on her bottom over 12 inches thick.
(iii) Heavy marine growth in her generators, coolers, resulting in all generators becoming defective.
(iv) Damage to condenser coils by mussels and marine life.

7. In the premises, the vessel could not be preserved from actual total loss without an expenditure which would exceed her value when the expenditure had been incurred.

8. Accordingly, the plaintiffs have suffered loss and damage and, by virtue of section 60 of the Marine Insurance Act 1906, the vessel has become a constructive total loss and the plaintiffs are entitled to recover the sum insured under the policy, but wrongfully and/or in breach of the policy the defendants have failed to pay the sum insured or any part thereof.

9. Further or alternatively, by virtue of section 56 of the Marine Insurance Act 1906, the plaintiffs are entitled to be indemnified by the defendants in respect of the partial loss of the said vessel.

And the plaintiffs claim:

(i) £500,000, or alternatively damages;

(ii) Interest.

Defence to Claim for Constructive Total Loss

155 POINTS OF DEFENCE

1. Paragraphs 1 and 2 of the Points of Claim are admitted. The defendants will refer to the policy for its full terms and effect.

2. Except that it is admitted that the policy was taken out in the name of the plaintiffs, no admission is made in respect of paragraph 3 of the Points of Claim.

3. It is admitted and averred that, on about June 5, 19—, war broke out between Israel and the Arab States and that, at about 6.00 p.m. on June 6, 19—, the Suez Canal was closed to all traffic. It is denied that no agreement with regard to the clearing of the Canal is likely to be reached in the foreseeable future. Save as aforesaid, paragraph 4 of the Points of Claim is not admitted.

4. Further or alternatively, the defendants will rely on the known current state of the political situation in the Middle East, as reported in the serious newspapers and periodicals, in support of their contention that an agreement with regard to the clearing of the Canal is foreseeable. In particular, the defendants will rely on the fact that the Arab States have accepted the United Nations Security Council's Resolution, put forward by the United States of America, who are known to be supporters of Israel, for the settlement of the dispute. Further, both the United States of America and the Union of Soviet Socialist Republics are reported as being anxious to avoid further conflict between Israel and the Arab States, and, together with the other members of the Security Council, have been considering ways in which the dispute can be brought to an end.

5. Paragraph 6 of the Points of Claim is not admitted.

6. If, which is not admitted, the vessel has suffered damage as alleged or at all, the defendants will contend that such damage can be repaired at a reasonable cost when the vessel is released. In the premises, paragraph 7 of the Points of Claim is denied.

7. Save that the defendants make no admission as to the plaintiffs' loss and damage and that they admit that they have failed to pay the whole sum insured under the policy, paragraph 8 of the Points of Claim is denied.

8. Paragraph 9 of the Points of Claim is admitted. On three separate occasions, namely by letters dated ——, addressed by one Jones, the managing director of the defendants to one Smith, the managing director of the plaintiffs, the defendants have offered to pay to the plaintiffs a reasonable sum in respect of the partial loss of the vessel, but the plaintiffs have rejected and continue to reject these offers, unless the defendants admit that the vessel has become a constructive total loss, within the terms of section 60 of the Marine Insurance Act 1906, which the defendants will not do.

Claim for Total/Constructive Total Loss

POINTS OF CLAIM

156 1. By a policy of marine insurance No. 12345, dated March 31, 19—, and subscribed by the defendants to the extent of 100 per cent., the plaintiffs were insured for the period of twelve calendar months commencing noon December 31, 19—, in respect of their motor vessel CAPULET, valued at £100,000 against total and/or constructive and/or arranged and/or compromised total loss including salvage and salvage charges (and subject to " total loss only " clauses as attached as far as applicable) caused by the insured perils, including fire.

2. The policy was further subject to the Institute Time Clauses as attached, as far as applicable, clause 17 whereof provides:

> " 17. In ascertaining whether the vessel is a constructive total loss, the insured value shall be taken as the repaired value and nothing in respect of the damaged or break-up value of the vessel or wreck shall be taken into account. No claim for constructive total loss based upon the cost of recovery and/or repair of the vessel shall be recoverable hereunder unless such cost could exceed the insured value."

3. The plaintiffs were, at all material times, the owners of the said vessel and were and are fully interested in the said policy of insurance.

4. On about February 2, 19—, the vessel sailed from Hong Kong for London carrying a cargo of 12,000 tons of copra of which about 500 tons were carried on deck.

5. At about noon on February 16, 19—, in the course of the said voyage, fire broke out in the deck cargo stowed above Nos. 3 and 4 holds. The officers and crew were unable to control the fire which spread to the extent that it became necessary to abandon ship. The master, officers and crew were subsequently taken on board by the South African trawler MONTAGUE, which vessel, together with three other South African tugs (hereinafter called collectively "the salvors"), towed the CAPULET into Cape Town on February 19, 19—. The fire continued to burn on board the vessel throughout the said period.

6. The vessel was destroyed and/or reduced to scrap value by the said fire. The plaintiffs by their agents, Messrs. Jones & Company, gave notice of abandonment thereof in writing to the defendants on February 18, 19—.

7. In the premises, the vessel was totally lost by a peril insured against, namely fire, during the currency of the policy of insurance.

8. Alternatively, the vessel was reasonably abandoned on account of its actual total loss by reason of fire appearing to be unavoidable, and/or the vessel was so damaged by fire during the currency of the policy of insurance that the cost of repairing the damage would have exceeded the insured value, namely £100,000, and the vessel was rendered a constructive total loss.

9. In the premises, and/or by reason of sections 56 and 60 of the Marine Insurance Act 1906, the plaintiffs are entitled to recover the sum insured under the policy but, wrongfully and/or in breach of the policy, the defendants have failed to pay the sum insured or any part thereof.

And the plaintiffs claim:

(i) £100,000, or alternatively damages;

(ii) Interest.

Defence to Claim for Total/Constructive Total Loss

POINTS OF DEFENCE

157 1. Paragraphs 1 and 2 of the Points of Claim are admitted. The defendants will refer to the policy for its full terms and effect.

2. Except that it is admitted that the policy was taken out in the name of the plaintiffs, no admission is made in respect of paragraph 3 of the Points of Claim.

3. It is admitted that on February 16, 19—, the South African trawler MONTAGUE, in response to distress signals sent out by the CAPULET, approached her and, discovering her to be on fire, offered every assistance. It is admitted that the master, officers and crew of the CAPULET were taken on board the MONTAGUE. It is further admitted that on February 19, 19—, the MONTAGUE, together with three salvage tugs, towed the CAPULET into Cape Town. Save as aforesaid, no admissions are made in respect of paragraphs 4 and 5 of the Points of Claim. The plaintiffs are put to strict proof of the facts alleged herein.

4. Save that the notice of abandonment is admitted and that it is denied that the plaintiffs were entitled to give such notice to the defendants, paragraph 6 of the Points of Claim is not admitted.

5. Paragraph 7 of the Points of Claim is denied. It is denied that the alleged loss was occasioned by an insured peril as alleged or at all.

6. Further or alternatively, the loss of the CAPULET was caused by the wilful misconduct of the plaintiffs in procuring or conniving at the casting away of the vessel.

7. Save that no admission is made as to the cost of repairing the alleged damage, paragraph 8 of the Points of Claim is denied.

8. The defendants admit that they have not paid the sum assured or any part thereof, save as aforesaid paragraph 9 of the Points of Claim is denied.

Claim for Damage to Ship by Fire

POINTS OF CLAIM

158 1. The plaintiffs are, and were at all material times, the owners of the steamship SIEVE.

2. By a Lloyd's policy of marine insurance No. 10101, dated January 1, 19—, the plaintiffs caused the said vessel to be insured against the perils therein enumerated, including perils of the seas,[6] for a period of twelve months beginning on October 1, 19—. The plaintiffs were at all material times fully interested in the said policy [7] and will refer to the same for its full terms and effect.

3. On February 1, 19—, while insured as aforesaid and lying at St. Katherine's dock in the Port of London, a fire broke out in the

[6] Particulars of perils of the seas are always necessary, *i.e.* the precise nature of the casualty must be stated.

[7] Both an interest in the subject-matter insured (insurable interest) and an interest in the policy must be pleaded, except when the latter is self-evident, *i.e.* the policy is in the assured's own name.

vessel's engine room, as a result of which she was severely damaged and the plaintiffs suffered loss and expense. Full particulars showing the extent of the said damage and the cost of repairing the same, are contained in the surveyors' reports and repairers' accounts, copies of which are delivered separately herewith.

4. The value of the said vessel was agreed by clause 9 of the said policy to be £1,000,000. The cost of the said repairs was £500,000.

5. The said policy was subscribed by the defendant (among others) for the sum of £2,000.

6. In the premises, the defendant became liable to pay to the plaintiffs his proportion of the aforesaid loss, the said proportion being £1,000. The defendant has failed to pay the said or any sum to the plaintiffs.

And the plaintiffs claim £1,000, or alternatively damages.

Defence to Claim for Damage to Ship by Fire

POINTS OF DEFENCE

159 1. Paragraphs 1 and 2 of the Points of Claim are admitted.

2. Paragraph 3 of the Points of Claim is denied. No fire occurred in the vessel's engine room as alleged or at all. The damage referred to in the said paragraph (if any) was the result of ordinary wear and tear. Further or alternatively, the said alleged damage was caused by a fire or series of fires which occurred while the vessel was at sea on various dates before the commencement of the policy sued on. The defendant is unable to give further particulars of the said fire or fires until after discovery herein.

3. Further or alternatively, if any fire occurred as alleged in paragraph 3 of the Points of Claim or at all, the damage caused thereby could have been repaired at a cost not exceeding £5,000.

4. The defendant admits the value of the said vessel and the amount of his subscription to the said policy.

5. The defendant denies that he is liable to pay the sum claimed, or any sum, to the plaintiffs. Alternatively, the defendant is not in any case liable to pay the sum claimed, or any sum, to the plaintiffs. Alternatively, the defendant is not in any case liable to pay more than £10 [8] to the plaintiffs.

[8] Based upon the cost of repair pleaded in paragraph 3.

Claim for General Damage to Cargo

POINTS OF CLAIM

160 1. By a policy of marine insurance dated June 20, 19—, the defendants insured 3,000 tons of maize in bags for a voyage Casablanca to Singapore per the motor vessel CORIOLANUS sailing on or about July 19—. The policy provided *inter alia* as follows:

> "Sue and Labour Clause: . . . and in case of any loss or misfortune, it shall be lawful to the assured, their factors, servants and assigns, to sue, labour, and travel for, in and about the defence, safeguards, and recovery of the said goods and merchandises and ship, etc., or any part thereof, without prejudice to this insurance; to the charges whereof, we, the assurers, will contribute each one according to the rate and quantity of his sum herein assured."

The policy further included the Institute Cargo Clauses (All Risks), clause 5 whereof provides:

> "This insurance is against all risks of loss of, or damage to, the subject-matter insured, but shall in no case be deemed to extend to cover loss, damage or expense proximately caused by delay or inherent vice or nature of the subject-matter insured. Claims recoverable hereunder shall be payable irrespective of percentage."

2. The plaintiffs were at all material times the owners of the said goods which were shipped on board the vessel at Casablanca on or about July 2–3, 19—. In the premises, the plaintiffs were fully interested in the goods and in the policy.

3. The maize was shipped in paper bags containing 56 lbs. On July 25, 19—, the vessel arrived at Singapore where the said cargo was discharged. During the course of the discharge, a number of bags in which the goods were packed, broke and a large quantity of the goods became loose in the lighters. The plaintiffs thereupon arranged for the cargo to be rebagged and thereby incurred expense, amounting to £0,000, in respect of the cost of such rebagging and of the additional lighterage and landing charges incurred by reason of the condition of the goods.

Particulars

[*Showing details of how the total figure of £0,000 is obtained*]

4. In the premises, by reason of the Sue and Labour Clause in the aforesaid policy, the plaintiffs are entitled to recover from the defendants the said expenditure of £0,000, which was incurred by them in

taking steps to safeguard and/or recover the goods insured and to avoid what would otherwise have been a loss or damage within the terms of the policy for which the defendants would have had to indemnify them.

5. Further or alternatively, on discharge, 500 tons of the said cargo in Nos. 2 and 3 lower holds were discovered to be damaged. The maize was wetted, rotting and fermenting. Full particulars of the damage are shown in Survey Report No. 12345 of Messrs. Jones & Co., Lloyd's agents, dated Singapore August 8, 19—.

6. The said damage occurred during the currency of the policy by reason of a peril or perils insured against.

Particulars

(i) The owners of the vessel, their servants or agents failed to load, and/or to stow, and/or to carry, the said cargo so as to provide sufficient ventilation for the same before and/or during the voyage. The hatches were laid and matted over. The 'tween-deck hatches were not opened during the voyage. By reason of the foregoing the cargo received no, or no adequate, ventilation particularly in way of the hatch coamings.

(ii) The vessel encountered heavy weather on July 18–20, 19—, whereby ventilation of the cargo was prevented or further restricted on the said dates.

(iii) The damaged cargo was situated in and beneath the hatch coamings and was damaged by the heating and lack of ventilation as aforesaid.

(iv) Further or alternatively, rainwater entered Nos. 1 and 4 lower holds by way of the 'tween-deck hatches, when the vessel was berthed at Casablanca during loading on July 2 or 3, 19—.

7. In the premises, the plaintiffs have suffered loss and damage and have incurred expense in respect of their said goods by reason of a peril insured against, and claim to be indemnified against the said loss, damage and expense by the defendants.

Particulars

[*Showing details of the loss, damage and expense*]

And the plaintiffs claim:

(i) Under paragraph 4, £0,000;
(ii) Under paragraph 7, £0,000;
(iii) Interest.

Defence to Claim for General Damage to Cargo

POINTS OF DEFENCE

161 1. Paragraph 1 of the Points of Claim is admitted. The defendants will refer to the said policy of marine insurance for its full terms and effect.

2. It is admitted that the said goods were shipped on board the vessel at Casablanca on or about July 2 or 3, 19—. Save as aforesaid, paragraph 2 of the Points of Claim is not admitted.

3. It is admitted and averred that the maize was shipped in bags containing 56 lbs. each and that the vessel arrived at Singapore on July 25, 19—. Save as aforesaid, paragraph 3 of the Points of Claim is not admitted.

4. Paragraph 4 of the Points of Claim is denied. The maize was packed in paper bags which were defective and inadequate to withstand the ordinary incidents of the insured transit, in that the seams opened because of no adhesive or inadequate adhesive matter to keep them firmly closed and the contents secure, during ordinary and necessary handling and carriage. In the premises, if (which is not admitted) the plaintiffs incurred expenditure in respect of the rebagging, and/or additional lighterage and landing charges, because of the aforesaid inherent vice of the cargo, the defendants are not liable to the plaintiffs as alleged or at all by virtue of section 55 (2) (*c*) of the Marine Insurance Act 1906 and clause 5 of the Institute Cargo Clauses (All Risks) set out in the Points of Claim.

5. Further or alternatively, the said expenses were not incurred by the plaintiffs in order to avert any loss or damage to or in and about the defence, safeguard or recovery of any part of the maize. The said expenses were solely incurred in order to discharge the maize or to discharge the same more easily from the said vessel and/or from a lighter into which it had been discharged and, in the premises, the expenditure does not fall within the Sue and Labour Clause in the said policy.

6. Further or alternatively, the said maize was packed wet or damp into the said bags before loading, and caused or contributed to the alleged weakness of the bags. In the premises, the alleged loss or damage occurred by reason of the inherent vice or the nature of the goods and the defendants are not liable for the reasons aforesaid.

7. Save that the Survey Report is admitted, paragraph 5 of the Points of Claim is not admitted.

8. No admission is made in respect of any of the allegations con-

tained in paragraph 6 of the Points of Claim. If (which is not admitted) the 500 tons of the said cargo were discharged damaged as alleged, the defendants will contend that the said damage was caused or contributed to by the inherent vice of the goods, in that the maize was loaded wet or damp.

9. Paragraph 7 of the Points of Claim is denied.

Cargo Owner's Claim for Partial Loss by Fire

POINTS OF CLAIM

162 1. By a policy of marine insurance dated —, 19—, and numbered 2468 and subscribed by the defendants, and a declaration thereunder, dated July 15, 19—, and numbered 2468A, the defendants agreed to insure 500 tons of ground nuts in bags, valued at £10,000, the property of the plaintiffs, from East Africa to the United Kingdom.

2. The said policy was in the sum of £7,000, being a part of policies totalling £35,000.[9] The plaintiffs were at all material times fully interested in the said policy and will refer to the same for its full terms and effect.

3. The said goods were insured by the said policy against the perils therein specified, including " fire . . . and all other perils, losses and misfortunes that have or shall come to the hurt, detriment or damage of the said goods."

4. The said goods, in a consignment of 11,217 bags, were loaded on board the ss. EMPIRE BUILDER at Dar es Salaam between July 20 and 27, 19—, and were thereafter carried in the said vessel on its voyage to the United Kingdom.

5. The weight of the contents of the said 11,217 bags on shipment was 500 tons 0.1.22. The weight of contents which ought to have been delivered from the said vessel was 496 tons 8.1.22. In fact, there were delivered from the said vessel only 274 tons 3.0.8 and the balance thereof, namely, 222 tons 5.1.14, was not delivered. The said 274 tons 3.0.8 actually delivered were damaged by fire to the extent of 50 per cent. of the arrived value thereof. In the premises, the plaintiffs suffered a loss in the sum of £7,749 for which they are entitled to be indemnified by their insurers.

Full particulars showing how the above figures are calculated are contained in the average statement of Messrs. Abacus & Co. dated July 31, 19—, a copy of which has been delivered to the defendants.

[9] Large risks are usually spread over several policies which may contain elaborate provisions for " averaging " losses between them.

6. Further or alternatively, the said loss of and damage to the said goods was caused by fire during the currency of the said policy, namely, a fire or series of fires which occurred in the cargo spaces of the said vessel in which the said goods were being carried, namely, Nos. 1 and 3 'tween-decks and Nos. 1 and 2 lower holds, at or about the time when the said vessel was at Suez in the course of the said voyage. In the premises, the defendants are liable under the said policy to indemnify the plaintiffs for their said loss.

7. The defendants' proportion of the said loss, which they are, in the premises, liable to pay to the plaintiffs, is £2,118. The defendants have wrongfully failed and refused to pay the said or any sum to the plaintiffs.

And the plaintiffs claim £2,118, or alternatively damages.

Defence to Cargo Owner's Claim for Partial Loss by Fire

POINTS OF DEFENCE

163 1. The policy of marine insurance and declaration referred to in paragraph 1 of the Points of Claim are admitted subject to production thereof. It is denied that the said ground nuts were at any material time the property of the defendants.

2. It is denied that the plaintiffs were interested in the said policy as alleged in paragraph 2 of the Points of Claim or at all. The said policy was taken out by the Omnium Trading Co. in their own name and no assignment of the said policy is averred to have been made or was made.

3. Paragraph 3 of the Points of Claim is admitted.

4. Paragraphs 4, 5 and 6 of the Points of Claim are denied. Further or alternatively, it is denied that any of the said goods were lost or damaged as alleged or at all, or that the said alleged loss occurred at any time during the currency of the said policy, or that any such loss was caused by any risk insured against by the said policy. Further or alternatively, none of the said goods that were lost (if any) were covered by the said policy.

5. Further or alternatively, the said ground nuts were the produce of the Republic of Canoodle-Dum. By a resolution of the Security Council of the United Nations, dated April 1, 19—, the carriage of any product of the said republic in any ship owned by nationals of, or registered under the flag of, any member of the United Nations, was prohibited. The EMPIRE BUILDER was a British owned and registered ship and Great Britain was, at the material time, a member

of the United Nations. In the premises, the said ship was engaged on an illegal voyage by the law of nations and the insurers are entitled to avoid the insurance policy.

6. In the premises, the defendants are under no liability to pay the plaintiffs the sum claimed or any sum.

Cargo Owner's Claim for Sue and Labour Expenses

POINTS OF CLAIM

164 1. By a policy of marine insurance dated May 4, 19—, and numbered 12345 and subscribed (*inter alios*) by the defendants, and a declaration thereunder numbered 6789, the defendants agreed to insure 1,000 tons of Chilean nitrates valued at £17,080, the property of the plaintiffs, on a voyage from Valparaiso to the United Kingdom, against all risks of loss and/or damage from whatsoever cause arising, irrespective of percentage. The plaintiffs were at all material times fully interested in the said policy.

2. The said policy further provided as follows:

> "... in case of any loss or misfortune, it shall be lawful to the assured, their factors, servants and assigns, to sue, labour and travel for, in and about the defence, safeguard and recovery of the said goods ... or any part thereof, without prejudice to this insurance; to the charges whereof, we, the assurers, will contribute, each one according to the rate and quantity of his sum herein insured."

3. The said goods were packed in paper sacks containing 56 lbs. each and were loaded in good order and condition in the ss. ADMIRAL BLIMP. The said vessel left Valparaiso on June 1, 19—, and arrived in London on July 18, 19—. On arrival as aforesaid, a large number of the said sacks were found to be torn and/or broken and a large quantity of the goods was loose, and the plaintiffs incurred expense in re-bagging and landing the same.

Particulars

Additional lighterage charges incurred by reason of the condition of the said goods	£2,510
Additional landing charges ditto	£7,010
20,000 paper sacks at £62 per 1,000	£1,240
Cost of re-bagging	£1,990
	£12,750

4. Had the plaintiffs not taken the above steps to safeguard and/or recover the said goods, the same would have suffered loss and/or damage within the terms of the aforesaid policies. In the premises, the defendants are liable to pay to the plaintiffs their proportion of the said expenses, namely, £1,690.

And the plaintiffs claim £1,690, or alternatively damages.

Defence to Cargo Owner's Claim for Sue and Labour Expenses

POINTS OF DEFENCE

165 1. Paragraphs 1 and 2 of the Points of Claim are admitted.

2. No admissions are made as to paragraphs 3 and 4 of the Points of Claim.

3. It is denied that the said goods encountered any insured peril or suffered, or were in danger of suffering, any loss or damage within the meaning of the said policy, as alleged or at all.

4. If the plaintiffs incurred expenses as alleged, the same was due to the inherent vice or nature of the goods themselves, and the defendants are not in any event liable therefor.

Particulars

The said goods, owing to their hygroscopic nature, were not suitable for packing in paper sacks. Further or alternatively, the sacks were inadequate in that, owing to defective stitching, the sides of the sacks were not firmly sewn together throughout their length. In the premises, the said goods were incapable of withstanding the ordinary incidents of the voyage.

5. In the premises, the defendants are under no liability to the plaintiffs herein.

Cargo Owner's Claim for Loss by Inherent Vice

POINTS OF CLAIM

166 1. The Plaintiffs were at all material times the owners of certain goods on which they caused themselves to be insured by a policy of marine insurance as particularised hereunder.

Particulars

Policy No. 90909, dated May 3, 19—, in the sum of £75,000 on "Interest as per schedule attached, valued as attached"; and a declaration thereunder dated May 8, 19—, in the following terms (so far as material):

> "Per rail and steamer and/or steamers. From Villa Mercedes (Argentine) to Flual Warehouse in United Kingdom via London. 390 cases Argentine corned beef. 24 tins each 2 lb. 14 oz. per case. Tins marked XYZ 1/2/3 etc. £9,475."

2. The perils insured against by the said policy were expressed as follows:

> "Being against risks of whatsoever nature and/or kind. Average irrespective of percentage. Including blowing of tins. Including inherent vice and hidden defect. Condemnation by authorities to take place within 3 months of the date of arrival in final warehouse in the United Kingdom but not exceeding 5 months in all from date of manufacture."

The said policy also contained the following clause:

> "Institute Cargo Clauses (All Risks): 1. This insurance attaches from the time the goods leave the warehouse at the place named in the policy for the commencement of the transit and continues until the goods are delivered to consignees or other final warehouse at the destination named in the policy."

3. The plaintiffs were at all material times fully interested in the said policy, and will refer to the same for its full terms and effect.

4. The said goods left the manufacturer's warehouse at Villa Mercedes in March 19— and reached their respective final warehouses in the United Kingdom at various dates in May and June 19—. Full particulars of the said dates of arrival are contained in the loss adjustment of Messrs. Laurel & Hardy, a copy of which has been delivered to the defendants.

5. In the course of the said transit and while insured as aforesaid, the said goods suffered loss or damage from one or more insured perils.

6. In the premises, the plaintiffs have suffered loss and damage and have been put to expense amounting in all to £5,680. Full particulars of the said loss damage and expense are contained in the said adjustment of Messrs. Laurel & Hardy.

7. The said policy was underwritten by the defendants in the sum of £6,500. The defendants' proportion of the said loss of £5,680 is therefore £3,900.

8. In the premises, the defendants are liable to pay the plaintiffs the sum of £3,900, but the defendants have wrongfully refused to pay the said or any sum.

And the plaintiffs claim £3,900, or alternatively damages.

120

Defence to Cargo Owner's Claim for Loss by Inherent Vice

POINTS OF DEFENCE

167 1. Except that the plaintiffs' ownership of the goods therein referred to is not admitted, and subject to production of the policy of marine insurance therein referred to, paragraphs 1, 2 and 3 of the Points of Claim are admitted.

2. Paragraphs 4 and 5 of the Points of Claim are denied.

3. If any of the said goods were lost or damaged as alleged or at all, such loss and damage was caused by the inherent vice of the goods themselves, in that the same were improperly manufactured, and, in the premises, occurred before the goods left the manufacturer's warehouse at the place named in the said policy for the commencement of the transit.

4. Alternatively, any such loss and damage was caused by condemnation of the said goods by the public health authorities of the places in which the consignees' final warehouses were situated, and such condemnation took place after delivery of the said goods to such warehouses, and/or more than 5 months from the date of manufacture of the said goods.

5. Further or alternatively, the alleged loss and damage (if any) was caused prior to shipment of the said goods in the said vessel. The plaintiffs had no insurable interest in the said goods, or under the said policies, prior to the shipment of the said goods and have not at any material time acquired any such interest.

6. In the premises, the defendants are not in any event under any liability to the plaintiffs herein.

7. Further or alternatively, the words in the said policy, "tins marked XYZ 1/2/3 etc.," amounted to a warranty that all the said tins would be so marked. In breach of the said warranty some of the said tins were not so marked. Alternatively, the plaintiffs represented to the defendants, before taking out the said policy and in order to induce the defendants to subscribe the said policy, that all the said tins would be marked with a code to enable the date of manufacture of the said goods to be verified. The said representation was material to the risk and was false, in that some of the said tins were not so marked.

8. Further or alternatively, the plaintiffs did not disclose to the defendants, before taking out the said policy, that the goods were not manufactured in accordance with the usual process for goods of the same class but were manufactured by a novel process which did not involve complete sterilisation of the said goods. The said fact was material to the risk and ought to have been disclosed.

9. In the premises, the defendants became entitled to avoid the said policy and are not in any event under any liability to the plaintiffs herein.

10. Paragraph 7 of the Points of Claim is admitted. Paragraphs 6 and 8 of the Points of Claim are denied.

Claim for Total Loss of Freight

POINTS OF CLAIM

168 1. The plaintiffs are and were at all material times the owners of the steamship SIEVE.

2. By a Lloyd's policy of marine insurance No. 98765 dated February 1, 19—, the plaintiffs caused the freight earned or expected to be earned by the said vessel during the period December 1, 19—, to November 30, 19—, to be insured against the perils therein specified including restraint of princes.

3. By a charterparty dated April 1, 19—, it was agreed between the plaintiffs and the Worldwide Trading Company Ltd., as charterers, that the said vessel should proceed to Havana and there load a full and complete cargo of cigars for carriage to London in consideration of a lump sum freight of £10,000 to be paid by the charterers to the plaintiffs on signing bills of lading.

4. The said vessel arrived at Havana on April 15, 19—. On April 16, 19—, while the vessel was waiting her turn to load, a number of ships of the United States Navy appeared off the said port and the officer commanding the said ships ordered all merchant vessels including the SIEVE to leave the port immediately.

5. In consequence of the said order, the said vessel sailed away from Havana without having loaded any cigars and no freight was paid to the plaintiffs under the said charterparty.

6. In the premises, there was a loss of freight within the terms of the said policy and the defendant became liable to pay the plaintiffs the proportion of the said loss underwritten by him, namely, £1,500. But the defendant has failed and refused to pay the said or any sum to the plaintiffs.

And the plaintiffs claim £1,500, or alternatively damages.

Defence to Claim for Total Loss of Freight

POINTS OF DEFENCE

169 1. Paragraphs 1, 2 and 3 of the Points of Claim are admitted.

2. It is admitted that the vessel arrived at Havana on April 15, 19—, and that ships of the United States Navy appeared off the said port on April 16, 19—. It is denied that the officer commanding the said ships issued any order as alleged or at all.

3. It is admitted that the vessel left Havana without having loaded any cigars and that no freight was paid to the plaintiffs under the said charterparty.

4. The said loss of freight was caused by the voluntary act of the master of the said vessel in sailing away from Havana. Had the vessel remained at Havana, her cargo could have been loaded and freight would have been earned.

5. Alternatively, the defendant will rely upon clause 13 (b) of the Institute Time Clauses: Freight,[10] which were incorporated in the said policy. If the departure of the vessel from Havana was caused by restraint of princes, the loss of freight was due to frustration of the charterparty voyage caused by such restraint and is consequently not within the terms of the said policy.

6. The defendant admits that his proportion of the loss (if any) is £1,500 and that he has not paid the said sum to the plaintiffs, but denies that he is liable to pay the said or any sum to the plaintiffs.

Insurer's Claim to be Subrogated to the Rights of the Assured

POINTS OF CLAIM

170 1. The defendants were at all material times the owners of the ss. DEVIOUS. On February 13, 19—, the DEVIOUS was in collision with the ss. ECCENTRIC. As a result of the said collision, the DEVIOUS became a total loss.

2. On July 1, 19—, the defendants received, from the owners of the ECCENTRIC, damages for the loss of the DEVIOUS amounting to £180,000.

3. By a policy of marine insurance dated November 30, 19—, the plaintiffs and other insurers insured the defendants against loss of or damage to the DEVIOUS by perils of the seas, in the sum of £75,000, on the terms and conditions therein contained. The DEVIOUS was valued in the said policy at £75,000.

4. As a result of the said loss of the DEVIOUS, the plaintiffs became liable to pay to the defendants the full amount of their subscription to the said policy, namely, £5,000, the plaintiffs paid the said sum to the defendants on July 4, 19—.

10 "Warranted free of any claim based on loss of or frustration of the insured voyage caused by arrests, restraints or detainments of kings, princes, peoples. . . ."

5. On paying for the total loss of the DEVIOUS as aforesaid, the plaintiffs became entitled to take over *pro tanto* the interest of the defendants in the subject matter insured. Further or alternatively, the plaintiffs were thereupon subrogated *pro tanto* to all the rights and remedies of the defendants in, and in respect of, the said subject matter. The plaintiffs will rely upon section 79 (1) of the Marine Insurance Act 1906. Further or alternatively, the defendants in recovering damages from the owners of the ECCENTRIC for the loss of the DEVIOUS were acting *pro tanto* as agents for the plaintiffs and are bound to account to the plaintiffs for the sums so recovered.

6. In the premises, the plaintiffs are entitled to receive such proportion of the aforesaid sum of £180,000 as their subscription to the said policy bears to the insured value of the DEVIOUS, namely, £12,000. And the plaintiffs claim £12,000, or alternatively damages.

Defence to Insurer's Claim to be Subrogated to the Rights of the Assured

POINTS OF DEFENCE

171 1. Paragraphs 1, 2, 3 and 4 of the Points of Claim are admitted.

2. The defendants make no admissions as to paragraph 5 of the Points of Claim.

3. Of the sum of £180,000 paid to the defendants by the owners of the ECCENTRIC, only £150,000 was referable to the value of the DEVIOUS, the remaining £30,000 being in respect of loss of profit. The actual value of the DEVIOUS at the time of her loss was £150,000.

4. Paragraph 6 of the Points of Claim is denied. If (which is denied) the plaintiffs are entitled to receive any sum from the defendants, they are entitled to the amount of their subscription to the said policy and no more. Alternatively, they are entitled only to such proportion of the sum of £150,000 as the amount of their said subscription bears to the insured value of the DEVIOUS, namely, £10,000.

Shipowner's Claim to Recover General Average Loss

POINTS OF CLAIM

172 1. The plaintiffs are, and were at all material times, the owners of the steamship SIEVE.

2. By a Lloyd's policy of marine insurance No. 999 dated Feb-

ruary 15, 19—, the plaintiffs caused the said vessel to be insured against the perils therein enumerated, including perils of the seas, for a period of 12 months from December 1, 19—. The plaintiffs were at all material times fully interested in the said policy and will refer to the same for its full terms and effect.

3. On February 29, 19—, while crossing the Indian Ocean on a voyage from London to Fremantle with a cargo of agricultural machinery, the said vessel encountered a tropical cyclone as a result of which she sustained damage and was likely to sustain further damage if she continued on her voyage.

4. As a result of the said damage, the said vessel took refuge in the port of Colombo. The decision to put into the said port was reasonably and voluntarily made by the Master for the common safety of ship and cargo, and the act of so putting in was, in the premises, a general average sacrifice.

5. As a result of the said vessel's taking refuge as aforesaid, the plaintiffs incurred extraordinary expenditure amounting to £8,000. Full particulars showing how the said sum is made up are delivered separately herewith.[11]

6. Alternatively, the plaintiffs will rely on section 66 (4) of the Marine Insurance Act 1906 and say that they are entitled to recover the proportion of the said expenditure falling upon them, namely, £5,000, as shown in the aforesaid particulars.

7. The said policy was subscribed by the defendant in the sum of £2,000.

8. In the premises, the defendant is liable to pay the plaintiffs the sum of £1,000, being his proportion of the said sum of £8,000; alternatively, the sum of £500, being his proportion of the said sum of £5,000.

And the plaintiffs claim £1,000, or alternatively damages.

Defence to Shipowner's Claim to Recover General Average Loss

POINTS OF DEFENCE

173 1. Paragraphs 1 and 2 of the Points of Claim are admitted.

2. Paragraphs 3 and 4 of the Points of Claim are denied.

3. The damage (if any) suffered by the SIEVE, while crossing the Indian Ocean, was of a trivial nature and she could safely have continued her voyage. It is denied that ship and cargo were at any material time in such danger as to necessitate a general average sacrifice.

[11] See note 5, *supra*.

4. It is admitted that the sums referred to in paragraphs 5, 6, 7 and 8 of the Points of Claim are correctly calculated. It is denied that the plaintiffs are entitled to the sums claimed therein or any sum.

Cargo Owner's Claim to Recover General Average Contribution

POINTS OF CLAIM

174 1. By a policy of marine insurance dated December 1, 19—, and subscribed by the defendants, the defendants agreed to insure certain agricultural machinery therein specified and valued at £150,000, the property of the plaintiffs, from the United Kingdom to Australia. The plaintiffs were at all material times fully interested in the said policy and will refer to the same for its full terms and effect.

2. The said machinery was insured by the said policy against the perils therein specified, including perils of the seas.

3. The said machinery was loaded in the ss. SIEVE for carriage from London to Fremantle, Australia. On February 29, 19—, while crossing the Indian Ocean the said vessel with the said machinery on board was severely damaged in a violent storm and took refuge in the port of Colombo for the common safety of ship and cargo.

4. As a result of the said vessel's taking refuge as aforesaid, her owners incurred extraordinary expenditure to which the plaintiffs were, in the premises, liable to contribute. The amount of the said expenditure was £7,911 and the amount of the plaintiff's contribution thereto was £2,309. Full particulars showing how the said amounts are calculated are contained in the average statement of Messrs. Abacus & Co., a copy of which is delivered herewith.

5. The plaintiffs will rely on section 66 (5) of the Marine Insurance Act 1906 and are, in the premises, entitled to recover the said sum of £2,309 from the defendants.

And the plaintiffs claim £2,309, or alternatively damages.

Defence to Cargo Owner's Claim to Recover General Average Contribution

POINTS OF DEFENCE

175 1. The defendants admit the policy of marine insurance referred to in paragraph 1 of the Points of Claim, subject to its production.

2. The said machinery was valued in the said policy at £150,000 " for the purposes of total loss only " but was otherwise unvalued.

3. The said machinery was not, at the material time, the property of the plaintiffs but was sold to the Billabong Development Co. (Pty.) Ltd., by a contract dated February 1, 19—, which provided, *inter alia*, that the property in the said machinery should pass to the buyers on loading into the ss. SIEVE.

4. The said machinery was not insured against perils of the seas. The said policy was expressed to be "against the risks of rust and/or corrosion, and fire only, unless the carrying vessel be totally lost."

5. Paragraph 3 of the Points of Claim is admitted. No admissions are made as to paragraph 4 of the Points of Claim.

6. Paragraph 5 of the Points of Claim is denied. If (which is denied) the defendants are liable to pay any sum to the plaintiffs, the true value of the said machinery was £75,000 and no more, and the defendants are not in any event liable to pay more than a contribution based on such value.

7. Except as above, each and every allegation in the Points of Claim is denied as if the same were herein set forth and traversed seriatim.

Shipowner's Claim for Return of Premium

POINTS OF CLAIM

176 1. By a policy of marine insurance dated February 2, 19—, it was agreed between the plaintiffs, as owners of the ss. SIEVE, and the defendants, as insurers, that the defendants would insure the said vessel against the perils specified in the said policy for a period of 12 months beginning on January 1, 19—.

2. In consideration of the said agreement, the plaintiffs paid the defendants a premium amounting to £2,800.

3. The said policy provided *inter alia* as follows: "To return 8 per cent. for each complete calendar month the vessel may be laid up in port."

4. The said vessel was laid up in the Port of Milford Haven from June 20, 19—, to December 31, 19—.

5. In the premises, the sum of £1,344 is due and owing from the defendants to the plaintiffs. But the defendants have failed and refused to pay the said or any sum to the plaintiffs.

And the plaintiffs claim £1,344, or alternatively damages.

Defence to Shipowner's Claim for Return of Premium

POINTS OF DEFENCE

177 1. Paragraphs 1, 2 and 3 of the Points of Claim are admitted.

2. Paragraph 4 of the Points of Claim is denied. From June 20 to August 30, 19—, the said vessel was lying at anchor in an open roadstead some 2 miles from Milford Haven. On August 30, 19—, the said vessel was secured to a jetty in the said port and was there used as a store ship until November 30, 19—. In the premises, the vessel was not laid up for the period between June 20 and November 30, 19—.

3. It is admitted that the defendants have not paid the sum of £1,344 to the plaintiffs. It is denied that the plaintiffs are entitled to the said sum. If the plaintiffs are entitled to recover any sum from the defendants, they are entitled to recover the sum of £224 and no more.

[The next paragraph is 190]

Chapter 6

ADMIRALTY PLEADINGS

1. Statements of Claim

Claim for Possession and Declaration of Ownership by Sole Owner

STATEMENT OF CLAIM

190 1. On or about January 1, 19—, the plaintiff negotiated with one Brown, a shipbroker, with a view to purchasing the motor yacht DAMON for the sum of about £50,000.

2. In the course of the said negotiations, the plaintiff instructed Brown that he did not wish to purchase DAMON in his own name, but requested Brown to procure some person to serve as the plaintiff's nominee, and, as such, to hold DAMON and all documents of title as trustee for the benefit of the plaintiff absolutely.

3. In accordance with the plaintiff's instructions and request, on or about January 10, 19—, the said Brown invited the defendant to act as nominee or trustee as aforesaid and the defendant agreed so to act.

4. Shortly thereafter, the plaintiff paid the said Brown the sum of £50,000 and instructed the said Brown to arrange for the purchase of DAMON in the name of the defendant.

5. DAMON was sold by Universal Steam Ships Company Limited as vendors to the defendant. By a cheque dated January 30, 19—, for £49,000 drawn by the said Brown, the vendors were paid the price, less broker's commission, out of the purchase-money which the plaintiff had provided.

6. Thereafter, on a date unknown to the plaintiff, the defendant took possession of DAMON and has since enjoyed her as if he were the beneficial owner. Further the defendant holds a bill of sale and other documents of title to DAMON. Despite demands made by the plaintiff in letters dated July 6 and 20, 19—, the defendant has failed and refused to yield up possession of DAMON and/or has failed and refused to transfer legal title to the said ship to the plaintiff and/or to deliver up to the plaintiff a bill of sale and all other documents of title necessary to enable the plaintiff to register himself as owner of DAMON.

7. Further or alternatively, in failing and refusing to yield up

possession of DAMON the defendant has wrongfully detained and detains DAMON whereby the plaintiff has suffered loss and damage.

Particulars

(i) Interest at 7 per cent. on £50,000 since the date upon which the defendant took possession of DAMON. £3,200

(ii) Insurance premiums, moorings, etc. £1,080

(iii) Further the plaintiff has been deprived of the pleasurable use of DAMON.

And the plaintiff claims:

(i) A declaration that the motor yacht DAMON is held by the defendant on trust for the plaintiff absolutely, and/or that the plaintiff is the beneficial owner of $^{64}/_{64}$ shares of DAMON;

(ii) Possession of the said ship;

(iii) An order that the defendant do transfer the legal title to DAMON to the plaintiff together with the bill of sale and all other documents of title relating to DAMON;

(iv) Damages for detention or, alternatively, judgment against the defendant for the loss sustained and a reference to the Registrar to assess damages;

(v) Interest;

(vi) Costs.

Claim in Co-ownership Dispute

STATEMENT OF CLAIM

191 1. The plaintiffs are the registered owners of $^{32}/_{64}$ shares of the vessel DAMON and the defendants are the registered owners of the other $^{32}/_{64}$ shares.

2. During the co-ownership of the plaintiffs and defendants, the defendants have acted as the managing owners of the vessel and have received the freights and earnings of the vessel.

3. The defendants rendered to the plaintiffs on January 1, 19—, certain particulars of the earnings and disbursements of the vessel, but, despite the frequent applications and requests of the plaintiffs, the defendants have neglected and refused to render to the plaintiffs proper accounts.

4. The defendants have frequently laden the vessel with their own goods when more profitable employment could have been found for

the vessel, and, although the plaintiffs on September 29, 19—, gave notice in writing to the defendants that they were no longer to act as managing owners, the defendants continue to act as managing owners and continue to employ the vessel in a manner not approved by the plaintiffs.

5. On September 29, 19—, the plaintiffs made an offer in writing to the defendants either to sell to the defendants the plaintiffs' $^{32}/_{64}$ shares in DAMON for £50,000, being the fair value of the shares, or to purchase the defendants' shares for the like amount; but the defendants refused either to buy or sell on the said terms.

And the plaintiffs claim:

(i) An order for an account to be taken of the vessel's earnings and disbursements to be referred to the Registrar;

(ii) Judgment against the defendants for the amount to be found due to the plaintiffs;

(iii) An order for the appraisement and sale of DAMON.

Claim in a Mortgage Action

STATEMENT OF CLAIM

192 1. The plaintiffs were at all material times the mortgagees of DAMON under a mortgage dated August 29, 19—, and executed at Bergen, Norway.

2. Under the said mortgage, instalments of the mortgage debt were to be paid by the defendants at half-yearly intervals on January 1 and July 1, the final instalment of Norwegian Kr. 100,000 being payable on January 1, 19—. The said mortgage further provided:

(i) that, with each instalment, interest should be paid on the outstanding balance for the half-year period preceding the date of payment at 6 per cent. per annum;

(ii) that amounts which were not paid on the due date should carry interest at 8 per cent. per annum.

The plaintiffs will further refer to the said mortgage as may be necessary for its full terms and effect.

3. All instalments due under the said mortgage were duly paid save for the final instalment of Norwegian Kr. 100,000, plus interest of Norwegian Kr. 15,000, which were due on December 1, 19—, and which the defendants have wrongfully failed and refused to pay. In the premises, there is due and owing to the plaintiffs Norwegian Kr. 115,000, plus interest at 8 per cent. per annum, from January 1, 19—, until the date of payment.

And the plaintiffs claim:

(i) Norwegian Kr. 115,000, at Norwegian Kr. 15 to £1=£7,666;

(ii) Interest thereon at 8 per cent. from January 1, 19—;

(iii) Costs.

Claim for Damage done by Ship

STATEMENT OF CLAIM

193 1. The plaintiffs are, and were at all material times, the owners and/or the persons in possession of installations known as the Universal Oil Terminal at Milford Haven (hereinafter referred to as " the said terminal ").

2. The defendants are, and were at all material times, the owners of the motor vessel DAMON registered in the Port of Panama, of 30,000 tons gross and 20,000 tons net register, some 700 feet in length and 100 feet in beam.

3. Shortly before 12.00 hours on January 1, 19—, DAMON was in the harbour of Milford Haven under the navigation or management of the defendants, their servants or agents, proceeding towards the said terminal where she intended to berth, laden with 60,000 tons of crude oil. Her draught was 40 feet forward and 41 feet aft. One tug was made fast forward. The weather was fine and clear. The wind was North-West, force 4. It was about 1 hour before high water and the flood tide was running at a rate of about 1½ knots.

4. Shortly after DAMON had passed the said terminal, she began to swing to starboard and, for a time, moved crabwise on the tide. When she had reached a position about 2 cables to the Eastward of the said terminal, heading approximately West-South-West, she began to move slowly ahead and thereafter to gather headway until her bow collided at a broad angle with the said terminal.

5. In consequence of the collision, the said stage was severely crushed, and the plaintiffs have suffered loss and damage and have been put to expense. Full particulars will be given on discovery.

6. The said collision, loss, damage and expense were solely caused by the negligence of the defendants, their servants or agents in the navigation and management of DAMON.

Particulars

(i) The plaintiffs will rely upon the facts hereinbefore set out as prima facie evidence of negligence and will, if necessary, rely upon the maxim *res ipsa loquitur*;

(ii) Further, the defendants, their servants or agents were negligent in the following particular respects:

(a) they failed to keep a good look-out;

(b) they proceeded at an excessive speed;

(c) they failed to ease, stop, or reverse their engines in due time or at all;

(d) they failed to make any adequate use of the assistance of tugs in manoeuvring;

(e) they attempted to swing when they were too close to the said terminal;

(f) they arrived off the said terminal too ear'y on the tide.

And the plaintiffs claim:

(i) Judgment against the defendants for damage sustained and costs;

(ii) A reference to the Registrar to assess the amount of such damage.

Claim for Damage Sustained by Ship on Collision

STATEMENT OF CLAIM [1]

194 1. The plaintiffs have suffered damage by reason of a collision between their steam tanker PYTHIAS and the defendants' steam tanker DAMON, which was solely caused by the negligence of the defendants, their servants or agents, as hereinafter appears.

2. Shortly before 03.57 hours on October 16, 19—, PYTHIAS, a steel single screw steam tanker, registered at Piraeus, of 40,043 tons gross, 26,908 tons net register, 778 feet in length, 116 feet in beam, fitted with turbines of 20,000 s.h.p. and manned by a crew of 38 hands all told, was in the Arabian Sea approaching a position reckoned to have been latitude 21°33′ North, longitude 59°43′ East, in the course of a voyage from Ras Tanura to Kalundborg, laden with 59,553 tons of crude oil. Her draught was about 37 feet 8 inches forward and 39 feet 6 inches aft. The wind was westerly, a light breeze, there was dense fog and there was no tide or current of any material force. PYTHIAS was on a course of 203° (true) and, with engines working at slow speed ahead on stand by (15 nozzles), was making about 6 to 7 knots through the water. Regulation masthead lights, side lights and

[1] This form is adapted from the Statement of Claim served in *The Almizar* [1969] 1 Lloyd's Rep. 1; [1970] 1 Lloyd's Rep. 67 (C.A.); [1971] 2 Lloyd's Rep. 290 (H.L.). For the Defence and Counterclaim, see § 220, *infra*. For the Preliminary Acts, see § 382, *infra*. For example of unrelated Defence and Counterclaim alleging negligence on the part of a third vessel joined as a defendant to the Counterclaim, see § 221, *infra*.

stern light, all of which were burning brightly, were being duly exhibited on board PYTHIAS. Prolonged blasts for fog were being sounded on her whistle at intervals in accordance with the Regulations and a good lookout was being kept.

3. In these circumstances, one prolonged blast was heard from a ship bearing on the starboard bow of PYTHIAS, which subsequently proved to be DAMON, whereupon the engines of PYTHIAS were immediately stopped and a signal of one prolonged blast was sounded on her whistle in reply. Immediately afterwards, her engines were put emergency full speed astern with a double ring and three short blasts were sounded on her whistle. After a short interval, during which no further signals had been heard from DAMON, PYTHIAS was stopped in the water and her engines were stopped and a signal of two prolonged blasts was sounded on her whistle. Then DAMON replied with one long blast from a much closer position but still on the starboard bow of PYTHIAS who immediately sounded a second signal of two prolonged blasts. Almost immediately afterwards, a single white light became visible over the top of the fog close to and bearing about two points on the starboard bow of PYTHIAS, whereupon a series of short blasts were immediately sounded on her whistle as a warning signal to the DAMON, which appeared to be heading easterly. The DAMON, however, came on at speed and, with her stem and starboard bow, struck the starboard side of PYTHIAS about 70 feet abaft her stem at an approximate angle of 50° to 60° leading aft on PYTHIAS, doing damage.

4. The defendants, their servants or agents were negligent in that they:

(i) Failed to keep a good lookout.

(ii) Failed to make proper and timely or any use of their radar, and/or failed to observe and/or act upon its indications in due time with proper seamanlike skill and care or at all.

(iii) Proceeded at an excessive speed in fog.

(iv) Having heard, forward of their beam, the fog signals of PYTHIAS, whose position was not ascertained, failed to stop their engines and then navigate with caution.

(v) Failed to ease, stop or reverse their engines in due time or at all.

(vi) Altered course in fog to port and/or to starboard at times when, and/or in circumstances where, it was not safe and proper so to do.

(vii) Failed to keep clear of PYTHIAS.

(viii) Failed to comply with Rules numbered 15, 16, 27 and 29 of the Collision Regulations 1965.

And the plaintiffs claim:

(i) Judgment against the defendants for the damage sustained and costs;

(ii) A reference to the Registrar to assess the amount of such damage.

Claim for Damage Sustained by Ship Otherwise than on Collision

STATEMENT OF CLAIM

195 1. The plaintiffs have suffered damage loss and expense by reason of the negligent navigation and management of the defendants' vessel DAMON by the defendants, their servants or agents, as hereinafter appears.

2. Shortly before about 18.20 hours on June 5, 19—, the plaintiffs' vessel PYTHIAS, a motor tanker of 700 tons gross and 500 tons nct register, some 200 feet in length and 35 feet in beam and powered by a diesel engine of 900 h.p., was at the Universal Oil Berth in the Manchester Ship Canal, having loaded a cargo of oil. She was securely moored, starboard side to, in the following manner:

forward: two head ropes and a rope spring

aft: two stern ropes and a rope spring.

All the said lines were hove tight and made fast on the bitts.

3. In these circumstances, DAMON was observed proceeding outward bound at high speed and causing an excessive swell. After DAMON had passed very close to the Universal Oil Berths, PYTHIAS surged heavily along the wharf and all her lines parted. As PYTHIAS was drawn away, her starboard anchor was let go but her stern grounded on the northern bank of the canal, causing damage to PYTHIAS and loss and expense to the plaintiffs.

4. The defendants, their servants or agents, were negligent in one or more of the following particular respects:

(i) They failed to keep a good look out;

(ii) They improperly caused an excessive swell;

(iii) They were proceeding at an illegal, and/or excessive, speed;

(iv) They failed to keep on their own starboard side of mid-channel;

(v) They failed to comply with Rule 25 of the Collision Regulations 1965 and the provisions of By-Laws 4, 7 and 11 of the Harbour and Port of Manchester By-Laws.

And the plaintiffs claim:

(i) Judgment against the defendants for the damage sustained and costs;

(ii) A reference to the Registrar to assess the amount of such damage.

Claim for Damage Sustained by Ship in Defective Berth

STATEMENT OF CLAIM [2]

196 1. The defendants are the owners of, and/or occupy and have control and management of, a wharf situate at Mudwater.

2. PYTHIAS is a steel motor vessel of 400 tons gross and 200 tons net register, some 150 feet in length and 25 feet in beam, and powered by a diesel engine of 300 h.p. At the times hereinafter mentioned PYTHIAS was bound for the said wharf to discharge a cargo of 500 tons of grain. Her draught was about 11 feet aft and 9 feet forward.

3. The defendants were the owners of the said cargo, and/or were the holders or indorsees of the bills of lading issued in respect of the same. In the premises, the said cargo was to be discharged for reward to the defendants and/or for their benefit and for the purposes of their business.

4. At about 17.30 hours (all times B.S.T.) on January 1, 19—, PYTHIAS came alongside the said wharf with her port side to, heading upstream. The vessel was thereupon securely moored as follows:

[*Set out particulars of moorings*]

At the time of the said mooring, the tide was nearly slack, high water being predicted for 18.30 hours. There was about 12 feet of water over the said berth.

5. At about 19.45 hours, all the said moorings parted, whereupon the vessel's head swung out in the channel and the stern of PYTHIAS struck the wharf. PYTHIAS came to rest at an angle of about 90° across the river, listing heavily to starboard. As the flood tide made, the vessel's head began to move towards the wharf, and by 05.00 hours the vessel refloated and proceeded under her own power. PYTHIAS was brought alongside the wharf, starboard side to, heading downstream, and, at about 06.00 hours, discharge of the cargo commenced. By about 09.00 hours, PYTHIAS was aground on an even keel.

6. In the premises, it was a term to e implied by law in the contract of carriage and/or discharge contained in, or evidenced by, the said bills of lading, that the defendants would take reasonable care to see that their berth was safe or to warn the plaintiffs of their failure to do so. Further or alternatively, by virtue of their duty as owners and/or consignees and/or receivers of the said cargo, the defendants warranted to the same effect.

7. Alternatively, the defendants owed a duty to the plaintiffs at common law and/or by virtue of the Occupiers' Liability Act 1957

[2] For Defence, see § 223, *infra*.

to take reasonable care to see that their berth was safe or to warn the plaintiffs of their failure to do so.

8. By virtue of the facts set out above, PYTHIAS sustained damage, causing loss and expenses to the plaintiffs.

9. The said damage, loss and expense were caused by the breach of the said contract and/or warranty and/or the said duty and/or the negligence of the defendants, their servants or agents.

Particulars

(i) They failed to take any, or any adequate, steps to ascertain the condition of the said berth before allowing PYTHIAS to come and lie thereon.

(ii) They failed to warn PYTHIAS that the said berth was not a safe and proper berth, and/or that they had not taken any, or any adequate, steps to ascertain the condition of the berth.

(iii) They failed to make or maintain the said berth in a safe and proper condition.

(iv) They caused or permitted the said berth to become covered with a deep layer of mud.

(v) They failed to construct and/or maintain the said berth with a hard base.

(vi) They so constructed and/or maintained the said berth so as to have a slope from the upstream end down to the downstream end and from the wharf side down to the river side of the berth.

(vii) The plaintiffs will further rely on the fact that PYTHIAS suddenly broke away from her moorings.

And the plaintiffs claim:

(i) Judgment against the defendants for the damage sustained together with interest and costs;

(ii) A reference to Registrar to assess damages.

Claim for Fatal Accident on Collision

STATEMENT OF CLAIM [3]

197 1. The plaintiff is the widow and, by virtue of Letters of Administration issued on November 5, 19—, the administratrix of

[3] For Defence, see § 222, *infra*.

the estate of John Smith deceased and she brings this action on behalf of herself as well as on behalf of the said estate.

2. At about 22.30 hours on July 12, 19—, the plaintiff and the said John Smith were lawfully on board the PYTHIAS crossing from Dover to Calais when PYTHIAS collided with DAMON. The said collision was caused by the negligent navigation and/or management of PYTHIAS and/or of DAMON. The plaintiff cannot give particulars of the negligence alleged in support of her claims until after discovery.

3. By reason of the matters aforesaid, the plaintiff sustained personal injuries and suffered loss and damage.

Particulars of injuries

The plaintiff sustained injuries to her right shoulder, bruising and shock.

Particulars of special damage

Expenses incurred in attending hospital	£40
Damage to clothing	£ 5
	£45

4. Further, the said John Smith during his lifetime suffered injuries as a result of the collision and in consequence thereof died on July 13, 19—, and by his death, his life has been shortened whereby his estate has suffered.

Particulars of special damage

Funeral expenses	£50

Particulars pursuant to the Fatal Accidents Acts 1846 to 1959.

This action is brought for the benefit of the plaintiff, now aged 63 years. The deceased was 69 years of age at the time of his death and had retired from work. He was in receipt of a pension of £250 per quarter from his former employers. He was the sole support of his wife and, by his death, she has suffered loss and damage.

And the plaintiff claims:

(i) Damages for personal injuries;

(ii) Damages under the Law Reform (Miscellaneous Provisions) Act 1934 for the benefit of the estate of the deceased;

(iii) Damages under the Fatal Accidents Acts 1846 to 1959 for the benefit of herself as widow.

Claim by Stevedore for Personal Injury Sustained when Struck by Falling Cargo

STATEMENT OF CLAIM [3a]

198 1. On November 8, 19—, the plaintiff was employed as a dock worker by the Universal Stevedores Company Limited and, in the course of his employment, was engaged in discharging wine casks from the motor vessel DAMON. The said vessel was owned and occupied by the defendants.

2. The provisions of the Docks Regulations 1934 applied to the said work and the defendants owed to the plaintiff the duty of care under the Occupiers' Liability Act 1957.

3. In the course of discharging the casks which were stowed in No. 4 'tween-deck, the plaintiff and one Labourer, a fellow employee, had removed some casks from a position about mid-length along the port side when the stack of barrels just aft of their position collapsed and one of the falling barrels struck the plaintiff.

4. The said accident was caused by the negligence and/or breach of statutory duty of the defendants, their servants or agents.

Particulars

(i) They failed to load DAMON and stow the said casks in a safe and secure manner.

(ii) They failed to warn the plaintiff that the said vessel was loaded and the said casks were stowed in an unsafe and insecure manner.

(iii) They failed to take reasonable measures, by shoring or otherwise, to guard against accident during the unloading and handling of the said cargo.

(iv) They failed to ensure that the casks were held in position by dunnage.

5. As a result of the said accident, the plaintiff suffered injury, loss and damage.

[3a] For Defence, see § 225, *infra*.

Particulars of injury

Dislocation of the left shoulder. Injury to the pelvis consisting of a fracture [*etc.*].

Particulars of special damage

Loss of earnings from November 10, 19—, to June 20, 19—, at £25 per week £800.
The plaintiff will give the appropriate credit for National Insurance benefits received.
And the plaintiff claims damages.

Claim by Cadet-hand Struck by Heavy Seas

STATEMENT OF CLAIM [3b]

199 1. The plaintiff, an infant, was born on June 1, 19—, and brings this action by James Smith, his father and next friend.

2. At all material times, the plaintiff was employed by the defendants to serve on board their ship DAMON as a cadet.

3. In the premises, it was the duty of the defendants to take reasonable care by their servants or agents for the plaintiff's safety while he went about his work and to make the ship, its fittings and equipment as safe a place for him to work in as they reasonably could.

4. During the morning of January 1, 19—, DAMON was in the course of a voyage from South American ports to European ports laden with cargo. The weather was deteriorating. At about 08.00 hours, the plaintiff was called out by the chief officer and instructed to rig a lifeline forward. The wind was Northerly force 8 to 9. Heavy seas were breaking over the deck, and water was washing down the port and starboard alleyways.

5. While the plaintiff was engaged in rigging the said lifeline, a heavy sea broke over the deck on the starboard side and washed the plaintiff against the forward part of the bridge and caused him serious injuries, loss and damage.

Particulars of injury

The plaintiff suffered a severe concussional brain injury and facial laceration. He has lost the sight of his right eye. There is a 10 per cent. risk of epileptic occurrences.

[3b] For Defence, see § 224, *infra*.

Particulars of loss and damage

The plaintiff was unfit for work until August 20, 19—. His employment with the defendants was terminated on the same day and he has been obliged to give up his career at sea. Since October 1, 19—, he has been employed as a salesman at a wage of £9 per week. Until his accident, the plaintiff was receiving from the defendants £30 a month gross, plus free board (valued at £5 per week).

Loss of wages and board from January 1 to October 1, less payments by defendants	£500
Less half of National Insurance benefits received and contributions unpaid.	£200
	£300

6. The said injuries, loss and damage were caused by the negligence and/or breach of duty of the defendants, their servants or agents.

Particulars

(i) They unnecessarily ordered the plaintiff to work in an area where he was exposed to the risk of being injured by heavy seas.

(ii) They failed to post a look-out to warn the plaintiff to take care for his own safety when heavy seas broke over the deck.

(iii) They failed to alter the course of the ship in order to make the starboard side a lee side while the plaintiff was at work.

And the plaintiff claims damages.

Claim for Damage to Cargo on Collision

STATEMENT OF CLAIM

200 1. The plaintiffs, as the owners of cargo laden on board the steam tanker PYTHIAS, have suffered damage by reason of a collision between PYTHIAS and the defendants' steam tanker DAMON, which collision was solely caused by the negligent navigation of DAMON by the defendants, their servants or agents as hereinafter appears.

[*For paragraphs 2, 3 and 4, continue as in § 194, supra, save that paragraph 3 should conclude*: "doing damage and causing the plaintiff's cargo or part thereof to escape and be lost whereby the plaintiffs have suffered loss and damage."]

Claim for Damage to Cargo During Voyage [4]

STATEMENT OF CLAIM

201 1. Under bills of lading dated January 1, 19—, issued by or on behalf of the defendants, there were shipped on board the defendants' vessel DAMON at Bangkok 1,000 bags of maize in good order and condition, for carriage for reward to Singapore and delivery there in like good order and condition.

2. The plaintiffs were the owners of the said cargo and/or were the holders or indorsees of the said bills of lading.

3. In breach of their duty as carriers, and/or as bailees for reward, and/or in breach of the contract contained in, or evidenced by, the said bills of lading, the defendants failed to deliver the said cargo in good order and condition but delivered the same damaged by sea water, whereby the plaintiffs have suffered loss and damage.

Particulars

[*Set out details of damage suffered*]

4. Further or alternatively, the said bills of lading expressly incorporated the Hague Rules as applied by the Hong Kong Carriage of Goods by Sea Ordinance. The said Rules provide *inter alia*:

[*Set out Article 3* (*1*) *and* (*2*)]

5. DAMON sailed from Bangkok on January 2, 19—. During January 5 and 6, 19—, the vessel experienced weather which was poor but not unusual for the China Sea in the month of November. By 18.00 hours on January 6, the vessel had developed a list to port. Soundings indicated water in the bilges to a depth of 3 feet. The vessel's pumps were started. The vessel arrived at Singapore on January 7, 19—. The cargo, which was seriously damaged by sea water, was discharged. On inspection of the vessel, it was discovered that the fabric of the vessel was wasted and heavily rusted. There were cracks in the shell plating on the port side.

6. In breach of the said Rules and the said contract, the defendants failed to exercise due diligence to make DAMON seaworthy and/or make the holds and all other parts of the ship fit and safe for their reception, carriage and preservation, and/or properly and

[4] For Defence, see § 226, *infra*. *Cf.* Points of Claim and Points of Defence for damage to cargo in Commercial Court, *supra*, §§ 122 and 123.

carefully to load, handle, stow, keep, or care for the goods, and/or by their negligence caused or permitted the said cargo to become damaged.

Particulars

(i) The plaintiffs will rely upon the facts and matters contained in paragraph 5 herein as evidence of unseaworthiness, breach of contract, breach of duty and negligence.

(ii) The defendants failed to maintain DAMON properly or at all.

(iii) The defendants failed to survey and/or dry dock DAMON regularly or at all.

(iv) The defendants failed to keep all parts of DAMON adequately protected and painted.

(v) The defendants failed to discover and weld up the said cracks in the side plating before or at the beginning of the voyage.

And the plaintiffs claim damages together with interest thereon and costs.

Claim for Breach of Charterparty—Unsafe Berth

STATEMENT OF CLAIM [4a]

202 1. The plaintiffs were at all material times the owners of the Greek tanker PYTHIAS.

2. By a time charterparty dated in London October 8, 19—, made between the plaintiffs and defendants, the plaintiffs agreed to charter the said vessel to the defendants upon the terms set out in the said charterparty.

3. The said charterparty provided *inter alia* as follows:

"3. . . . The vessel shall be employed between safe ports, berths and places where she can always be safely afloat. . . .

11. The master shall be furnished by charterers from time to time with all requisite instructions and sailing directions. . . .

13. The master (although appointed by the owners) shall be under the orders and direction of charterers as regards employment of the vessel, agency or other arrangements. . . . Charterers hereby indemnify owners against all consequences or liabilities that may arise from the master, charterers or their agents signing bills of lading or other documents, or from the master otherwise complying with charterers' or their agents' orders. . . ."

[4a] For Defence, see § 227, *infra*.

4. There were further implied in the said charterparty one or other or both of the following terms:

(a) That the defendants should exercise reasonable care for the safety of the said vessel while at any port, berth or place to which they had ordered her.

(b) That the defendants should give the master of the vessel full and sufficient warning of any dangers or difficulties at any such port, berth or place, or, alternatively, of any such dangers or difficulties of which they knew or ought to have known.

5. On March 16, 19—, the vessel berthed at No. 1 berth, Holiday Bay, pursuant to the orders of the defendants, to load a cargo of petroleum products.

6. Holiday Bay and/or No. 1 berth was not a safe port, berth or place for the said vessel to load in March. In the premises, the defendants, by ordering the vessel to the said port, berth or place, were in breach of clause 3 of the said charterparty.

Particulars

(i) In the event of strong winds or gales from the Southerly quadrant, such as can be expected in the month of March, heavy seas and swell enter and/or arise within Holiday Bay. The said seas and swell cause a vessel such as PYTHIAS to range and work heavily against No. 1 berth.

(ii) By the time the said wind, sea and swell have arisen or are arising, it is extremely hazardous, if not impossible, for a vessel such as PYTHIAS to leave the said berth unassisted by tugs, without doing and sustaining damage.

(iii) No tugs are available to assist a vessel in leaving the said berth in the aforesaid conditions of sea and swell.

(iv) The breasting wires laid to the West of the said berth are not sufficiently strong and/or adequate in number to hold a vessel off the wharf in the aforesaid conditions of sea and swell.

7. By reason of the unsafeness of Holiday Bay and/or No. 1 berth, the said vessel sustained serious damage on March 18, 19—.

Particulars

(i) The vessel was moored port side to, with 3 head ropes, 3 stern ropes, fore and aft springs, and 2 breasting wires. All the said moorings were properly adjusted and tended.

(ii) During the night of March 16/17, the vessel discharged ballast. The wind was Westerly force 4 and the vessel lay comfortably at her berth.

(iii) Loading commenced at about 07.30 on March 17. During the day, the wind remained about West to West-South-West, increasing at times to a strong breeze. At about 16.00 hours, the master put out 3 further stern ropes and 2 further head ropes.

(iv) At about 23.15 hours, the wind and swell had increased and the master decided to suspend further loading and gave orders to ballast the vessel down, and put the engines in readiness. A pilot was called.

(v) At about 01.00 hours on March 18, the wind suddenly backed to the South and South East increasing in strength to a near gale. Ballasting continued until, at about 04.00, the moorings of PYTHIAS began to part. It was impossible to prevent the vessel being thrown against the wharf sustaining and doing damage. Thereafter all lines were cast off and the vessel was manoeuvred clear of the wharf.

8. Further or alternatively, the said casualty and the consequent loss and damage were caused as a result of the master complying with the defendants' orders to load at No. 1 berth, Holiday Bay. In the premises, the plaintiffs are entitled to be indemnified by the defendants under clause 13 of the said charterparty in respect of the said loss and damage.

9. Further or in the further alternative, the said casualty and the said loss and damage were caused by the defendants' failure to furnish the master with all instructions and sailing directions in breach of clause 11 of the said charterparty.

Particulars

(i) They failed to give the master any warning of the risks of bad weather and/or heavy seas and swell.

(ii) They failed to give the master any warning during March 17 that the wind might back to the South or East and increase to gale force, and/or that heavy seas and swell could be expected in the said Bay and at the said berth.

10. Further or in the further alternative, the said casualty and the said loss and damage were caused by the defendants' breach of the implied terms of the said charterparty in paragraph 4 hereof.

And the plaintiffs claim:

(i) Judgment against the defendants in respect of the said damage, together with interest and costs.

(ii) If necessary, a reference to the Registrar to assess damages.

(iii) An order that the defendants indemnify the plaintiffs for any damages which the plaintiffs may become liable to pay to the owners of the said wharf in respect of the damage done to the said wharf, as a result of the aforesaid casualty. Alternatively an order that the question of the defendants' liability to indemnify the plaintiffs for such damages be left over until the liability of the plaintiffs to the owners of the wharf for damages, if any, and their assessment be finally decided.

(iv) Such further or other relief as may seem fair and just.

Claim for Towage

STATEMENT OF CLAIM

203 1. By a contract made orally on or about October 18, 19—, the plaintiffs undertook to provide their motor tug PULLER to tow the defendants' motor vessel DAMON to a berth in the port of Sydney, in consideration of payment by the defendants of the plaintiffs' scale of charges for such services. The said contract was made between one Jones acting for and on behalf of the plaintiffs and one Smith acting for and on behalf of the defendants.

2. Further, the said contract was subject to the plaintiffs' conditions of towage known as the United Kingdom Standard Towage Conditions,[4b] which provide *inter alia* as follows:

> " 3. The tugowner shall not, whilst towing, bear or be liable for damage of any description done by or to the tug . . . arising from any cause, including negligence at any time of the tugowners' servants or agents . . . and the hirer shall pay for all loss or damage . . . and shall also indemnify the tugowner against all consequences thereof. . . ."

3. In pursuance of the said contract, PULLER, a motor tug of about 50 feet in length and 20 feet in beam, powered by diesel engines developing about 500 h.p., and manned by a crew of 5 hands all

[4b] For the full terms of these standard conditions, see *Collisions at Sea* (B.S.L. Vol. 4), § 1304.

told, left her berth in Sydney at about 09.40 hours on May 19 and thereafter came up with DAMON in the approaches to the port. PULLER was instructed by those on board DAMON to make fast to the port bow. The towage connection was completed by about 11.25 hours, and the towage commenced shortly thereafter. During the course of the tow, PULLER struck an unidentified submerged obstruction in the limits of the port, whereby PULLER sustained damage causing loss and expense to the plaintiffs. DAMON was thereafter brought to her berth, and the towage connection was let go at about 14.30 hours.

4. By reason of the said towage services, there is due and owing to the plaintiffs the sum of £100, being the standard charge therefor.

5. Further, by virtue of the said conditions of towage, the defendants are liable to pay for the aforesaid damage, loss and expense, and the plaintiffs are entitled to be indemnified therefor.

And the plaintiffs claim:

(i) Under paragraph 4, £100;
(ii) under paragraph 5, a declaration that they are entitled to an indemnity for the said damage;
(iii) a reference to the Registrar to assess damages;
(iv) interest;
(v) costs.

Claim for Pilotage

STATEMENT OF CLAIM

204 1. The plaintiff is a Certificated Pilot of Trinity House and a member of the Deep Sea Pilots Association.

2. On or about April 8, 19—, it was agreed between Messrs. Universal Ships Agents Company, for and on behalf of the defendants, and the secretary of the Deep Sea Pilots Association, for and on behalf of the plaintiff, that the plaintiff would render pilotage services for the defendants on board the defendants' ship DAMON, on a voyage from the Folkestone pilot station to Leningrad, commencing on April 20, 19—. It was further agreed that, in consideration of the said services, the defendants would pay to the plaintiff a fee of £750.

3. In pursuance of the said agreement, the plaintiff boarded DAMON on April 20, 19—, and rendered pilotage services, as aforesaid, to Leningrad in the U.S.S.R., but the defendants have failed to pay the said fee of £750.

And the plaintiff claims £750 with interest thereon and costs.

Claim for Goods and Materials Supplied

STATEMENT OF CLAIM

205 1. Pursuant to an agreement in writing dated January 1, 19—, made by and between the plaintiffs and the defendants, the plaintiffs supplied to and installed in the defendants' vessel DAMON, a Radio Transmitter Receiver Type A100 for the vessel's operation and maintenance. It was agreed between the plaintiffs and defendants that the plaintiffs would let and the defendants would hire the equipment for a period of 5 years at an annual rental of £300, payable quarterly in advance commencing January 1, 19—.

2. The said agreement expressly provided *inter alia* as follows:

"3. The shipowner shall keep the equipment in his own possession and control.

4. If the shipowner shall commit any breach of this agreement, the company shall be entitled without notice to terminate the hiring forthwith and may retake possession of the equipment.

5. The shipowner shall not be liable for loss of the equipment unless caused by pilferage or theft not attributable to the act or neglect of the company or its servants or agents.

6. Upon the termination of the hiring under any clause in this agreement, the shipowner shall remain liable to pay to the company all arrears of hire or rent due hereunder and all other sums due by way of damages or otherwise."

3. The defendants have failed and refused to pay the following hire payments.

Particulars

From January 1, 19— to December 31, 19—, £900.

4. On or about December 31, 19—, the equipment was stolen from DAMON, whilst the vessel was lying in the port of Liverpool. The said theft was not due to the act or neglect of the plaintiffs, their servants or agents. In the premises, the plaintiffs have suffered loss and damage:

Particulars

2 years' hire		£600
Less cost of maintenance	£200	
Less credit for early payment	£ 50	
		£350
Plus value of equipment at end of 5 years		£100
		£450

And the plaintiffs claim:

(i) £900, under paragraph 3;
(ii) Damages, under paragraph 4;
(iii) Interest;
(iv) Costs.

Claim for Repairs to Ship

STATEMENT OF CLAIM [5]

206 1. The plaintiffs carry on business as ship repairers at Hull.

2. On or about January 7, 19—, the plaintiffs agreed with Messrs. Jones & Company, acting for and on behalf of the defendants, to repair and to supply materials to DAMON. The said contract was contained in a letter dated January 1, 19—, from Messrs. Jones & Company to the plaintiffs and in a letter dated January 7, 19—, from the plaintiffs to Messrs. Smith & Company.

3. Between February 14, 19—, and March 10, 19—, the plaintiffs executed certain work on DAMON in pursuance of the aforesaid contract.

4. There is due and owing to the plaintiffs, in respect of the said work, the sum of £5,000. Particulars of the said work and the cost thereof have been delivered to the defendants and exceed 3 folios in length.

And the plaintiffs claim:

(i) judgment for the said sum of £5,000;
(ii) interest;
(iii) costs.

Claim for Seaman's Wages

STATEMENT OF CLAIM

207 1. By a written contract of service, dated January 1, 19—, made between the plaintiff and the Universal Steamship Company Limited (hereinafter referred to as " Universal "), the plaintiff was employed to serve the said company as a seaman, in accordance with the terms of the National Maritime Board Agreement, for a period of two years commencing July 30, 19—.

2. At the conclusion of the said period, the parties to the said contract, expressly or by implication, agreed that the said employment should continue until determined by mutual agreement or by reasonable notice to be given by either party.

[5] For Defence and Counterclaim, see § 231, *infra*. For Reply and Defence to Counterclaim, see § 240, *infra*. For Rejoinder, see § 241, *infra*.

3. On March 5, 19—, the parties to the said contract determined the said employment by mutual agreement.

4. Between June 10, 19—, and March 5, 19—, Universal appointed the plaintiff to serve as seaman on board their vessel DAMON. During the said period, the plaintiff faithfully and diligently served on DAMON and performed all his obligations under the said contract.

5. In the premises, on March 5, 19—, there was due and owing to the plaintiff the sum of £200 as wages and emoluments:

Particulars

(i) Voyage No. 8 from June 10 to December 5, 19—		£1,000
(ii) Voyage No. 9 from January 20 to March 5, 19—		£ 500
Gross wages		£1,500
less		
Income Tax	£400	
National Insurance Benefit	£ 20	
Sums paid	£880	
		£1,300
Balance due		£ 200

6. The plaintiff claims and is entitled to exercise a maritime lien upon the said vessel DAMON (now known as PYTHIAS) to secure payment of the said sum of £200.

7. Notice in writing of the institution of this action was sent to the Panamanian Consul General in London on November 16, 19—.[5a]

And the plaintiff claims:

(i) £200;
(ii) Interest;
(iii) Costs.

Claim for Master's Wages and Disbursements

STATEMENT OF CLAIM

208 1. The plaintiff claims in respect of the balance of wages and other emoluments due to him and earned by him on board DAMON and/or in the service of the defendants, together with additional sums and/or compensation due to him under his contract of service and/or under the provisions of Greek maritime law, in consequence of the

[5a] See R.S.C., Ord. 75, r. 5 (5). See also the Consular Relations Act 1968, s. 4.

termination thereof, together with his costs of repatriation and maintenance upon repatriation.

2. Further, the plaintiff, as Master of DAMON, in the course of his duties as master and as the authorised agent of the defendants, has expended and disbursed various sums of money for the benefit and on behalf of the defendants. The defendants are liable to reimburse the plaintiff in respect of the said sums but have failed to do so. The plaintiff claims and is entitled to be repaid the said sums by the defendants.

3. The plaintiff was engaged by the defendants under a contract of service which incorporated the provisions of the collective agreement made in Athens on February 17, 19—. The rate of his remuneration was agreed by an exchange of letters with the defendants' agents, Messrs. Universal Agents & Company, dated January 5 and January 10, 19—. In accordance with the said provisions, the plaintiff faithfully and diligently performed his obligations under the said contract.

4. On August 18, 19—, at the port of London, DAMON was put under the arrest of this Court. The plaintiff continued to serve on board DAMON until September 21, 19—, when his contract was determined.

5. On September 21, there was due and owing to him the following amounts:

(i) Wages and emoluments £3,000;

(ii) Disbursements £1,850.

6. Further, there is due and owing to the plaintiff the sum of £120 under, and by virtue of, the provisions of Greek maritime law as compensation payable in respect of the termination of his contract, and the sum of £75, in respect of his cost of repatriation and the costs of maintenance during repatriation.

7. Notice in writing of the institution of this action was given to the Greek Consul General on January 1, 19—.

And the plaintiff claims:

(i) £5,045;

(ii) Interest;

(iii) Costs.

Claim for Agent's Disbursements

STATEMENT OF CLAIM [5b]

209 1. The defendants' vessel DAMON was in the port of Fowey between January 1 and 10, 19—.

[5b] For Defence, see § 232, *infra*.

2. Between those dates, the plaintiffs expended certain sums, and/or made certain disbursements, on account of the said ship at the request of, and as agents for, the defendants.

Particulars

Harbour dues	£55
Light dues	£10
Fresh water	£ 3
Cash for master	£20
Ship's stores	£ 2
Agency fees	£10
	£100

3. The defendants have failed to pay the sum of £100 and, in the premises, the said sum is due and owing to the plaintiffs.

And the plaintiffs claim £100, or alternatively damages, together with interest and costs.

Claim for General Average Contribution [6]

STATEMENT OF CLAIM

210 1. The plaintiffs are the owners of the vessel PYTHIAS.

2. The defendants were the owners of the cargo laden on PYTHIAS for and during the voyage hereinafter described, and/or were the holders or indorsees of the bills of lading, issued by or on behalf of the plaintiffs, whereunder the said cargo was shipped.

3. On January 1, 19—, whilst PYTHIAS was proceeding through the Panama Canal on a voyage from Rotterdam to San Francisco, trouble was experienced with the vessel's steering. A tug assisted PYTHIAS to Panama. The vessel's steering gear and rudder headpiece and mainpiece were twisted so that the rudder was about 10° to starboard when the helm was in mid-position. It was decided to effect temporary repairs. Repairs commenced on January 5, 19—, and were completed on January 12, 19—. The repairs were inspected on January 13, and were found to be satisfactory. PYTHIAS proceeded on her voyage the same day.

4. On or about January 15, the plaintiffs declared general aver-

[6] *Cf.* Points of Claim in Commercial Court, § 138, *supra*.

age. It was an express provision of the aforesaid bills of lading that general average should be adusted according to the York-Antwerp Rules 1950.

5. The defendants failed and refused to give security for any general average contribution that might become due from them or to sign a general average bond. By letter dated November 17, 19—, the defendants undertook to pay any general average contribution that might become due from them. As a consequence of the said undertaking and in reliance thereon, the said cargo was discharged and released at San Francisco.

6. The general average adjustment was published on July 30, 19—. The defendants' contribution thereunder was £2,000. Particulars of the said adjustment were sent to the defendants on August 5, 19—. The defendants have failed and refused to pay the said contribution.

And the plaintiffs claim:

(i) Under paragraph 6, £2,000;
(ii) Interest;
(iii) Costs.

Claim for Salvage by Pilot

STATEMENT OF CLAIM [6a]

211 1. The plaintiff rendered salvage services to the motor vessel DAMON, her cargo and freight, in Gravesend Reach of the River Thames on January 1, 19—, as hereinafter appears.

2. The plaintiff is an experienced Trinity House River Pilot and had held his licence for 10 years. The plaintiff has also held a Foreign-Going Master's Certificate of Competency since 1950, and has served 10 years at sea.

3. DAMON is a steel motor vessel of 10,000 tons gross and 6,500 tons net register, 300 feet in length and 40 feet in beam, and fitted with steam turbine engines developing 2,500 b.h.p. At all material times, she was laden with a full cargo of coal. Her draught was 25 feet forward and 25 feet 6 inches aft. Her salved value was £600,000 or more. The plaintiff does not know at the present time the salved value of her cargo and freight.

4. At the time of the plaintiff's services, the weather was fine and clear. The wind was South-Westerly, force 3 to 4. The tides were springs. Low tide was predicted for 21.06 hours, and high water was predicted for 03.10 hours on the following morning.

5. At about 18.30 hours on January 18, it was reported that

[6a] This form is adapted from the Statement of Claim served in *The Hudson Light* [1970] 1 Lloyd's Rep. 166. For unrelated Defences to claims for salvage, see §§ 228, 229 and 230, *infra*.

HUDSON LIGHT had gone aground in the vicinity of the Lower Tier. The plaintiff was on turn at the pilot station. At the request of the Thames Navigation Service, the plaintiff boarded the pilot cutter, and subsequently boarded HUDSON LIGHT at 19.55 hours. She was heading 240° true, with her stern in line with the Lower Tier and 300 feet down river of the lower bow. She had a list of at least 5° to starboard. She was attended by four tugs, PULLER, PUSHER, TOWER and TUGGER. PULLER and PUSHER were made fast to the starboard bow and were towing abeam. TOWER and TUGGER were made fast aft and were towing in the line of the vessel. The tide was ebbing.

6. On boarding DAMON, the plaintiff ordered soundings to be taken. These showed that she was aground over her entire length. The plaintiff estimated that the vessel would not refloat before 22.30 hours and ordered the engines to be made ready by 22.00 hours. The plaintiff ordered the tugs to stop towing. At about 21.00 hours, the plaintiff ordered PULLER and PUSHER to come inside DAMON and to lay aft on the port bow to stop DAMON moving ahead on the flood tide.

7. At 22.35 hours, the head of DAMON began to alter to port, whereupon the plaintiff ordered the engines to be worked half-astern and the tugs to tow at maximum power. DAMON thereafter began to move astern and refloated at about 22.40 hours. Thereafter DAMON was safely moored to a buoy at 23.15 hours and the plaintiff came ashore.

8. DAMON was heavily aground over the whole of her length and was exposed to the risks of bottom damage, structural strains and damage to her rudder and propeller. She was awkwardly angled across the flood tide. As the tide made, there was the danger that she would move ahead and higher up the bank.

9. The plaintiff's services were promptly and efficiently rendered. The plaintiff took effective command of DAMON and gave all necessary orders for directing the tugs. His services enabled DAMON to be refloated and moored as quickly and as safely as possible.

And the plaintiff claims salvage.

Claim for Salvage by Tug

STATEMENT OF CLAIM [6b]

212 1. The plaintiffs rendered salvage services to DAMON, her cargo and freight in the circumstances hereinafter appearing.

6b For unrelated Defences to claims for salvage, see §§ 228, 229 and 230, *infra.*

2. SPRAYER is a steel screw tug of 126 tons gross and 26 tons net register, 84 feet in length and 22 feet in beam, fitted with diesel engines of 1,000 h.p. and an auxiliary diesel engine for operating her fire and salvage pumps, and was manned, at the time of the services, by a crew of 10 hands all told. Her fire pump delivers 90 tons of water an hour through standard fire hose. The value of SPRAYER was £40,000.

3. DAMON is a steel screw motor vessel of about 2,800 tons gross and 1,170 tons net register, some 300 feet in length and 40 feet in beam, powered by diesel engines of 1,200 b.h.p. and manned by a crew of 20 hands all told. At the time of the services DAMON was laden with a cargo of 3,000 tons of wood pulp. The value of DAMON was £60,000 and the value of her cargo, including freight was £38,000.

4. SPRAYER was stationed at Rochester on the morning of January 21, 19—. At about 03.15 hours on that day, those on board SPRAYER heard a ship blowing several SOS signals on her whistle and thereafter observed DAMON, which was berthed at No. 5 buoy, was on fire. The engines of SPRAYER were immediately made ready and her moorings cast off. SPRAYER then proceeded up river about 800 feet to DAMON. The wind was Southerly, a light breeze, the weather fine and clear and the tide about 3 hours ebb.

5. SPRAYER arrived alongside DAMON at about 03.30 hours and made fast to one of the dumb barges lying along the starboard side of DAMON. The master then boarded the barge, carrying with him a fire hose consisting of 200 feet of 2½ inch hose, fitted with a nozzle and handed the hose up to a member of DAMON's crew. The amidships accommodation was on fire throughout and burning fiercely with flames reaching up to the bridge. Pumping began at about 03.35 hours and members of the crew of DAMON directed the hose through each of the starboard port holes of the accommodation in turn.

6. SPRAYER continued pumping until about 04.50 hours, at which time the fire was nearly out and under sufficient control to be extinguished by the use of buckets. SPRAYER was requested to remain alongside DAMON until 06.00 hours, when the master of DAMON said SPRAYER could leave. SPRAYER then cast off and returned to her mooring where she made fast at 06.50 hours.

7. The said services were promptly and efficiently rendered and were entirely successful. No other effective fire fighting assistance was available and the Fire Brigade were unable to get a hose run off from shore to ship. SPRAYER got under way very promptly and arrived alongside DAMON within a very short time of her sounding

SOS. All necessary equipment on SPRAYER was ready for immediate use.

8. By reason of the services, DAMON and her cargo were saved from sustaining very serious additional damage and from possible total loss. In the absence of assistance from SPRAYER, the fire would have spread rapidly and destroyed DAMON and her cargo and might have affected the dumb barges alongside her. The conditions on board DAMON would have deteriorated rapidly and her crew would have been forced to abandon her.

And the plaintiffs claim salvage.

Claim on Salvage Dispute between two Salvors

STATEMENT OF CLAIM

213 1. The plaintiffs are skilled and experienced salvage contractors of high standing and repute who carry on business at Marseilles in France.

2. The defendants are the owners of the tug DAMON and the employers of her master and crew.

3. At about 12.00 hours on January 1, 19—, fire broke out on board the motor tanker PYTHIAS of about 50,000 tons gross, which was then in the Mediterranean, approximately in position latitude 42° North, longitude 8° East. The fire spread rapidly and on January 2 the crew of PYTHIAS left the vessel. Thereafter PYTHIAS was in need of professional salvage assistance. The plaintiffs had available the tug TOWER in the port of Marseilles.

4. By an exchange of cables on January 2, the master of PYTHIAS accepted the services of the plaintiff upon the terms of Lloyd's open form of salvage agreement (No Cure-No Pay). In the premises, the Plaintiffs contracted to use their best endeavours to salve PYTHIAS, and the owners of PYTHIAS undertook to pay to the plaintiffs salvage remuneration in the event of success. By necessary implication, it was a term of the contract that the owners of PYTHIAS licensed the plaintiff to take possession of PYTHIAS and her cargo, and to go aboard for the purpose of salving her.

5. The defendants were informed of the existence of the said contract by a telex message sent at about 19.00 hours on January 2. The master of DAMON was likewise informed of the said contract by cable sent at that time and at regular intervals thereafter.

6. At about 17.00 on January 2, the salvage tug TOWER of 1,000 tons gross, about 250 feet in length and 40 feet in beam, powered by engines of 9,000 i.h.p. and manned by a crew of 20 hands all told,

sailed from Marseilles for the purpose of rendering salvage assistance to PYTHIAS.

7. At about 05.00 hours on January 3, TOWER arrived in the vicinity of PYTHIAS. Thereafter, the plaintiffs and the said tug were ready able and willing to render salvage assistance to PYTHIAS and to take her in tow.

8. The plaintiffs and their tug were prevented from performing their obligations under the said contract and from rendering salvage services, by reason of the malicious and wrongful interference by the defendants, their servants or agents with the said contract and further by reason of the false representation of the master of DAMON.

Particulars

(i) Between the time of arrival of TOWER and 10.00 hours on January 12, the defendants, well-knowing of the said contract and, with the intention of depriving the plaintiffs of their rights and benefits under the said contract, failed and refused to allow the plaintiffs and their tug to approach PYTHIAS, and/or take possession of her, and/or to board her or to make fast to her, and/or to perform any salvage services which the plaintiffs were bound and entitled to render.

(ii) When TOWER arrived in the vicinity of PYTHIAS, the defendants' tug DAMON was already made fast to PYTHIAS and towing her in a North-Westerly direction. The master of DAMON, despite several demands and protests, failed and refused to hand over PYTHIAS to TOWER. The defendants retained exclusive possession of PYTHIAS and ordered TOWER to keep clear and not interfere.

(iii) Further, the master of DAMON, in a radio message to TOWER at about 12.00 hours on January 3, falsely and maliciously represented to the plaintiffs that the owners of PYTHIAS had contracted with the defendants on the terms of the said Lloyd's open form of salvage agreement. The said representation was untrue and was made by the master of DAMON fraudulently, well-knowing that the same was false, or recklessly not caring whether the same was true or false. Relying upon the truth of the said representations, the master of TOWER kept the tug well clear of PYTHIAS and made no attempt to take possession of her.

(iv) PYTHIAS was towed by DAMON to Marseilles and there delivered to her owners at about 10.00 hours on January 12.

(v) On August 5, 19—, an action was commenced in this Court against the owners of the PYTHIAS by the defendants claiming salvage in respect of events referred to herein. The said action was tried on March 8, 19—, and judgment in the sum of £30,000 was pronounced in favour of the defendants.

9. In the premises, and, as a consequence of the said malicious and wrongful interference and/or the said false representation, the plaintiffs lost the chance of salving PYTHIAS and thereafter recovering a salvage award. The plaintiffs will contend that, if they had been able to take possession of PYTHIAS, she would have been safely towed to Marseilles by TOWER. The plaintiffs thereafter would have expected to recover a substantial proportion of the salved value of PYTHIAS as salvage remuneration or, alternatively, the sum of £30,000.

And the plaintiffs claim:

(i) £30,000, or alternatively damages;
(ii) Interest;
(iii) Costs.

[The next paragraph is 220]

2. Defences

Defence and Counterclaim in Collision Action

DEFENCE AND COUNTERCLAIM [7]

220 1. The defendants admit that the plaintiffs have suffered damage by reason of a collision between their steam tanker PYTHIAS and the defendants' steam tanker DAMON, but deny that the same was caused by the alleged or any negligence on the part of the defendants, their servants or agents. Further, the said collision and damage were solely caused by the negligence of the plaintiffs, their servants or agents, in the navigation of PYTHIAS as hereinafter appears. Save as herein expressly admitted, each and every allegation contained in the Statement of Claim is denied.

2. Shortly before about 04.03 hours (G.M.T. + 4) on October 16, 19—, DAMON a steam tanker registered in the port of Monrovia, of 30,599 tons gross and 18,977 tons net register, 760 feet in length and 105 feet 2 inches in beam, powered by a Westinghouse steam

[7] This form is adapted from the Defence and Counterclaim in *The Almizar* [1969] 1 Lloyd's Rep. 1. For the Preliminary Acts see § 382, *infra*. For Statement of Claim, see § 194, *supra*.

turbine double reduction geared engine of 19,000 s.h.p. and manned by a crew of 52 hands all told, was in the Arabian Sea in the course of a voyage from Europe to the Persian Gulf in ballast. Her draught was 21 feet 9 inches forward and 25 feet aft. There was little or no wind, the weather was apparently fine and clear and there was no material current. DAMON was proceeding on a course of 23° (true) and, with her engines working at full speed ahead, she was making good about 16 knots through the water. Two white masthead lights, red and green side lights and a fixed white stern light were burning brightly in accordance with the Collision Regulations. A good look-out was being kept on board her. Her radar set had been switched on and was warming up so as to enable the position of the ship to be fixed accurately at the end of the watch.

3. In these circumstances, a radar echo from another vessel which subsequently proved to be PYTHIAS was observed on the screen dead ahead of DAMON and distant about 5 miles. Those on watch on board DAMON looked carefully ahead but were unable to sight the other vessel. When, shortly thereafter, the radar echo was observed still dead ahead but having closed to a distance of about 3 miles, the course of DAMON was altered by 40° to starboard in two successive steps. Very shortly after DAMON had begun to swing to starboard, the lights of a vessel proceeding in the same direction as DAMON, distant about 1 mile on the port bow, disappeared from view, whereupon the presence of fog was apprehended, the engine room telegraphs of DAMON were rung to "stop," and a fog signal of one prolonged blast was sounded upon her whistle at frequent and diminishing intervals until the collision. Shortly after the engine room watch had shut off the ahead valve and opened the astern valve, the engine room telegraphs were rung to "stand by."

4. When, shortly thereafter, the said radar echo from PYTHIAS had disappeared from the screen (having been observed for the last time well on the port bow) the engine room telegraphs were again rung to "stop" but the said order was not carried out by those in the engine room. Those on board DAMON continued to listen carefully for fog signals. The first two signals of one prolonged blast that were heard appeared to come from the port side forward of DAMON's beam, and were thought to have been sounded by the vessel proceeding in the same direction as DAMON. Thereafter two or three more fog signals were heard on the port side, but those on board DAMON were unable to tell which ship had sounded them. DAMON by this time had been steadied up on a course of between 60° and 65°. Very shortly after the radar echo of a vessel bearing about 30° on the port bow had been observed on the screen distant about half a

mile, the loom of a white light high up was seen on a bearing between 1 and 2 points on the port bow, distant about 3 ships' lengths and apparently closing rapidly, whereupon the engine room telegraphs on board DAMON were at once put "full speed astern" and two signals, each of three short blasts were sounded upon the whistle in quick succession. The engine room watch, which had only just opened the ahead valve in response to the order "stand by," promptly executed the order "full speed astern."

5. Very shortly afterwards, a green light and the bridge lights of PYTHIAS came into view as that vessel came on rapidly, and, with her starboard side in way of Nos. 1 and 2 wing tanks, struck the stem and starboard bow of DAMON at an angle of about 70° to 80° leading aft on PYTHIAS, causing damage to DAMON and loss and expense to the defendants. The said collision occurred in dense fog approximately in position latitude 21° 23′ North and longitude 59° 36′ East.

6. The plaintiffs, their servants or agents were negligent in the following particular respects:

(i) They proceeded at an excessive speed in or in the vicinity of fog.

(ii) They failed to ease, stop or reverse their engines in due time or at all.

(iii) Having heard apparently forward of their beam the fog signals of a vessel whose position was not ascertained, they failed to stop their engines and thereafter to navigate with caution.

(iv) They improperly, and/or at an improper time, altered course to port.

(v) They failed to keep a good look-out.

(vi) They failed to make proper or any use of the radar equipment on board PYTHIAS.

(vii) They failed to sound fog signals.

(viii) They failed to comply with rules 15, 16, 27, and 29 of the Collision Regulations 1965.

COUNTERCLAIM

7. The defendants repeat the allegations contained in paragraphs 1, 2, 3, 4, 5 and 6 of the Defence herein,

And counterclaim:

(i) Judgment against the plaintiffs and their bail for the damage sustained, and costs;

(ii) If necessary, a reference to the Registrar to assess damages.

Defence and Counterclaim in Collision Action Alleging Negligence on Part of Third Vessel

DEFENCE AND COUNTERCLAIM

221 1. The defendants deny that the collision between their ship, DAMON, and the ship PYTHIAS was caused by the negligence of the defendants, their servants or agents. It is denied that the defendants or their servants or agents were negligent as alleged or at all. The said collision, and any damage suffered by the plaintiffs in consequence, were caused by the negligence of the plaintiffs, their servants or agents and/or the owners of the ship or vessel ROGUE, their servants or agents as hereinafter appears. Save as hereinafter expressly admitted or stated to be not admitted, each and every allegation contained in the Statement of Claim is denied.

2. Shortly before about 22.10 hours on October 8, 19—, DAMON, a steel single screw tanker of the Port of Monrovia, of 25,000 tons gross and 1,700 tons net register, about 700 feet in length and 90 feet in beam, powered by steam turbines of 15,000 s.h.p., and manned by a crew of 30 hands all told, was in the Straits of Dover, in the course of a voyage from Caracas to Rotterdam, with a cargo of 40,000 tons of crude oil. Her draught was 36 feet forward and 35 feet aft. The wind was North-Westerly, force 6, the weather was fog, and the tide was setting in a South-Westerly direction at the rate of about 1 knot. DAMON was on a course of 50° (true) and, with her engines working at full speed ahead, was making about 10 knots through the water. Two white masthead lights, red and green side lights and a fixed white stern light were burning brightly in accordance with the Collision Regulations. A good look-out was being kept on board her, her radar was in operation, and single prolonged blasts for fog were being automatically sounded on her whistle, in accordance with the Collision Regulations.

3. In those circumstances, the radar echo of a vessel that later proved to be PYTHIAS was first observed distant about 10 miles and bearing about 10° on the port quarter of DAMON. The echo was carefully watched and from subsequent observations, it became apparent that PYTHIAS was coming up on DAMON. After a period, the radar echo of another vessel, which subsequently proved to be ROGUE, was particularly observed distant about 9 miles and bearing about 5° on the port bow of DAMON.

4. When ROGUE had closed to a distance of about 4 miles, her bearing had not apparently changed. Accordingly the course of DAMON was altered to 70° (true). Following that manoeuvre, it was observed that PYTHIAS was distant about 1½ to 2 miles and bearing

about 10° to 15° on the starboard quarter of DAMON. Thereafter, ROGUE was observed to alter course to port. Her radar echo approached the heading marker on DAMON's radar, whereupon the engines of DAMON were put dead slow ahead. PYTHIAS was observed to continue to come up on the starboard quarter of DAMON, sounding fog signals. Shortly thereafter, the engines of DAMON were stopped in order to afford ROGUE a wide berth. As soon as DAMON was stopped in the water, DAMON commenced to sound several signals of two prolonged blasts. ROGUE crossed ahead of DAMON at speed and went clear.

5. Very shortly afterwards, the foremast light of PYTHIAS was seen high up, distant about half a cable, bearing about 4 points on the starboard quarter and indicating a heading of about 60° (true), whereupon the wheel of DAMON was put hard-a-port and her engines full ahead in an attempt to manoeuvre clear. But PYTHIAS came on and, as her mainmast light and red sidelight came into view, the stem and port bow of PYTHIAS struck the starboard side of DAMON about abreast the funnel at an angle of about 10° leading forward on DAMON. As a consequence, of the said collision, DAMON was damaged, whereby the defendants have suffered loss and expense.

6. The said collision occurred approximately in position latitude 50° 10′ North, longitude 1° 30′ West.

7. The plaintiffs, their servants or agents were negligent in the following particular respects:

(i) They proceeded at an excessive speed in fog.

(ii) They failed to ease, stop or reverse their engines in due time or at all.

(iii) They failed to keep a proper look-out.

(iv) They failed to make proper use of their radar and/or failed to act upon its indications with seamanlike skill and care.

(v) Having heard, apparently forward of their beam, the fog signals of a vessel whose position was not ascertained, they failed to stop their engines and navigate with caution.

(vi) Alternatively, having detected the presence of another vessel forward of their beam, before hearing her fog signals or sighting her, they failed to take such action as would have avoided a close quarters situation.

(vii) They improperly, or at an improper time, altered course to starboard and, further or alternatively, they thereafter improperly, or at an improper time, altered course to port.

(viii) They failed to comply with Rules 16, 24, and 27, as qualified by Rule 29 of the Collision Regulations 1965 and/or the recommendations contained in the annex thereto.

8. Further or alternatively, the said collision and the consequent damage were caused by the negligence of the owners of ROGUE, their servants or agents.

Particulars

(i) They proceeded at an excessive speed in fog.
(ii) They failed to ease, stop or reverse their engines in due time or at all.
(iii) They failed to keep a proper look-out.
(iv) Having heard, apparently forward of their beam, the fog signals of a vessel whose position was not ascertained, failed to stop their engines and navigate with caution.
(v) Alternatively, having detected the presence of another vessel forward of their beam, before hearing her fog signals or sighting her, they failed to take such action as would have avoided a close quarters situation.
(vi) They improperly, or at an improper time, altered course to port.
(vii) They failed to sound fog signals.
(viii) They failed to comply with Rules 15, 16, 27 and 29 of the Collision Regulations 1965.

COUNTERCLAIM

9. The second-named defendants by Counterclaim are the owners of the vessel ROGUE.

10. The plaintiffs, by Counterclaim, repeat the allegations contained in paragraphs 1 to 8 inclusive of the Defence herein.

And counterclaim:

(i) Judgment against the first and second defendants by Counterclaim for the damage sustained together with interest and costs;
(ii) If necessary, a reference to the Registrar to assess damages;
(iii) A declaration that the second-named defendants by Counterclaim are bound to indemnify the plaintiffs by Counterclaim, in respect of any sums that might be found due to the plaintiffs from the defendants in the original action, or, alternatively, that the second-named defendants by Counterclaim contribute to the same.

To Universal Steam Ships Company Limited of Monrovia, Liberia.

Take notice that, if you intend to defend this counterclaim, an appearance must be entered to the counterclaim on your behalf [*insert time fixed by Rules or by order for service out of jurisdiction*] after service of this defence and counterclaim upon you, inclusive of the day of service, otherwise judgment may be given against you without further notice.

DIRECTIONS FOR ENTERING APPEARANCE

[*As on Writ of Summons*]

Defence to Claim in Respect of Fatal Accident with Plea of Exemption under Ticket Conditions

DEFENCE OF FIRST DEFENDANTS [8]

222 1. Paragraph 1 of the Statement of Claim is admitted.

2. Save that it is denied that the collision referred to in the Statement of Claim was caused or contributed to by the first defendants, their servants or agents, paragraph 2 of the Statement of Claim is admitted. The said collision was solely caused by the negligence of the second defendants, their servants or agents as hereinafter appears.

3. Shortly before about 22.32 hours on July 12, 19—, PYTHIAS, a single screw motor vessel registered in the Port of London, of 5,000 tons gross and 2,300 tons net register, some 400 feet in length and some 52 feet in beam, powered by diesel engines of 3,500 h.p. and manned by a crew of 50 hands all told, was in the English Channel in the course of a voyage from Dover to Calais. PYTHIAS was carrying 120 passengers and her draught was about 18 feet forward and 20 feet aft. The wind was Northerly, force 2. The weather was fine and clear. The tide was setting West-South-Westerly, at a rate of about half a knot. PYTHIAS was on a course of 120° (true) and, with her engines working at full speed ahead, she was making about 11 knots through the water. She was exhibiting two white masthead lights, red and green sidelights, and a white stern light, in accordance with the Regulations. A good look-out was being maintained on board her.

4. In those circumstances, the silhouette of a vessel, which later proved to be the second defendants' vessel DAMON, was observed distant about 200 to 300 metres, bearing about 50° on the starboard bow of PYTHIAS and heading across the bow of PYTHIAS at about a right angle, whereupon the helm of PYTHIAS was put hard-a-port and

[8] For Statement of Claim, see § 197, *supra*.

her engines were stopped. DAMON came on at speed, and, with her stem and port bow, struck the starboard side of PYTHIAS in way of the bridge at an angle of about 80° leading forward on PYTHIAS, causing extensive damage to PYTHIAS.

5. The said collision occurred aproximately in a position latitude 51° 05′ North, longitude 1° 05′ East.

6. The second defendants, their servants or agents, were negligent in the following particular respects:

(i) They failed to exhibit the appropriate or any proper lights whilst under way at night.

(ii) They failed to devise and/or maintain any, or any proper system to ensure that their vessel's regulation steaming lights were burning brightly and/or were being exhibited.

(iii) They failed to keep any or any proper look-out.

(iv) They failed to ease, stop or reverse their engines in due time or at all.

(v) They improperly attempted to cross ahead of PYTHIAS.

(vi) They failed to keep their course and speed.

(vii) They altered course improperly and/or at an improper time.

(viii) They failed to comply with Rules 1 (b), 2 (a), 10, 21, 27, 28 and 29 of the Collision Regulations 1965.

7. Further or alternatively, the carriage of the plaintiff and the said John Smith on board PYTHIAS was subject to the conditions contained in the first defendants' standard form of passenger ticket which provide *inter alia* as follows:

> "9. The shipowners shall not be liable to any passenger carried under this contract for loss, damage or delay to the passenger arising from . . . collision, . . . perils of the sea, river or of navigation of any kind, . . . even though the loss damage or delay may have been caused or contributed to by the neglect or default of the shipowners' servants or of other persons for whose acts he would otherwise be responsible."

8. In the premises, if (which is denied) the said collision was caused or contributed to by the negligence of the first defendants, their servants or agents in the navigation or management of PYTHIAS, the first defendants are not liable to the plaintiff therefor as alleged or at all.

9. No admissions are made as to paragraphs 3 and 4 of the Statement of Claim.

Defence to Claim for Damage Sustained by Ship in Defective Berth

DEFENCE [9]

223 1. Paragraph 1 of the Statement of Claim is admitted.

2. Save that no admissions are made as to the draught of PYTHIAS, paragraph 2 of the Statement of Claim is admitted.

3. Paragraph 3 of the Statement of Claim is denied.

4. By letter dated December 8, 19—, from the defendants to the plaintiffs, the plaintiffs were instructed to berth their vessel PYTHIAS starboard side to the defendants' wharf, heading downstream. The master of PYTHIAS was orally instructed to the same effect by one Jones, the defendants' foreman, at about 15.00 hours on January 1.

5. Save that it is admitted that PYTHIAS came alongside the said wharf with her port side to, heading upstream, at about 17.00 hours on January 1, no admissions are made as to paragraph 4 of the Statement of Claim.

6. Save that no admissions are made as to the moorings of PYTHIAS which parted, paragraph 5 of the Statement of Claim is admitted.

7. Paragraphs 6 and 7 of the Statement of Claim are denied.

8. Paragraph 8 of the Statement of Claim is admitted.

9. Paragraph 9 of the Statement of Claim is denied. The said damage, loss and expense was solely caused by the plaintiffs' improperly berthing PYTHIAS port side to the wharf, contrary to the defendants' instructions.

COUNTERCLAIM

10. The defendants repeat the allegations contained in the Defence.

11. As a consequence of the breaking away of PYTHIAS from the wharf, the said wharf was damaged, causing loss and expense to the defendants.

12. The said loss, damage and expense was caused by the negligence of the plaintiffs, their servants or agents.

Particulars

(i) They failed to obey or heed the instructions of the defendants.

(ii) They negligently caused or allowed PYTHIAS to be berthed port side to the berth.

[9] For Statement of Claim, see § 196, *supra*.

(iii) They negligently ran the engines of PYTHIAS while still aground.

And the defendants counterclaim:

(i) Judgment against the plaintiffs for the loss and damage sustained together with interest and costs;

(ii) A reference to assess damages.

Defence to Claim for Personal Injuries Sustained by Cadet-hand Struck by Heavy Seas

DEFENCE [10]

224 1. Paragraphs 1 and 3 of the Statement of Claim are admitted.

2. Paragraph 3 of the Statement of Claim is denied.

3. DAMON was proceeding from Buenos Aires to London. She was laden to a draught of about 30 feet forward and 31 feet aft. Her course was 64° (true) and, with her engines working at full speed ahead, she was making about 13 knots through the water. The wind was North-North-Easterly. It was increasing in strength. At 09.00 hours, it was variously estimated between force 6 and 8. The weather was cloudy but clear between rain showers. The sea was becoming rough. Spray from broken waves occasionally came on deck, but no seas had broken over the foredeck.

4. In these circumstances, at about 08.20 hours, while the plaintiff was forward on the starboard side of DAMON, engaged in rigging a life line in the course of his employment, an exceptionally heavy and freak sea broke over the port shoulder of the vessel and swept the deceased away.

5. It is denied that the plaintiff was injured by reason of the negligence of the defendants, their servants or agents in the navigation or management of DAMON.

6. Further, the defendants will contend that the injuries sustained by the plaintiff were solely caused by perils of the sea over which the defendants, their servants or agents had no control. Alternatively, the said accident could not have been prevented by the exercise of reasonable care and skill on the part of the defendants, their servants or agents.

7. Save as aforesaid, the allegations contained in paragraphs 4 to 6 inclusive of the Statement of Claim are denied.

[10] For Statement of Claim, see § 199, *supra*.

Defence to Claim for Personal Injuries Sustained by Stevedore

DEFENCE [11]

225 1. Save as is herein expressly admitted, the defendants deny each and every allegation in the Statement of Claim as if set out herein and traversed seriatim.

2. DAMON is a steel motor ship of 5,000 tons gross and 3,000 tons net register, some 300 feet in length and 45 feet in beam. DAMON left Antwerp on January 1, 19—, with some 5,000 tons of general cargo, including 350 casks of wine. The vessel reached London on November 5 and unloading of the said casks began.

3. The casks were laden in No. 4 'tween-deck and were stowed lying fore and aft, on their side, some 3 tiers high. Each line of casks was held in position by dunnage. The plaintiff was engaged *inter alia* in the discharge of the said casks in the service of Messrs. Universal Stevedores Company Limited. After some casks had been removed from the top two tiers, the plaintiff, together with other employees of the said company began to remove some casks from the bottom tier. The chief officer of DAMON complained to the said company's superintendent about this manner of discharge, fearing damage to the casks and injury to the stevedores in the event of a fall. But no steps were taken to change the method of discharge. Shortly thereafter, some casks on the top tiers fell, causing the plaintiff to be thrown on his back.

4. No admissions are made as to the extent of the plaintiff's injuries. In any event, it is denied that the same were caused by the negligence of the defendants, their servants or agents. It is denied that the defendants, their servants or agents were negligent as alleged or at all.

5. The alleged accident was solely caused by the negligence of the said company, their servants or agents including the plaintiff:

Particulars

(i) They discharged the casks in an improper manner.
(ii) They failed to discharge the casks tier by tier.
(iii) They attempted to discharge the casks too fast.
(iv) They failed to have proper regard for their own safety.
(v) They failed to heed or act upon the complaint and/or warning of the chief officer of DAMON.

[11] For Statement of Claim, see § 198, *supra*.

Defence to Cargo Claim

DEFENCE [12]

226 1. Save that no admissions are made as to the number of bags or as to their order and condition on shipment, paragraph 1 of the Statement of Claim is admitted.

2. No admissions are made as to paragraph 2 of the Statement of Claim.

3. Paragraph 3 of the Statement of Claim is denied.

4. Paragraph 4 of the Statement of Claim is admitted. The said Rules further provide *inter alia* as follows:

[*Set out Article IV, r. 2* (*c*), (*p*) *and* (*q*)]

5. Paragraph 6 of the Statement of Claim is denied.

6. Further or alternatively, if, which is denied, any of the said bags were damaged by water, the same was caused by the entry of sea-water through a crack in the shell plating sustained during the vessel's passage through heavy weather during January 5 and 6, 19—. In the premises, and by virtue of Article IV of the said Rules, the defendants are not liable therefor.

Particulars

(i) DAMON was built in 19— and, at all material times, was classified 100 A1 by Lloyd's Register of Shipping. Prior to January 19—, the vessel last underwent a special survey in February 19— and an annual survey in May 19—.

(ii) DAMON commenced loading on December 28, 19—. The holds were carefully swept and inspected and found to be clean and dry. The vessel sailed on January 2, 19— and, during January 5 and 6, experienced very heavy seas with wind of force 9 to 10. The vessel received heavy pounding from the waves and was rolling and pitching in a violent manner.

(iii) By 18.00 hours on January 6, the vessel had developed a list to port. Soundings indicated water in the port bilge to a depth of 100 centimetres. The pumps were started. The cargo was discharged at Singapore on January 7 and about 12 centimetres of water was found at the bottom of the hold on the starboard side.

(iv) It was thereafter discovered that, on the port side, the welding

12 For Statement of Claim, see § 201, *supra*. *Cf*. Points of Defence in cargo claim in Commercial Court, § 122, *supra*.

on the common seam between plates B-4 and D-1 was cracked between frames 26 and 27 for a length of about 2 feet.

(v) At no time before 18.00 hours on January 6, did anything occur which caused or could reasonably have caused the defendants to believe that the said welding was in any way defective and/or liable to crack.

7. Save as is hereinbefore expressly admitted or stated to be not admitted, each and every allegation contained in the Statement of Claim is denied.

Defence to Breach of Charterparty—Unsafe Berth

DEFENCE [13]

227 1. The defendants do not admit and put the plaintiffs to proof of the facts alleged in paragraph 1 of the Statement of Claim.

2. Paragraph 2 of the Statement of Claim is admitted.

3. Paragraph 3 of the Statement of Claim is admitted. Further, the said charterparty provided:

"1 (b) The vessel shall be in every way fit to carry crude petroleum and/or its producer.

(c) The vessel shall be tight, staunch, strong, in good order and condition, in every way fit for the service, with her machinery, boilers and hull in such a state as to obtain the most economic working. . . .

9. . . . The vessel shall load and discharge cargo as rapidly as possible, by night as well as by day, when required by charterers or their agents to do so.

10. The master shall prosecute his voyages with the utmost dispatch and shall render all reasonable assistance with the vessel's deck and engineer officers and crew and equipment."

The defendants will refer, at the arbitration, to the said charterparty for its full terms and effect.

4. The defendants deny that the terms alleged in paragraph 4 of the Statement of Claim were implied terms of the charterparty.

5. The facts alleged in paragraph 5 of the Statement of Claim are admitted.

6. The matters alleged in paragraph 6 of the Statement of Claim (including the particulars therein set out) are denied. It is denied that the defendants were in breach of clause 3 of the said charterparty as alleged or at all.

7. If (which is denied) it was a term of the charterparty that the

[13] For Statement of Claim, see § 202, *supra*.

defendants would not order PYTHIAS to an unsafe port or place and if (which is also denied) the port or place of Holiday Bay and/or No. 1 berth was unsafe, the plaintiffs, by their conduct, waived performance of that term and/or are estopped from alleging the existence and/or breach of that term.

Particulars

Pursuant to the defendants' orders under the said time charterparty, PYTHIAS berthed at No. 1 berth in Holiday Bay to load a cargo on several previous occasions. Accordingly, the master of PYTHIAS had ample opportunity to consider and investigate the safety of the place to which his vessel had been ordered. Furthermore, the characteristics of the said place are fully apparent upon examination of published charts, and on inquiry of the Admiralty Pilot. In the premises, the plaintiffs, by their servant or agent, the master, were aware, or ought reasonably to have been aware, of the unsafe characteristics (if any) of Holiday Bay and/or No. 1 berth, but at no time before PYTHIAS berthed on March 16, 19—, did the plaintiffs raise any objection to the nomination of Holiday Bay and/or No. 1 berth under the charterparty, nor did they complain or protest to the defendants that the said ports or places were unsafe, nor did they request the defendants to nominate some other port or place. In consequence, the plaintiffs led the defendants to believe that the plaintiffs approved of the nomination of the said ports and/or places (whatever their characteristics in fact) and that they waived any objection on the ground of unsafety that they might otherwise have had. In consequence, the defendants ordered PYTHIAS to return to Holiday Bay and/or No. 1 berth for the voyage in question, and/or made arrangements for a cargo to be shipped there, and/or took no steps to nominate or provide a cargo at any other port or place, as they might have done if the plaintiffs had made such an objection of complaint or protest or request.

8. Further, if the defendants were not entitled by the original terms of the charterparty to order PYTHIAS to Holiday Bay and/or No. 1 berth in March, there was an implied agreement arising out of the facts alleged in paragraph 7 hereof that the defendants should be so entitled, and that, by reason of those facts, and/or of the master of PYTHIAS returning to Holiday Bay and/or No. 1 berth in the voyage in question, and berthing there and remaining there when he knew or ought to have known of the characteristics of the port or place, and of the risk to the safety of his vessel while at the said port or place, the plaintiffs impliedly consented to accept the said risk

of damage arising from the unsafety of the port and the presence of PYTHIAS thereat.

9. The matters alleged in paragraphs 7, 8, 9, and 10 of the Statement of Claim (including the particulars therein) are denied.

10. Alternatively, any loss or damage which the plaintiffs or any of them or PYTHIAS may prove to have sustained by reason of events on March 18, 19—, while the vessel was at Holiday Bay and/or No. 1 berth, were solely or proximately caused by the negligent navigation or management of PYTHIAS by the plaintiffs, their servants or agents, and/or by the plaintiffs' breach or breaches of the terms of the said charterparty and/or in law is too remote from the alleged cause to be recoverable.

Particulars

The master and/or chief officer of PYTHIAS failed to take proper and seamanlike care of their vessel and/or were negligent in the following particular respects:

(i) They failed properly or at all to make seamanlike plans or preparations in good time to take PYTHIAS to sea temporarily, in order to avoid the risk of causing or sustaining damage while remaining in her berth during the said night.

(ii) They failed to keep a proper look-out with seamanlike care and skill and vigilance. In particular, they failed to observe weather, sea and swell conditions, and changes therein and barometric indications during March 17 and 18, 19—.

(iii) They failed to obtain, and/or consider, and/or heed, and/or act upon, the weather forecasts and synoptic information prepared and issued from local meteorological sources which were available to those on board PYTHIAS, during March 17, 19—.

(iv) They failed to leave their berth during the evening of March 17, 19—, or, alternatively, at some time earlier than 01.00 hours on March 18, 19—, in order to shelter at sea from the bad weather that was forecast and/or expected to reach Holiday Bay during the night of March 17 and 18.

(v) They failed to consider, and/or to heed, and/or to follow, the example of the master of the vessel DAMON which berthed at No. 2 berth at about 13.30 hours on March 17, but whose master decided at about 14.30 hours to leave again and, in fact, left again at 18.21 hours the same day on account of the approach of bad weather.

(vi) They failed to consider and/or to heed and act upon suggestions by the Harbourmaster to the master at about 16.00

hours that PYTHIAS (like DAMON) might have to leave her berth because of the approaching bad weather.

(vii) They failed to load cargo at a sufficiently fast rate. The master and/or chief officer unreasonably failed and/or refused to load in accordance with good tankship practice or procedures, and/or to load more than one product at a time. Accordingly, PYTHIAS loaded at a rate much slower than the rate at which the shippers could provide cargo and/or in a manner which left her trimmed by the head. As a result, the master neglected the opportunity to complete loading substantially before 23.00 hours and/or to improve the vessel's trim as soon as possible.

(viii) They failed to take any, or any proper, steps (such as ballasting or loading additional cargo, which was suggested to the officer of the watch by one Smith at about 14.00 hours on March 17) to reduce the vessel's windage and/or to bring the vessel to a seaworthy trim at the earliest possible time.

11. By reason of the matters alleged in sub-paragraphs (vi) and (vii), the plaintiffs were in breach of clauses 9 and 10 of the said charterparty.

12. If it be the fact (contrary to the defendants' contentions) that PYTHIAS was not capable of loading more than one product at a time and/or was not capable of loading at a faster rate than that at which she in fact loaded on March 17, 19—, the plaintiffs were in breach of clause 1 (b) and (c) of the said charterparty. By reason of the said breaches, the time for loading was longer, and/or PYTHIAS was deprived of a seaworthy trim for a longer period, than the plaintiffs and defendants contemplated.

13. The defendants deny that the plaintiffs, or any of them, are entitled to the relief claimed.

14. Save as is hereinbefore expressly admitted, each and every allegation contained in the Statement of Claim is denied as if set out and traversed seriatim.

Defence in Salvage Action Denying Salvage

DEFENCE

228 1. The defendants do not admit that the plaintiffs or any of them rendered salvage services to DAMON as alleged in the Statement of Claim or at all. Save as hereinafter appears, the defendants deny each and every allegation in the Statement of Claim.

2. Save that the horsepower of PULLER and her value are not admitted, the defendants admit paragraph 2 of the Statement of Claim.

3. DAMON is a steel single screw motor vessel of 2,873 tons gross and 1,893 tons net register, 327 feet in length and 46 feet in beam and fitted with triple expansion engines of 1,750 i.h.p. At the material time, DAMON was inward bound to Dagenham with a cargo of 4,000 tons of sugar in bulk. She was lying at a tier on Erith Reach waiting for a berth. She was manned by a crew of 20 hands all told, and her draught was 20 feet forward and 21 feet aft. The values alleged in paragraph 3 of the Statement of Claim are agreed.

4. At about 16.00 hours on December 8, 19—, when DAMON was moored heading down river with wires and ropes out to the head buoy and the after buoy, one of the starboard bow wires parted. DAMON then began sounding signals of two long blasts followed by two short blasts, indicating that she required boatmen to attend upon her. The wind was then Southerly force 5 to 6. The force of the wind increased thereafter and at about 17.35 hours, one of the port bow ropes parted. By 18.30 hours, the wind had increased to force 7 with squalls. At about this time, further forward moorings parted. Thereafter, both anchors were let go as the last of the forward moorings parted. The vessel's head was brought up not more than two points to port of her original heading. In the meantime, two starboard quarter ropes parted.

5. In these circumstances, PULLER came up to DAMON and asked whether her services were required. PULLER was thereupon requested to run out a 4½ inch insurance wire to the head buoy. This task was duly carried out and occupied a total of 20 to 30 minutes. The wire was hove tight on the windlass of DAMON. Shortly afterwards, PULLER was observed with her stem in contact with the port bow of DAMON and with her engines working ahead apparently trying to push. PULLER had not been requested to execute any such manoeuvre, did not meet with any success and did not benefit DAMON in any way. After about 10 minutes, PULLER abandoned her efforts. Shortly afterwards, boatmen arrived and PULLER left.

6. It is specifically denied that DAMON was in a position of danger when PULLER came up or at any time thereafter. She was securely held by her anchors and her remaining moorings on the after buoy. It is specifically denied that, even in the unlikely event of the anchors dragging or the after moorings parting, DAMON would have been in any danger of being driven aground. DAMON had the full use of her engines and could, if necessary, have counteracted any excessive strain on her anchors or moorings. Alternatively, if any real danger of

breaking adrift had arisen, DAMON could have slipped her anchors and cut her moorings and proceeded under her own power.

7. The taking out and securing of the forward insurance wire were ordinary boatmen's services. The alleged or any risk of personal injury or loss of life to the crew of PULLER is denied. PULLER's attempt to push was ineffective and rendered no benefit to DAMON.

Defence in Salvage Action Admitting Salvage

DEFENCE

229 1. The defendants admit that the plaintiffs rendered salvage services to DAMON, but say that the account of such services set out in the Statement of Claim is exaggerated and in some respects inaccurate. Save as is hereinafter expressly admitted, the defendants deny each and every allegation in the Statement of Claim.

2. Save that their values are not admitted, the defendants admit the particulars of the tugs contained in paragraphs 2, 3 and 4 of the Statement of Claim.

3. DAMON is a steel twin screw motor vessel of 50,000 tons gross and 20,000 tons net register, some 900 feet in length and 100 feet in beam and is fitted with engines of 4,000 h.p. At the time of the services DAMON was manned by a crew of 800 hands all told and was in the course of a voyage from Southampton to New York carrying passengers. Her draught was 30 feet forward and 32 feet aft. The value of DAMON was £6,000,000.

4. At about 19.40 hours on April 27, 19—, DAMON was in the approach roads to New York when she fouled No. 27 buoy with her starboard side and dragged it with her. Her engines were stopped at the time and DAMON was making about 4 knots over the ground. Shortly afterwards, the port anchor was let go and DAMON came to rest heading about due West, with her starboard side aft touching the starboard margin of the dredged channel. The tide was flooding at the rate of about half to one knot and the wind was westerly, force 5. Sounding all round, the vessel showed deep water except over the starboard side aft.

5. The tugs PULLER, PUSHER and TOWER were asked by V.H.F. to come down to DAMON. The tug PUSHER was ordered to tow the No. 27 buoy clear of DAMON and then to take up position on the starboard quarter and push with her stem fender. PULLER and TOWER were made fast aft and ordered to tow on the port quarter. Shortly thereafter, DAMON swung clear into the channel, with her own engines working at slow speed ahead. The port anchor of

DAMON was hove up and, with the three tugs in attendance, proceeded into the port of New York.

6. The defendants specifically deny that DAMON was in a position of danger from which she could not have extricated herself without assistance, or in which she would have sustained damage as alleged. The edge of the channel is steep, and the stern of DAMON was at no time in danger of being driven farther to starboard. There is no doubt that the stern of DAMON would have swung clear without assistance as soon as the tide made. Her port engine was at all times available for use.

7. The services of all the tugs were performed under the directions of the pilot on board DAMON, were of a simple character and did not involve any of the tugs or those on board them in any difficulty or danger as alleged.

Defence of Cargo Interests in Salvage Action Alleging Consecutive Risks and Negligence

DEFENCE

230 1. It is admitted that the plaintiffs rendered salvage services to the cargo laden on board the ship DAMON.

2. At the inception of the plaintiffs' services, the carriage of the said cargo was delayed and the said cargo was temporarily immobilised because DAMON was disabled by damage. The whole, or alternatively the greater part, of the cargo was in no, or no appreciable, danger of loss or damage. The said cargo was capable of being discharged from DAMON into another vessel.

3. In the premises, it is denied that the said cargo was in danger. Alternatively, it is denied that the said cargo was in the same danger as DAMON. The risks and perils to ship and cargo respectively were different in kind.

4. Further or alternatively, the plaintiffs' services were, from the outset, rendered to ship and cargo separately and the benefits conferred upon each were distinct. Alternatively, if (which is denied) the said services were undertaken for the joint benefit of ship and cargo, they ceased to be a joint operation either (i) at about 12.00 hours on January 1, 19—, when the said cargo had been discharged from DAMON, or (ii) at about 16.00 hours on February 20, when serious damage was caused to DAMON by the negligence of the plaintiffs.

5. Further, it is denied that any of the services rendered by the plaintiffs after 12.00 hours on January 1, or alternatively after 16.00 hours on February 20, were for the benefit of the said cargo.

6. If (which is denied) these defendants are liable to pay remuneration in respect of the alleged or any services rendered by the plaintiffs after the said cargo had been discharged, these defendants will, in diminution thereof, rely upon the want of skill and care on the part of the plaintiffs, their servants or agents when, at about 16.00 hours on February 20, an explosion and fire causing serious damage occurred on board DAMON as a result of a spanner being negligently dropped into one of her empty cargo tanks when it contained inflammable and dangerous gases.

7. The value of crude oil cargo preserved for the benefit of these defendants by reason of the contractors' services was £50,000.

Defence and Counterclaim in Claim for Repairs

DEFENCE AND COUNTERCLAIM [14]

231 1. Paragraphs 1, 2 and 3 of the Statement of Claim are admitted.

2. It was a term of the contract, to be implied by law, that the plaintiffs would provide good and skilful workmanship and material and parts of good quality and reasonably fit for their purpose. Further, it was an implied term of the contract that the plaintiffs would exercise all reasonable skill and care in performing the said agreement.

3. In breach of the said implied terms, the plaintiffs failed to provide good and skilful workmanship and/or materials and parts of good quality and/or reasonably fit for their purpose, and/or the plaintiffs were negligent in performing the said agreement. Particulars of the defects in the work done and material supplied for the repair of DAMON are contained in the report of survey of James Smith dated May 3, 19—, already supplied to the plaintiffs.

4. The defendants admit that they have not paid the plaintiffs the sum of £5,000, being the sum claimed as the cost of the work done and material supplied by way of repairs to the defendants' vessel DAMON, but say that they are entitled to set up against the plaintiffs the matters hereinafter set out in extinction of the said sum, or such sum as may be found due to the plaintiffs, and/or to set off against the plaintiffs' claim such part of the damages hereinafter counterclaimed as may be necessary to extinguish the plaintiffs' claim.

5. By reason of the aforesaid breaches of contract, the defendants have suffered loss and damage.

[14] For Statement of Claim, see § 206, *supra*. For Reply and Defence to Counterclaim, see § 240, *infra*. For Rejoinder, see § 241, *infra*.

Particulars

Following the said survey and in accordance with its recommendations the defendants engaged the International Ship Repair Company Limited to execute repairs to DAMON in order to remedy the said defects. In consequence DAMON was detained from May 18 to May 29, 19—.

Cost of repairs	£4,000
Detention at £100 per day for 10 days	£1,000
	£5,000

6. By way of Counterclaim, the defendants repeat the allegations contained in paragraphs 1 to 5 inclusive of the Defence.

And counterclaim damages.

Defence to Claim for Agent's Disbursements

DEFENCE [15]

232 1. Paragraph 1 of the Statement of Claim is admitted.

2. Save for the sum of £20 advanced as cash to the master, paragraph 2 of the Statement of Claim is denied. All the other items of expenditure were incurred at the request of the time charterers of DAMON, Messrs. Universal Charterers, and for their account.

3. The defendants paid to the plaintiffs the said sum of £20 by cheque No. 1111 dated March 8, 19—.

4. In the premises, the plaintiffs are not entitled to the sum of £100 or any sum from the defendants.

[The next paragraph is 240]

15 For Statement of Claim, see § 209, *supra*.

3. Further Pleadings

Reply and Defence to Counterclaim in Claim for Repairs

REPLY AND DEFENCE TO COUNTERCLAIM [16]

240 1. Save as hereinafter appears and save as the same consists of admissions of matters expressly alleged in the Statement of Claim, the plaintiffs join issue with the defendants on their defence.

2. The said contract was subject to the plaintiffs' standard conditions of business which provide *inter alia* as follows:

> "4. Save as provided in clause 2, the contractor shall not be under any liability to the customer, either in contract or for delict or quasi-delict or otherwise, except for negligence, and such liability shall itself be subject to the following over-riding limitations and exceptions, namely:
>
> . . .
>
> (b) In no circumstances whatsoever, shall the liability of the contractor or any sub-contractor include any sum in respect of loss of profit or loss of use of the vessel or damages consequential on such loss of use. . . ."

The said conditions were contained in a letter dated January 7, 19—, from the plaintiffs to the defendants. The plaintiffs will further rely on the course of dealing between the parties since October 7, 19—.

3. In the premises, if (which is denied) the defendants have suffered any loss or damage as a consequence of the alleged breaches of contract, the plaintiffs are not liable for the same.

DEFENCE TO COUNTERCLAIM

4. The plaintiffs repeat the allegations in paragraphs 1 to 3 hereof and deny that the defendants are entitled to the relief claimed or to any relief.

Rejoinder in Action for Repairs

REJOINDER [17]

Served pursuant to order of Mr. Justice ————
dated the twenty-first day of February, 19—.

241 1. Save insofar as the same consists of admissions of matters

[16] For Statement of Claim, see § 206, *supra*; for Defence and Counterclaim, see § 231, *supra*, and for Rejoinder, see § 241, *infra*. In collision and similar actions, a Reply or Defence to Counterclaim can only be served with the leave of the court: see R.S.C., Ord. 75, r. 20 (1).

[17] For Statement of Claim, see § 206, *supra*; for Defence and Counterclaim, see § 231, *supra*; and for Reply and Defence to Counterclaim, see § 240, *supra*.

expressly alleged in the Defence and Counterclaim, and save as is hereinafter admitted, the defendants join issue with the plaintiffs upon their Reply and Defence to the Counterclaim herein.

2. It is denied that the plaintiffs agreed to carry out the work upon the defendants' vessel subject to the plaintiffs' standard conditions of business.

3. The defendants admit that the letter written by the plaintiffs, dated January 7, 19—, referred to in paragraph 2 of the Reply and Defence to Counterclaim, was delivered to their offices on or after May 3, 19—. But their servant, Jones, to whom the said letter was addressed, did not see the letter nor was he aware of its reference to the said standard conditions of business, until after he had visited the plaintiffs' officers on July 3, 19—. In the premises, the alleged notice of the said conditions was ineffective, because the defendants had already contracted with the plaintiffs without knowledge of the said conditions.

4. It is further denied that the said conditions were incorporated into the contract by virtue of the alleged or any course of dealing between the parties. The defendants put the plaintiffs to proof of each and every fact relied upon in support of the alleged course of dealing.

5. Further or alternatively, if (which is denied) the said conditions were (as is alleged) incorporated into the contract, then the defendants will contend that, by reason of the defective work done and materials supplied by the plaintiffs under the said agreement, it became the duty of the plaintiffs, in accordance with clause 2 of the said conditions, to remedy the said defects and replace the said materials. The sums claimed herein by the plaintiffs are wholly or partly attributable to the cost of work done and materials supplied necessary to remedy the said defects and replacing the said parts and, in the premises, are not recoverable from the defendants.

[The next paragraph is 250]

Part Three

ADMIRALTY FORMS

CHAPTER 7

THE WRIT

1. WRIT IN REM

Writ of Summons in Admiralty Action in Rem Issued out of the Admiralty Registry [1]

250 In the High Court of Justice 19—, Folio —–
Queen's Bench Division
Admiralty Court
Admiralty action in rem against:

[The ship DAMON [2]]
[The owners of the ship PYTHIAS] Plaintiffs
and
[The owners of the ship DAMON [2]] Defendants

ELIZABETH THE SECOND, by the Grace of God, of the United Kingdom of Great Britain and Northern Ireland and of Our other realms and territories Queen, Head of the Commonwealth, Defender of the Faith:

To the [owners of and other] persons interested in [the ship DAMON of the Port of London],

We command you that within 14 days after the service of this writ, inclusive of the day of service, you do cause an appearance to be entered for you in an action at the suit of [the owners of the ship PYTHIAS]; and take notice that in default of your so doing the Plaintiffs may proceed therein, and judgment may be given in your absence, and if the *res* described in this writ is then under arrest of the Court it may be sold by order of the Court.

Witness ——, Lord High Chancellor of Great Britain, the —— day of ——, 19—.

Note: This writ may not be served later than 12 calendar months beginning with the above date unless renewed by order of the Court.

1 See generally *Admiralty Practice* [B.S.L. 1, § 151 *et seq.*]. For a writ *in rem* issued out of District Registry, see § 251, *infra*. For a writ in a sister-ship action, see § 252, *infra*, and also *Admiralty Practice* [B.S.L. 1, §§ 65 and 260]. In possession actions, the defendants should be named as "All other persons interested in the ship."

2 Or as may be, describing the res.

DIRECTIONS FOR ENTERING APPEARANCE

The defendants may enter an appearance in person or by a solicitor either (1) by handing in the appropriate forms, duly completed, at the Admiralty Registry, Royal Courts of Justice, Strand, London, WC2A 2LL, or (2) by sending them to that office by post. The appropriate forms may be obtained by sending a postal order for [*insert current price*] with an addressed envelope, foolscap size, to the Clerk of Accounts, Vote Office, Royal Courts of Justice, Strand, London, WC2A 2LL.

Indorsement of claim[3]

The plaintiffs' claim is for ——.

[The plaintiffs are resident [*or* are acting by order or on behalf of ——who resides] at [*address*] outside the scheduled territories as defined by the Exchange Control Act 1947.]

This writ was issued by [A.B. & Co.,] of [*address*] solicitors for the said plaintiffs, whose address is —— [*or*

This writ was issued by [A.B. & Co.,] of [*address*] agent for [C.D. & Co.,] of [*address*], solicitors for the said plaintiffs, whose address is —— *or*

This writ was issued by the said plaintiffs who reside at [*address*] [*If the plaintiffs do not reside within the jurisdiction add*: and whose address for service is ——.]].

Indorsement as to service

This writ was served by me at [*address*] on [*person or property served*] on [Monday] the —— day of ——, 19—, by [*method of service*].

Signed ——
Address ——

Writ of Summons in Admiralty Action in Rem Issued out of District Registry

251 In the High Court of Justice 19—, No. ——
Queen's Bench Division
Admiralty Court
[Liverpool] District Registry.

[3] For precedents of indorsements, see §§ 270 *et seq.*, *infra.*

Admiralty action in rem against:

[The ship DAMON [4]]

[The owners of the ship PYTHIAS] Plaintiffs

and

[The owners of the ship DAMON [4]] Defendants

[*As in § 250, supra, substituting the following for the directions for entering appearance.*]

DIRECTIONS FOR ENTERING APPEARANCE

If the defendants reside or carry on business, or (in the case of a limited company) have a registered office, within the district of the above-named District Registry or the writ is indorsed with a statement that any cause of action in respect of which the plaintiffs claim relief wholly or in part arose in that district, the defendants must enter an appearance in person or by a solicitor in the District Registry and may do so either (1) by handing in the appropriate forms, duly completed, at the office of the District Registrar [*insert address of office*], or (2) by sending them to that office by post.

If the defendants neither reside or carry on business nor (in the case of a limited company) have a registered office within the district of the above-named District Registry and the writ is not indorsed with a statement that any cause of action in respect of which the plaintiffs claim relief wholly or in part arose in that district, the defendants may enter an appearance in person or by a solicitor either (1) by handing in the appropriate forms, duly completed, at the office of the District Registrar, or by sending them to that office by post, or (2) by handing in the said forms, duly completed, at the Admiralty Registry, Royal Courts of Justice, Strand, London, WC2A 2LL, or by sending them to that office by post.

The appropriate forms may be obtained by sending a postal order for [*insert current price*] with an addressed envelope, foolscap size, to (1) the District Registrar, High Court of Justice, [*insert address*] if the appearance is to be entered in the District Registry, or (2) the Clerk of Accounts, Vote Office, Royal Courts of Justice, Strand, London, WC2A 2LL, if the appearance is to be entered in London.

Writ of Summons in Admiralty Action in Rem issued out of the Admiralty Registry in a Sister-ship Action

252 In the High Court of Justice 19—, Folio ——
Queen's Bench Division

4 Or as may be, describing the res.

Admiralty Court
Admiralty action in rem against:

[The ships DAMON, DEMOS and DEMON]

[The owners of the ship PYTHIAS] Plaintiffs

and

[The owners of the ships DAMON, DEMOS and DEMON] Defendants

ELIZABETH THE SECOND [*continue as in* § 250, *supra*].

To the [owners of and other] persons interested in the ships DAMON of the Port of London and DEMOS and DEMON of the Port of Liverpool.

We command you [*continue as in* § 250, *supra*].

Indorsement of claim

The plaintiffs' claim is for compensation from the defendants who are [*or* were at all material times] the owners [*or* the charterers *or* in possession *or* in control] of the ship DAMON, for the damage suffered by the plaintiffs by reason of a collision between the plaintiffs' ship PYTHIAS and the defendants' ship DAMON in the Baltic Sea on or about the —— day of —— 19—, such collision being caused by the negligence of the defendants, their servants or agents.

[*Conclude as in* § 250, *supra*].

Writ of Summons in Admiralty Action in Rem in Respect of Loss of Life

253 In the High Court of Justice 19—, Folio ——
Queen's Bench Division
Admiralty Court
Admiralty action in rem against:

The ship DAMON

A.B. (Widow) and Executrix
[*or* Administratrix] of the
Estate of B.B. deceased Plaintiff

and

The owners of the ship DAMON Defendants

ELIZABETH THE SECOND [*continue as in* § 250].

Indorsement of claim [4a]

The plaintiff, as Executrix [*or* Administratrix] of the estate of B.B. deceased, claims damages on behalf of herself and her infant son

[4a] For Statement of Claim in similar action, see § 197, *supra*.

C.B., under the Fatal Accidents Acts 1846 to 1959, and damages, on behalf of the estate of the said B.B. deceased, under the Law Reform (Miscellaneous Provisions) Act 1934, in respect of the death of her husband B.B. who was killed as a result of a collision between the ship PYTHIAS and the defendants' ship DAMON in the English Channel, on or about the —— day of ——, 19—, which was caused by the negligence of the defendants, their servants or agents.

[The next paragraph is 260]

2. Writ in Personam [5]

Writ of Summons in Admiralty Action in Personam

260 In the High Court of Justice 19—, Folio ——
Queen's Bench Division
Admiralty Court
Between:

[A.B.C. Company Limited] Plaintiffs
and
[D.E.F. Company Limited] Defendants

ELIZABETH THE SECOND, by the Grace of God, of the United Kingdom of Great Britain and Northern Ireland and of Our other realms and territories Queen, Head of the Commonwealth, Defender of the Faith:

To [D.E.F. Company Limited] of [*address*].

We command you that within 14 days after the service of this writ on you, inclusive of the day of service, you do cause an appearance to be entered for you in an action at the suit of [A.B.C. Company Limited]; and take notice that in default of your so doing the plaintiffs may proceed therein, and judgment may be given in your absence.

Witness ——, Lord High Chancellor of Great Britain, the —— day of ——, 19—.

Note: This writ may not be served later than 12 calendar months beginning with the above date unless renewed by order of the Court.

DIRECTIONS FOR ENTERING APPEARANCE

[*As in* § 250, *supra.*]

[5] See generally *Admiralty Practice* [B.S.L. 1, §§ 421 *et seq.*].

Indorsement of claim

The plaintiffs' claim is for ——.[6]

[*If the plaintiffs' claim is for a debt or liquidated demand only, the following indorsement must be added*:]

And £—— (or such sum as may be allowed on taxation) for costs, and also, if the plaintiffs obtain an order for substituted service, the further sum of £—— (or such sum as may be allowed on taxation). If the amount claimed and costs be paid to the plaintiffs, their solicitor or agent within —— days after service hereof (inclusive of the day of service), further proceedings will be stayed, but if it appears from the indorsement on the writ that the plaintiffs are resident outside the scheduled territories, as defined by the Exchange Control Act 1947, or are acting by order or on behalf of a person so resident, proceedings will only be stayed if the amount claimed and costs are paid into court within the said time, and notice of such payment in is given to the plaintiffs, their solicitor or agent.

[*Continue with indorsements as to scheduled territories, solicitor and address, and service as in* § 250, *supra.*]

Writ of Summons in Admiralty Action in Personam Issued out of District Registry

261 In the High Court of Justice 19—, No. —
Queen's Bench Division
Admiralty Court
[Liverpool] District Registry.

Between: [A.B.C. Company Limited] Plaintiffs

and

[D.E.F. Company Limited] Defendants

[*Continue as in* § 252, *supra, substituting the following for the directions for entering appearance.*]

DIRECTIONS FOR ENTERING APPEARANCE

If the defendants reside or carry on business, or (in the case of a limited company) have a registered office within the district of the above-named District Registry, or the writ is endorsed with a statement that any cause of action in respect of which the plaintiffs claim relief wholly or in part arose in that district, the defendants must enter an appearance in person or by a solicitor in the District Registry, and may do so either (1) by handing in the appropriate

[6] For precedents of indorsements, see §§ 270 *et seq.*, *infra.*

forms, duly completed, at the office of the District Registrar [*insert address of office*], or (2) by sending them to that office by post.

If the defendants neither reside or carry on business nor (in the case of a limited company) have a registered office within the district of the above-named District Registry and the writ is not indorsed with a statement that any cause of action in respect of which the plaintiffs claim relief, wholly or in part, arose in that district, the defendants may enter an appearance in person or by a solicitor either (1) by handing in the appropriate forms, duly completed, at the office of the District Registrar, or by sending them to that office by post, or (2) by handing in the said forms, duly completed, at the Admiralty Registry, Royal Courts of Justice, Strand, London, WC2A 2LL, or by sending them to that office by post.

The appropriate forms may be obtained by sending a postal order for [*insert current price*] with an addressed envelope, foolscap size, to (1) the District Registrar, High Court of Justice [*insert address*], if the appearance is to be entered in the District Registry, or (2) the Clerk of Accounts, Vote Office, Royal Courts of Justice, Strand, London, WC2A 2LL, if the appearance is to be entered in London.

Writ of Summons in Admiralty Action in Rem and in Personam Issued out of the Admiralty Registry [6a]

262 In the High Court of Justice 19—, Folio ——
Queen's Bench Division
Admiralty Court
Admiralty action in rem against:
The ship DAMON and in personam against A.B. Limited.
[The owners of the ship PYTHIAS] Plaintiffs
and
[The owners of the ship DAMON and A.B. Limited] Defendants
ELIZABETH THE SECOND [*continue as in* § 250, *supra*].

To the [owners of and other] persons interested in [the ship DAMON of the Port of London] and to [A.B. Limited] of [*address*].

We command you [*continue as in* § 250, *supra*].

[The next paragraph is 270]

6a This form, although regularly used, is not in strict accordance with the Rules of the Supreme Court: see R.S.C., Ord. 6, r. 1, and Ord. 75, r. 3. However, see also Ord. 1, r. 9 and Ord. 2.

3. Indorsement of Writ [6b]

Indorsement on Writ of Claim by Sole Owner for Possession [7]

270 The plaintiff, as sole owner of the ship DAMON, claims possession thereof.

Indorsement on Writ of Claim by Part Owner for Possession

271 The plaintiff, as owner of $^{52}/_{64}$ shares in the ship DAMON, claims possession thereof.

Indorsement on Writ of Claim by Sole Owner for a Declaration of Ownership [8]

272 The plaintiff's claim is for a declaration that he is the owner of $^{64}/_{64}$ shares in the ship DAMON of the Port of Liverpool and is entitled to be registered as the sole owner thereof.

Indorsement on Writ of Claim by Part Owner for a Declaration of Ownership

273 The plaintiff's claim is for a declaration that he is the owner of $^{32}/_{64}$ shares in the ship DAMON of the Port of Liverpool.

Indorsement on Writ of Claim by Part Owners for Restraint [9]

274 The plaintiffs, as owners of $^{30}/_{64}$ shares in the ship DAMON, being dissatisfied with the management of the said ship by their co-owners, claim that their said co-owners do give bail or other satisfactory security in the sum of £——, being the value of the plaintiffs' said shares, for the safe return of the said ship to London.[10]

Indorsement on Writ of Claim in Respect of a Mortgage or Assignment of a Mortgage

275 The plaintiffs' claim is for the sum of £—— together with interest thereon being the amount due and owing to them as mortgagees under [an assignment of] a [registered] mortgage on the ship DAMON, dated the —— day of ——, 19—.

6b For Statements of Claim in similar actions, see *supra*, §§ 192–213.
7 For another example, see prayer to § 190, *supra*.
8 For another example, see prayer to § 190, *supra*.
9 See § 191, *supra*, for Statement of Claim in co-ownership dispute.
10 *i.e.* her port of registry.

Indorsement on Writ of Claim for Damage done by a Ship

276 The plaintiffs' claim is for damage caused to the sheer legs on the plaintiffs' jetty by the negligent navigation or management of the defendants' ship DAMON on the —— day of ——, 19—.

Indorsement on Writ of Claim for Damage Received by a Ship in Collision

277 The plaintiffs' claim is for damage to their ship PYTHIAS and loss and expense sustained by them by reason of a collision with the defendants' ship DAMON, which occurred in the English Channel on or about the —— day of ——, 19—, as a result of the negligence of the defendants, their servants or agents.

Indorsement on Writ of Claim for Damage Received by Ship and Cargo in Collision

278 The plaintiffs' claim is for damages in respect of damage to their ship PYTHIAS and loss and expense sustained by them, and also in respect of damage to cargo laden thereon of which they were, at all material times, bailees in possession, arising out of a collision between the PYTHIAS and the defendants' ship DAMON which occurred in the River Thames on the —— day of ——, 19—, by reason of the negligence of the defendants, their servants or agents in the navigation or management of the DAMON.

Indorsement on Writ of Claim for Damage Received by a Ship Otherwise than by Collision

279 The plaintiffs' claim is for damage to their ship PYTHIAS and loss and expense sustained by them in consequence of the negligent navigation of the defendants' ship DAMON in the Bristol Channel on the —— day of ——, 19—.

Indorsement on Writ of Claim for Damage to Ship Lying in Defective Berth

280 The plaintiffs' claim is for damage to their ship PYTHIAS on or about the —— day of ——, 19—, and loss and expense sustained by them by reason of the breach of contract and/or duty of the defendants, whereby the said ship was caused or permitted to lie at an unsafe berth at the Port of Shoreham.

Indorsement on Writ of Claim for Personal Injuries

281 The plaintiff's claim is for damages for personal injuries sustained and loss and expense incurred by him, arising out of an accident sustained on board the defendants' ship DAMON, on or about the —— day of ——, 19—, such accident being caused by the negligence and/or breach of duty and/or breach of contract of the defendants, their servants or agents.

Indorsement on Writ of Claim for Damage Sustained by Cargo in Collision

282 The plaintiffs' claim is for loss and damage arising out of and occasioned by a collision between the defendants' ship DAMON and the PYTHIAS which occurred on the —— day of——, 19—, in the English Channel by reason of the negligence of the defendants, their servants or agents.

Indorsement on Writ of Claim for Damage to Cargo

283 The plaintiffs, as the owners of cargo lately laden on board the the defendants' ship DAMON of the Port of Monrovia, and/or as holders and/or indorsees of the bills of lading whereunder the said cargo was shipped, claim damages from the defendants for loss of and/or damage to the said cargo during the voyage from Lattakia to Colombo in or about the month of ——, 19—, sustained by reason of the defendants' breach of contract and/or duty and/or negligence in and about the carriage thereof.

Indorsement on Writ of Claim for Damage to Cargo and for Declarations as to General Average and Salvage

284 The plaintiffs' claim is for:

(a) Damages for breach of contract and/or duty in and about the loading, handling, custody, care and discharge of the plaintiffs' cargo and the carriage thereof on board the defendants' ship DAMON, in the year 19—;

(b) A declaration that the plaintiffs are not and were never liable to contribute any sum in respect of the general average of the DAMON, her cargo and freight;

(c) A declaration that the plaintiffs are entitled to the cancellation of the bond and guarantee given to the defendants by way of general average security;

(d) The return of and cancellation of the bond and guarantee given to the defendants by or on behalf of the plaintiffs by way of general average security, and

(e) A declaration that the plaintiffs are entitled to be indemnified by the defendants against liability for salvage, including interest and costs incurred by the plaintiffs, and damages for the equivalent of the sums attributable to the plaintiffs by way of salvage, including interest and costs, together with the costs incurred by the plaintiffs in connection with the claim for salvage and interest thereon.

Indorsement on Writ of Claim for Breach of Charterparty

285 The plaintiffs claim damages as charterers of the defendants' ship DAMON under a charterparty dated the —— day of ——, 19—, for the loss suffered by them in consequence of the defendants' breach of the said charterparty.

Indorsement on Writ of Claim for Salvage

286 The plaintiffs' claim is for remuneration for salvage services rendered by them to the defendants' ship DAMON, her cargo and freight, in the English Channel off the Isle of Wight in the month of ——, 19—.

Indorsement on Writ of Claim for Salvage of Aircraft

287 The plaintiffs' claim remuneration for salvage services rendered by them to the defendants' aircraft G-ABGL and everything in and on board her at Southend, in the County of Essex, on or about the —— day of ——, 19—, and thereafter.

Indorsement on Writ of Claim for Towage

288 The plaintiffs' claim is for £—— for towage of the defendants' ship DAMON by the plaintiffs' tug HERO in the Thames Estuary on the —— day of ——, 19—, pursuant to an agreement dated the —— day of ——, 19—, and made between the plaintiffs and defendants herein.

Indorsement on Writ of Claim for Pilotage

289 The plaintiffs' claim is for the sum of £—— for services performed as pilot on board the defendants' ship DAMON in the River Thames, pursuant to a contract dated the —— day of ——, 19—, and made between the plaintiffs and the defendants.

Indorsement on Writ of Claim for Goods and Materials Supplied

290 The plaintiffs' claim is for the sum of £—— for goods and/or materials supplied to the defendants' ship DAMON for her operation or maintenance at the Port of Liverpool, during the month of ——, 19—, at the request of the defendants, their servants or agents.

Indorsement on Writ of Claim for Repair to Ship

291 The plaintiffs' claim is for the sum of £—— for repairs carried out to the ship DAMON at Dover between the —— day of ——, 19—, and the —— day of ——, 19—, [pursuant to a contract made between the plaintiffs and defendants and dated the —— day of ——, 19—, *or* at the request of the defendants *or as the case may be*].

Indorsement on Writ of Claim for Construction or Equipping of Ship

292 The plaintiffs' claim is for £—— for work performed and materials supplied in the [construction *or* equipping] of the defendants' ship DAMON during the period from the month of —— to the month of ——, 19—, pursuant to a contract made between the plaintiffs and defendants and dated the —— day of ——, 19—.

Indorsement on Writ of Claim for Dock Charges or Dues [11]

293 The plaintiffs' claim is for £—— for [dock charges *or* dues] incurred by the defendants as owners of the ship DAMON at the Port of Boston, in the months of —— and ——, 19—.

Indorsement on Writ of Claim of Master for Wages, Social Security Payments, etc., and Disbursements [12]

294 The plaintiff's claim is for wages together with bonuses, overtime and leave pay due to him, including all pension fund contributions, taxes, union fees and social security payments payable out of his earnings,[13] together with disbursements made by him as master and an indemnity in respect of all sums which he has paid or is liable to pay to the appropriate authorities in respect of all taxes, pension fund contributions and social security payments due and payable out of the earnings of the officers and crew of the ship DAMON, or by the defendants, in respect of the service on board the DAMON of her officers and crew.

Indorsement on Writ of Claim of Master for Wages and Disbursements [14]

295 The plaintiff's claim is for £——, for wages [15] due to him and earned

11 See *The Charger* (*No.* 2) [1966] 3 All E.R. 117; [1966] 1 Lloyd's Rep. 670; *The Queen of the South* [1968] P. 449; [1968] 1 Lloyd's Rep. 182.

12 See the Consular Relations Act 1968, s. 4, which provides that Orders in Council may be made to exclude or limit the jurisdiction of the Court to entertain proceedings relating to the remuneration or contract of service of the master or crew of any ship or aircraft belonging to a State specified in the Order, unless the Consul has first been notified of the intention to invoke the jurisdiction and has not objected. Orders have been made in respect of Austria, Belgium, Bulgaria, Denmark, Federal Republic of Germany, Greece, Hungary, Italy, Japan, Mexico, Norway, Poland, Romania, Spain, Sweden, U.S.S.R., and Yugoslavia. See § 306 and also *The Andrea Ursula* [1971] 1 Lloyd's Rep. 145.

13 See *The Arosa Kulm* (*No.* 2) [1960] 1 Lloyd's Rep. 97; *The Acrux* [1965] P. 391; [1965] 1 Lloyd's Rep. 565; *The Fairport* [1965] 2 Lloyd's Rep. 183; *The Westport* (*No.* 4) 1968) 2 Lloyd's Rep. 559.

14 See n. 12 to § 294, *supra*.

15 See n. 13, *ibid*.

by him as master of the defendants' ship DAMON, from the —— day of ——, 19—, to the —— day of ——, 19—, together with £—— for disbursements made by him as master on account of the said ship and on behalf of the defendants.

Indorsement on Writ of Claim for Seamen's Wages [16]

296 The plaintiffs' claim is for wages [17] earned as seamen on board the defendants' ship DAMON and due to them as follows:

To A.B., mate, £——, for wages from the —— day of ——, 19—, to the —— day of ——, 19—.

To E.F., able seaman, £——, for wages from the —— day of ——, 19—, to the —— day of ——, 19—.

To G.H., greaser, £——, for wages from the —— day of ——, 19—, to the —— day of ——, 19—.

Indorsement on Writ of Claim for Social Insurance Contributions [18]

297 The plaintiffs as master, officers and crew of the ship DAMON claim the sum of £——, being the sterling equivalent of French francs ——, in respect of social insurance contributions due from the owners of the DAMON for the benefit of the plaintiffs pursuant to an agreement entered into by the defendants with the Etablissement National des Invalides de la Marine.[19]

Indorsement on Writ of Claim for Agents' Disbursements

298 The plaintiffs' claim is for the sum of £—— in respect of disbursements made by them as agents for and on behalf of the defendants and at their request in respect of the ship DAMON.

Indorsement on Writ of Claim for General Average Contribution

299 The plaintiffs claim from the defendants contribution to a general average loss incurred during a voyage from Cuba to China in or about the month of ——, 19—.

Indorsement on Writ of Claim for Stevedoring

300 The plaintiffs' claim is for £——, being their account in respect of services rendered by them as stevedores in the discharging of cargo

[16] A claim for wages may be made either for a liquidated or unliquidated sum. See also n. 12 to § 294, *supra*, and *The Fairport* (*No.* 2) [1966] 2 Lloyd's Rep. 7.

[17] See n. 13 to § 294, *supra*.

[18] See n. 12 to § 294, *supra*.

[19] See n. 13 to § 294, *supra*.

from the defendants' ship DAMON in the Port of London, in the month of ——, 19—.

Indorsement on Writ of Claim under Lloyd's Form of Salvage Agreement [20]

301 The plaintiffs' claim is for a declaration that the parties are bound by an agreement upon the terms of Lloyd's form of salvage agreement (No Cure—No Pay) made between one C.D., on behalf of the plaintiffs, and the master of the ship DAMON, on behalf of the defendants, at about 10.00 hours, on the —— day of ——, 19—, whereby it was agreed, *inter alia*, that the plaintiffs would use their best endeavours to salve the ship DAMON, then in distress in the North Atlantic, or, alternatively, for salvage remuneration in respect of salvage services rendered by the plaintiffs to the ship DAMON between the —— day of —— and the —— day of ——, 19—.

Indorsement on Writ of Claim against Owners for Damage Occasioned by Oil Pollution

302 The plaintiffs claim, pursuant to the Merchant Shipping (Oil Pollution) Act 1971, for the damage, loss and expense sustained or incurred by the plaintiffs by reason of the discharge or escape of crude oil from the defendants' ship DAMON in the Bristol Channel on or about January 1, 19—.

Indorsement on Writ of Claim against Charterers for Damage Occasioned by Oil Pollution

303 The plaintiffs' claim is for:

(a) Damages from the defendants for the damage, loss and expense sustained or incurred, or which may be sustained or incurred, by the plaintiffs by reason of the leakage of large quantities of oil into the sea following a collision between the ship PYTHIAS and the defendants' ship DAMON in the English Channel, on or about the —— day of ——, 19—, which said nuisance was caused by the negligence and/or breach of duty of the defendants, their servants or agents, in the navigation or management of the DAMON and/or

(b) Reimbursement of loss and expenditure reasonably and necessarily incurred by the plaintiffs for the benefit of the defendants, and/or at their implied request, in preventing or reducing damage consequent upon the said leakage of oil which said loss and expenditure is continuing.

[20] See Kennedy, *Civil Salvage*, 4th ed., p. 292.

Praecipe for Service of Writ in Rem by the Admiralty Marshal

[*Heading as in action.*]

304 We, A.B. & Co., of ——, [solicitors for] the plaintiffs, request that the writ of summons left herewith be duly served on [the ship DAMON].

Dated the —— day of ——, 19—.

[*Signature*]

Indorsement on Writ of Acceptance of Service

305 We hereby accept service of this writ of summons on behalf of the defendants [and undertake to enter an appearance hereto [and provide bail in an amount not exceeding the statutory limit of liability of the DAMON] in due course].

[*Signature*]
Solicitors for the defendants

Notice to be Indorsed on Writ Pursuant to Consular Relations Act 1968

306 Notification of the intention to invoke the jurisdiction of this court was sent to the [Greek] Consul on the —— day of —— 19—, more than 14 days before the date hereof. No objection has been made to the institution of these proceedings.

Solicitor's Letter of Undertaking to Accept Service of Writ and Give Security

307 Dear Sirs,

The PYTHIAS and DAMON

We have been instructed by the owners of the DAMON in connection with the collision between that ship and the PYTHIAS which occurred in the Thames Estuary on January 1, 19—.

In consideration of your refraining from arresting the DAMON or any other ship in the same ownership in connection with the abovementioned collision, we undertake to accept service of any proceedings and to provide security to an amount not exceeding [the statutory limit of liability of DAMON *or* the value of DAMON *or as may be*].

Yours faithfully,
[*Signature*]

[The next paragraph is 320]

CHAPTER 8

ARREST

1. WARRANT OF ARREST [1]

Praecipe for Caveat against Arrest

320 In the High Court of Justice
Queen's Bench Division
Admiralty Court

[The DAMON [or description of property]]

We, A.B. & Co., of [*address*], [solicitors for the owners of the ship DAMON] request a caveat against the arrest of [the ship DAMON] and hereby undertake to enter an appearance in any action that may be begun in the High Court of Justice against the said [ship] and, within 3 days after receiving notice that such an action has been begun, to give bail in the action in a sum not exceeding £—— or to pay that sum into court.

We consent that the writ of summons and any other document in the action may be left for us at [*address*].

Dated the —— day of ——, 19—.

[*Signature*]

Praecipe for Warrant of Arrest

[*Heading as in action*]

321 We, A.B. & Co., of [*address*], [solicitors for] the plaintiffs, request a warrant to arrest [*description of property to be arrested, giving name if a ship*].

Dated the —— day of ——, 19—.

[*Signature*]

Warrant of Arrest [2]

[*Heading as in action*]

322 ELIZABETH THE SECOND, [*continue as in* § 250, *supra*].

1 See generally *Admiralty Practice* [B.S.L. 1, §§ 251 *et seq.*].
2 Two copies of this document are required by the Admiralty Marshal.

To the Admiralty Marshal of Our High Court of Justice and to all and singular his substitutes, Greeting. We hereby command you to arrest the ship DAMON of the Port of London [and the cargo now or lately laden therein, together with the freight due for the transportation thereof, *or* the freight due for the transportation of the cargo now or lately laden therein] and to keep the same under safe arrest until you shall receive further orders from Us.

Witness (*as in* § 250, *supra*).

The plaintiffs' claim is for [*copy indorsement of claim from the writ*].

Taken out by A.B. & Co., of [*address*], [solicitors for] the plaintiffs.

Marshal's indorsement as to service

On ——, the —— day of ——, 19—, the within-named [ship] lying at —— was arrested by virtue of —— for a short time on —— of the said ship, and on taking off the process, by leaving a copy thereof fixed in its place.

Memorandum of Particulars of Property to be Arrested [3]

323 In the High Court of Justice 19—, Folio—
Queen's Bench Division
Admiralty Court
Admiralty action in rem against:

The Admiralty Marshal is requested to execute the Warrant lodged herewith by the arrest of [*here insert description of property to be arrested*] lying [*name the dock and the port*].

An undertaking is hereby given that the Admiralty Marshal shall be indemnified in respect of all charges and expenses that may be incurred in consequence of these instructions.

Dated the —— day of ——, 19—.

[*Signature of solicitor or his clerk*]

Notice of Arrest by Admiralty Marshal [4]

324 In the High Court of Justice
Queen's Bench Division
Admiralty Court

[3] This form is provided by the Admiralty Registry when the warrant is issued in that registry.

[4] This notice is prepared by the Admiralty Registry and is affixed to arrested property.

NOTICE

The DAMON

The above-named vessel, her tackle, apparel and furniture [and her cargo and freight] being in the custody or possession of the Admiralty Marshal by virtue of a warrant from the said Court, all persons are hereby cautioned not to attempt to remove the same or interfere therewith, without the authority in writing of the said Marshal or of his substitute, otherwise they will be immediately proceeded against for contempt of Court.

[*Signature*]
Admiralty Marshal

Admiralty Marshal's Office,
Royal Courts of Justice,
London, WC2A 2LL.
—— day of ——, 19—.

2. Affidavit to Lead Warrant of Arrest [5]

Affidavit to Lead Warrant of Arrest in Action for Possession [6]

[*Heading as in action*]

325 I, A.B., of [*residence*], a solicitor of the Supreme Court, make oath and say as follows:

1. I am a partner in the firm of C.D. & Co., of [*address*], solicitors for the plaintiff.

2. I am informed by the plaintiff and verily believe that by an oral agreement made on the —— day of ——, 19—, between the plaintiff of the one part, and one E.F. of the other part, the said E.F. agreed to act as nominee of the plaintiff in the purchase of the ship DAMON.

3. By an agreement made on the —— day of ——, 19—, between the said E.F., acting as aforesaid of the one part, and G.H., of the

[5] See *Admiralty Practice* [B.S.L. 1, § 259].
[6] Except with the leave of the court, a warrant of arrest shall not be issued in a possession action in rem against a foreign ship belonging to a port of a State having a consulate in London, until notice that the action has been begun has been sent to the consul. Every affidavit to lead a warrant of arrest in such an action must state the nationality of the ship against which the action is brought and that the notice has been sent. A copy of the notice must be exhibited to the affidavit. For form of notice, see § 339, *infra*.

other part, the said G.H. agreed to sell to the said E.F., acting as nominee as aforesaid, the ship DAMON for the sum of £——.

4. The said E.F. has refused and/or neglected to hand over possession of the said ship DAMON and the documents of title relating thereto to the plaintiff.

5. The ship DAMON is registered at the Port of Southampton.

6. The aid and process of this Honourable Court are required to enable the plaintiff to obtain possession of the said ship DAMON and the documents of title thereto.

Sworn [*etc.*].

This affidavit is filed on behalf of the plaintiff.

Affidavit to Lead Warrant of Arrest in Action for Restraint

[*Heading as in action*]

326 I, A.B., of [*residence*], a solicitor of the Supreme Court, make oath and say as follows:

1. I am a partner in the firm of C.D. & Co., of [*address*], solicitors for the plaintiff.

2. From information obtained from the plaintiff and the ship's certificate of registry and other documents in this matter I verily believe that the plaintiff is the owner of 32/64 shares in the ship DAMON of the Port of Hull.

3. The said ship DAMON is now lying at Hull under the command and control of P.Q., who is the owner of the remaining 32/64 shares therein. The DAMON is about to proceed on a voyage to the Far East against my wish or consent.

4. Security in the sum of £——, which is estimated to be the plaintiff's interest in the said ship DAMON, has been demanded in writing by me from the said P.Q. Such demand has not been satisfied.

5. The aid and process of this Honourable Court are required by the arrest of the DAMON to prevent her from proceeding to sea until the plaintiff's demand for security has been satisfied.

Sworn [*etc.*].

This affidavit is filed on behalf of the plaintiff.

Affidavit to Lead Warrant of Arrest in Action for Mortgage

[*Heading as in action*]

327 I, A.B., of [*residence*], a solicitor of the Supreme Court, make oath and say as follows:

1. I am a partner in the firm of C.D. & Co., of [*address*], solicitors for the plaintiffs.

2. I am informed by F.G., a director of the plaintiffs, and verily believe that the plaintiffs are the mortgagees of the ship DAMON of the Port of London under a mortgage deed dated the —— day of ——, 19—, and made between the said plaintiffs and defendants. The said mortgage deed was duly registered at the Port of London pursuant to Section 31 of the Merchant Shipping Act 1894.

3. I am informed by the said F.G. and verily believe that the sum secured by the mortgage deed is £—— exclusive of interest and this sum has not been paid and is now due from the said defendants and owing to the said plaintiffs together with interest thereon.

4. The aid and process of this Honourable Court are necessary to enforce the payment of the plaintiffs' claim by the arrest of the ship DAMON.

Sworn [*etc.*]

This affidavit is filed on behalf of the plaintiffs.

Affidavit to Lead Warrant of Arrest in Action for Damage or Loss of Ship

[*Heading as in action*]

328 I, A.B., of [*residence*], a solicitor of the Supreme Court, make oath and say as follows:

1. I am a partner in the firm of C.D. & Co., of [*address*], solicitors for the plaintiffs.

2. I am informed by a report received from the master of the ship PYTHIAS and verily believe that, on the —— day of ——, 19—, a collision occurred in the English Channel between the plaintiffs' ship PYTHIAS and the defendants' ship DAMON of the Port of London whereby the PYTHIAS was [damaged *or* sunk].

3. The plaintiffs' claim for compensation for the loss or damage occasioned by the collision remains unsatisfied.

4. The aid and process of this Honourable Court are necessary to enforce the payment of such compensation by the arrest of the DAMON.

Sworn [*etc.*]

This affidavit is filed on behalf of the plaintiffs.

Affidavit to Lead Warrant of Arrest in Action for Damage to Cargo

[*Heading as in action*]

329 I, A.B., of [*residence*], a solicitor of the Supreme Court, make oath and say as follows:

1. I am a partner in the firm of E.F. & Co., of [*address*], solicitors for the plaintiffs.

2. The plaintiffs are the [owners of *or* consignees of *or* indorsees of 10 bills of lading in respect of] a number of consignments of oranges, melons and almonds shipped from Spain in good order and condition in the defendants' ship DAMON for carriage for reward to the United Kingdom and delivery in the like good order and condition.

3. I am informed by G.H., marine consultant and cargo surveyor for the plaintiffs, and verily believe that, during the said voyage, the said cargo sustained damage.

4. The plaintiffs' claim [arises out of agreements relating to the use or hire of the DAMON, contained in a time charterparty dated the —— day of ——, 19—, *or* relates to the carriage of goods in the DAMON pursuant to bills of lading dated the —— day of ——, 19—].

5. I verily believe that the defendants were, at the time when the cause of action arose, [the owners *or* the charterers *or* in possession or control] of the ship DAMON and are the persons who would, apart from section 4 of the Administration of Justice Act 1956, be liable to the plaintiffs in an action in personam and were also at the date of the issue of the writ in this action the beneficial owners of the DAMON as respects all the shares therein. The grounds for my belief are that it appears from Lloyd's Register of Shipping for 19— -19— that the owners of the DAMON are described as X.Y.Z. Ltd., of [*address*], and I am informed by J.K., of Lloyd's Register of Shipping that no change of ownership has taken place since the cause of action arose.

6. The plaintiffs have been unable to obtain any compensation from the defendants for the said damage and the aid and process of this Court are required to enforce payment thereof by the arrest of the ship DAMON of the Port of Genoa.

Sworn [*etc.*]

This affidavit is filed on behalf of the plaintiffs.

Affidavit to Lead Warrant of Arrest in Action for Salvage

[*Heading as in action*]

330 I, A.B., of [*residence*], managing clerk to Messrs. C.D. & Co., of [*address*], solicitors for the plaintiffs, make oath and say as follows:

1. I have the conduct of this action on behalf of the plaintiffs. The matters to which I depose in this affidavit are true to the best of my knowledge, information and belief, being based on documents and instructions received from E.F., the plaintiffs' managing director.

2. On the —— day of ——, 19—, certain salvage services were rendered by the plaintiffs to the ship DAMON of the Port of London and her cargo and freight.

3. The plaintiffs' claim for a salvage reward in respect of such services has not been satisfied.

4. The aid and process of this Honourable Court are required to enforce the payment of such reward by the arrest of the ship DAMON her cargo and freight.

Sworn [*etc.*]

This affidavit is filed on behalf of the plaintiffs.

Affidavit to Lead Warrant of Arrest in Action for Towage

[*Heading as in action*]

331 I, A.B., of [*residence*], a solicitor of the Supreme Court, make oath and say as follows:

1. I am a partner in the firm of C.D. & Co., of [*address*], solicitors for the plaintiffs.

2. The plaintiffs are the owners of the tug HERO of the Port of London.

3. I am informed by E.F., the plaintiffs' managing director, and verily believe that, pursuant to an agreement dated the —— day of ——, 19—, and made between the plaintiffs and the defendants, the plaintiffs' tug HERO on the —— day of ——, 19—, towed the defendants' ship DAMON from Dover to London Bridge for an agreed sum of £——.

4. Request for payment of the said sum of £—— has been made to the defendants but the said sum still remains owing.

5. The property to be arrested is the ship DAMON of the Port of Liverpool.

6. The said ship DAMON is the ship in connection with which the claim in this action arose.

7. I verily believe that the defendants were, at the time when the cause of action arose, [the owners *or* the charterers *or* in possession or control] of the ship DAMON, and are the persons who would apart from section 4 of the Administration of Justice Act 1956, be liable to the plaintiffs in an action in personam and were also, at the date of the issue of the writ in this action, the beneficial owners of the

DAMON as respects all the shares therein. The grounds for my belief are that it appears from Lloyd's Register of Shipping for 19— - 19— that the owners of the DAMON are described as X.Y.Z. Ltd., of [*address*], and I am informed by G.H., of Lloyd's Register of Shipping that no change of ownership has taken place since the cause of action arose.

8. The aid and process of this Honourable Court are required to enforce payment of the sum due to the plaintiffs in this action by the arrest of the ship DAMON.

Sworn [*etc.*]

This affidavit is filed on behalf of the plaintiffs.

Affidavit to Lead Warrant of Arrest in Action for Repairs

[*Heading as in action*]

332 I, A.B., of [*residence*], a solicitor of the Supreme Court, make oath and say as follows:

1. I am a partner in the firm of C.D. & Co., of [*address*], solicitors for the plaintiffs.

2. The plaintiffs are a company incorporated in Belgium and carry on business as ship repairers at Antwerp.

3. I am informed by E.F., the plaintiffs' managing director in London, and verily believe that the plaintiffs effected repairs to the defendants' ship DAMON at Antwerp on the —— day of ——, 19—, at the defendants' request.

4. The plaintiffs' charges and disbursements for the said repairs amount to £——, and such sum remains due and owing to the plaintiffs.

5. The said ship DAMON is the ship in connection with which the claim in this action arose.

6. I verily believe that the defendants were at the time when the cause of action arose [the owners *or* the charterers *or* in possession or control] of the ship DAMON and are the persons who would, apart from section 4 of the Administration of Justice Act 1956, be liable to the plaintiffs in an action in personam and were also, at the date of the issue of the writ in this action, the beneficial owners of the DAMON as respects all the shares therein. The grounds for my belief are that it appears from Lloyd's Register of Shipping for 19— - 19—, that the owners of the DAMON are described as X.Y.Z. Ltd., of [*address*], and I am informed by J.K. —— of Lloyd's Register of Shipping that no change of ownership has taken place since the cause of action arose.

7. The aid and process of this Honourable Court are required to enforce payment of the sum due to the plaintiffs in this action by the arrest of the ship DAMON of the Port of London.
Sworn [*etc.*].
This affidavit is filed on behalf of the plaintiffs.

Affidavit to Lead Warrant of Arrest in Action for Master's Wages and Disbursements

[*Heading as in action*]

333 I, A.B., of [*residence*], a solicitor of the Supreme Court, make oath and say as follows:

1. I am a partner in the firm of C.D. & Co., of [*address*], solicitors for the plaintiff.

2. I am informed by the plaintiff and verily believe that he was lately the master of the ship DAMON and that there is due and owing to him the sum of £—— in respect of wages earned by him in that capacity and also on account of disbursements made by him as master in respect of the said ship DAMON.

3. The property to be arrested is the ship DAMON of the Port of Genoa.

4. Notice of commencement of this action has been sent to the Consul General of Italy by letter dated the —— day of ——, 19—.[7] There is now produced and shewn to me a true copy of such letter marked " A.B.1." and exhibited hereto.
Sworn [*etc.*].
This affidavit is filed on behalf of the plaintiff.

Affidavit to Lead Warrant of Arrest in Action for Seamen's Wages

[*Heading as in action*]

334 I, A.B., of [*residence*], a solicitor of the Supreme Court, make oath and say as follows:

[7] Except with the leave of the court, a warrant of arrest shall not be issued in a wages action *in rem* against a foreign ship belonging to a port of a state having a consulate in London, until notice that the action has been begun has been sent to the consul. Every affidavit to lead a warrant of arrest in such an action must state the nationality of the ship against which the action is brought and that the notice has been sent. A copy of the notice must be exhibited to the affidavit. For form of notice, see § 339, *infra*.

1. I am a partner in the firm of C.D. & Co., of [*address*], solicitors for the plaintiffs.

2. I am informed by E.F., the second officer of the DAMON and one of the plaintiffs in this action, and verily believe that the plaintiffs have a claim against the defendants in this action in respect of wages due and owing to them for their services on board the ship DAMON for various periods between the —— day of ——, 19—, and the —— day of ——, 19—, and such claim has not been satisfied.

3. The property to be arrested is the ship DAMON of the Port of Genoa.

4. Notice of commencement of this action has been sent to the Consul-General of Italy by letter dated the —— day of ——, 19—.[8-9] There is now produced and shewn to me a true copy of such letter marked " A.B.1." and exhibited hereto.

Sworn [*etc.*].

This affidavit is filed on behalf of the plaintiffs.

Affidavit to Lead Warrant of Arrest in Action for Disbursements by Agent

[*Heading as in action*]

335 I, A.B., of [*residence*], a solicitor of the Supreme Court, make oath and say as follows:

1. I am a partner in the firm of C.D. & Co., of [*address*], solicitors for the plaintiffs.

2. The plaintiffs are ship agents in Liverpool and, at the request of the defendants, the plaintiffs acted as agents in respect of the call at that port of the defendants' ship DAMON in the month of ——, 19—. The plaintiffs incurred disbursements at Liverpool to the extent of £——. The defendants paid £—— on account, and, in the plaintiffs' account to them, dated the —— day of ——, 19—, were debited with the balance of £—— due.

3. The said sum of £—— remains due and owing to the plaintiffs and the aid and process of this Honourable Court are required to enforce payment of the sum due by the arrest of the DAMON of the Port of Monrovia.

4. The said ship DAMON is the ship in connection with which the claim in this action arose.

5. I verily believe that the defendants were, at the time when the cause of action arose, [the owners *or* the charterers *or* in possession

[8-9] See n. 7 to § 333, *supra.*

or control] of the ship DAMON and are the persons who would, apart from section 4 of the Administration of Justice Act 1956, be liable to the plaintiffs in an action in personam and were also at the date of the issue of the writ in this action the beneficial owners of the DAMON as respects all the shares therein. The grounds for my belief are that it appears from Lloyd's Register of Shipping for 19— -19— that the owners of the DAMON are described as X.Y.Z. Ltd., of [*address*], and I am informed by J.K. of Lloyd's Register of Shipping that no change of ownership has taken place since the cause of action arose.
Sworn [*etc*.].
This affidavit is filed on behalf of the plaintiffs.

Affidavit to Lead Warrant of Arrest in a Sister-Ship Action

[*Heading as in action*]

336 I, A.B., of [*residence*], a solicitor of the Supreme Court, make oath and say as follows:

1. I am a partner in the firm of C.D. & Co., of [*address*], the solicitors for the plaintiffs in this action, instituted by them against the owners of the ship DAMON for salvage services rendered by them to the defendants' ship DEMOS, on the —— day of ——, 19—.

2. The plaintiffs' claim for a salvage reward in respect of their services to the DEMOS has not been satisfied.

3. The property to be arrested is the ship DAMON of the Port of Mariehamn, Finland, and is not the ship in connection with which the claim in this action arose.

4. I verily believe that the persons who would, apart from section 4 of the Administration of Justice Act 1956, be liable to the plaintiffs in an action in personam were, when the cause of this action arose, [the owners *or* the charterers *or* in possession or control] of the ship in connection with which this claim arose, and were also, at the date of the issue of the writ in this action, the beneficial owners of the DAMON as respects all the shares therein. The grounds for my belief are that it appears from Lloyd's Register of Shipping for 19— - 19—, that the owners of the DAMON and DEMOS are described as X.Y.Z. Ltd., of [*address*].
Sworn [*etc*.].
This affidavit is filed on behalf of the plaintiffs.

[The next paragraph is 339]

3. Ancillary Forms

Notice to Consul of Commencement of Proceedings in Respect of a Claim for Possession or for Wages

339 Dear Sir,

The Italian ship MICHELANGELO

Please take notice that we have today instituted proceedings in the Admiralty Court of the High Court of Justice against the above-named ship of the Port of Genoa and now lying in Nelson Dock, Liverpool, in respect of a claim [by C.D. for possession of the said ship *or* by the master and crew of the MICHELANGELO for wages due and owing to them].

Yours faithfully,

[*Signature*]

Solicitors for the said [C.D. *or* master and crew]

To ——————

Consul-General of Italy.

Agreement for Trial as an Admiralty Short Cause

340 We, the undersigned solicitors for the above-named plaintiffs and defendants respectively, hereby consent that this action be tried as an Admiralty Short Cause pursuant to R.S.C., Ord. 75, r. 31.

[The next paragraph is 342]

4. Release from Arrest [10]

Praecipe for Caveat against Release and Payment out of Court [11]

342 In the High Court of Justice.
Queen's Bench Division.
Admiralty Court.

[10] See generally *Admiralty Practice* [B.S.L. 1, §§ 351–362; §§ 639 *et seq.*].
[11] See generally *Admiralty Practice* [B.S.L. §§ 280, 281].

[The DAMON]

We, A.B. & Co., of [*address*], [solicitors for the owners of the ship PYTHIAS] of [*address*], request a caveat against the issue of a release with respect to [the ship DAMON [12]] now under arrest, and should the said property be sold by order of the court, a caveat against payment out of court of the proceeds of sale.

The intending caveator claims to have an interest [to the extent of approximately £—— *if known*] in the above-mentioned property in respect of [*state nature of claim, e.g. salvage, collision damage*].

Dated the —— day of ——, 19—.

[*Signature*]

Praecipe for Withdrawal of Caveat

343 In the High Court of Justice
Queen's Bench Division
Admiralty Court

[The DAMON [13]]

We, A.B. & Co., of [*address*], [solicitors for the owners of the ship PYTHIAS] of [*address*], request that the caveat against [arrest *or* release and payment] entered on the —— day of ——, 19—, on behalf of [the owners of the ship PYTHIAS] be withdrawn.

Dated the —— day of ——, 19—.

[*Signature*]

Letter Submitting Names of Proposed Sureties

344 Dear Sirs,

The DAMON

We hereby submit the names of the undermentioned as sureties to bail on behalf of the [plaintiffs *or* defendants] in this action:

A.B. of [*address*], [*description*].

C.D. of [*address*], [*description*].

We shall be obliged if you will inform us as soon as possible whether or not the proposed sureties are satisfactory to your clients. If they are, we will have the bail completed forthwith.

Yours faithfully,

[*Signature*]

12 Description of property giving name, if a ship
13 Description of property giving name, if a ship

Letter Approving or Objecting to Proposed Sureties

345 Dear Sirs,

The DAMON

Thank you for your letter of the —— day of ——, 19—.

[We have been instructed that the proposed sureties to bail are acceptable to our clients, *or* We have been instructed to object to the proposed sureties to bail on the grounds that [*give reasons*].]

Yours faithfully,

[*Signature*]

Notice of Bail [14]

[*Heading as in action*]

346 Take Notice that bail has been given on behalf of the above-named [defendants], in the sum of £——, to answer judgment in this action, by A.B. of [*address*], [*description*], and C.D. of [*address*], [*description*], and that such bail has been taken before E.F., a Commissioner for Oaths.

Dated the —— day of ——, 19—.

[*Signature*]

Solicitors for the [defendants]

To Messrs. G.H. & Co.,
Solicitors for the [plaintiffs].

Bail Bond [15]

[*Heading as in action*]

347 Whereas this Admiralty action in rem against the above-mentioned property is pending in the High Court of Justice and the parties to the said action are the above-mentioned plaintiffs and defendants:

Now, therefore, we, A.B. of [*address*], and C.D. of [*address*],

[14] This notice must be served 24 hours before the bail bond can be filed unless a consent to filing the bail bond within 24 hours has been obtained from the opposite party. For form of consent, see § 350, *infra*.

[15] *Cf.* form in *Admiralty Practice* [B.S.L. 1, § 330]

hereby jointly and severally submit ourselves to the jurisdiction of the said Court and consent that, if they, the above-mentioned [defendants] [*or, in the case of a counterclaim, plaintiffs*] do not pay what may be adjudged against them in this action, with costs, or do not pay any sum due to be paid by them in consequence of any admission of liability therein, or under any agreement by which this action is settled before judgment and which is filed in the said Court, execution may issue against us, our executors or administrators, goods and chattels, for the amount unpaid or an amount of £—— whichever is the less.

This bail bond was signed by the said A.B. and C.D., the sureties, the —— day of ——, 19—.	[*Signatures of sureties*]

Before me [*Signature*]

a Commissioner for Oaths.

Affidavit of Justification [16]

[*Heading as in action*]

348 I, A.B., of [*residence*], [Chairman of Messrs. C.D. & Co. Ltd., of [*address*]] one of the proposed sureties for the [plaintiffs *or* defendants] in this action, make oath and say that I am worth more than the sum of [*the amount in words of the bail given*] after the payment of all my debts.

Sworn [*etc.*].

This affidavit is filed on behalf of the [plaintiffs *or* defendants]

Affidavit of Service of Notice of Bail

[*Heading as in action*] [17]

349 I, D.E., of [*residence*], clerk to Messrs. E. F. & Co. of [*address*], solicitors for the [plaintiffs *or* defendants] in this action, make oath and say as follows:

16 See *Admiralty Practice* [B.S.L. 1, § 329]. *Cf. ibid.* § 333 for suggested alternative form. Where a corporation is a surety to a bail bond given on behalf of a party, no affidavit of justification shall be made unless the opposite party requires it. Where such an affidavit is required it must be made by a director, manager, secretary or other similar officer of the corporation.

17 See *Admiralty Practice* [B.S.L. 1, § 334].

That I did on [Monday] the —— day of ——, 19—, between the hours of —— and —— o'clock in the [forenoon] serve on Messrs. A.B. & Sons, solicitors for the [plaintiffs *or* defendants] in this action, a notice of bail in the words and figures as follows:

"Take notice that bail has been given in the sum of [*state the amount*] on behalf of the above-named [plaintiffs *or* defendants] to answer judgment in this action by P.Q. of [*address*], [chairman of Messrs. X.Y. & Co. Ltd., of [*address*], and S.T. of [*address*], managing director of Mesrs. F.G. & Co. of [*address*]]. And that such bail has been taken before a Commissioner for Oaths.

Dated this —— day of ——, 19—.

[*Signature*]

Solicitors for the
[plaintiffs *or* defendants]

To: Messrs. A.B. & Sons,

Solicitors for the [plaintiffs *or* defendants]."

Sworn [*etc.*].

This affidavit is filed on behalf of the [plaintiffs *or* defendants].

Consent to Filing of Bail Bond within 24 Hours of Service of Notice of Bail

[*Heading as in action*]

350 We, A.B. & Co., solicitors for the [plaintiffs or defendants], hereby consent to the bail bond in this action being immediately filed notwithstanding that 24 hours have not elapsed since the service of notice of bail upon us.

Dated the —— day of ——, 19—.

[*Signature*]

Undertaking in Lieu of Bail

The PYTHIAS and DAMON. Collision
in the Mediterranean in January, 19—.

351 In consideration of your [releasing *or* refraining from arresting or otherwise detaining] the ship DAMON or any other property belonging to her owners or charterers or to any person who has, or had at any time, the management, possession or control of the DAMON in connection with any claim arising out of the above-mentioned colli-

sion, and, whereas you have demanded that the owners of the DAMON should cause security to be furnished in the sum of £—— in respect of your said claim, we hereby undertake upon demand to pay to you, or as you may direct, in sterling in London, any sum of sums including damages, interest and costs which may be found due to you from the owners of the DAMON by judgment of a court, agreement between the parties, award of an arbitrator or otherwise in consequence of the above mentioned collision, provided that our total liability hereunder shall not exceed the sum of £——, inclusive of interest and costs, and provided further that our liability hereunder shall be additional to and not in substitution for liability of any other person for or in connection with your claim, whether by way of undertaking or otherwise, and shall not be reduced or extinguished while any sum or sums found due to you as aforesaid from the owners of the DAMON remain unpaid save to the extent of such sum or sums.

This undertaking is to be governed by and construed in accordance with English law and is given without prejudice to any question of liability or of limitation of liability.

[*Signature*]

To ——

Notice of Motion to Release Part of Property under Arrest

[*Heading as in action*]

352 TAKE NOTICE that this Honourable Court will be moved on [Monday] the —— day of ——, 19—, at [10.30] o'clock, or so soon thereafter as counsel can be heard by counsel on behalf of the interveners in this action, the time charterers of the ship DAMON, for an order that the fuel oil contained in the bunker tanks of the ship DAMON, now lying under the arrest of this Honourable Court, be released from arrest and delivered up to the said interveners.

[*Signature*]

Solicitors for the interveners

To the plaintiffs and to Messrs. C.D. & Co., their solicitors.

Notice of Motion to Release Vessel under Arrest

[*Heading as in action*]

353 TAKE NOTICE [*continue as in* § 352, *supra*] on behalf of the defen-

dants, for an order that the vessel DAMON be released from the arrest of this Honourable Court.

[*Signature*]

Solicitors for the defendants

To the plaintiffs and to Messrs. A.B. & Co., their solicitors.

Affidavit in Support of Motion to Release Vessel under Arrest

354 I, A.B., of [*residence*], Solicitor of the Supreme Court, make oath and say as follows:

1. I am a partner in the firm of Messrs. A.B. & Co., of [*address*]. I have the conduct of this action on behalf of the defendants.

2. The claim endorsed on the writ of summons herein is for the sum of £5,000 for repairs executed to the motor vessel DAMON at the Port of Hull during February and March, 19—.

3. I am informed by the defendants and verily believe that the plaintiffs have not so far complied with a request of the defendants to furnish an itemised account in respect of the repairs, the subject of this claim, and until the said account is delivered by the plaintiffs, the defendants are unable to agree or admit the plaintiffs' claim.

4. The defendants have this day paid into this Honourable Court the sum of £5,000 in accordance with R.S.C. Ord. 75, r. 24 as security for the plaintiffs' claim, without prejudice to their liability and my firm has also furnished the plaintiffs' solicitors with an undertaking to pay such sum as may be due to them in respect of the costs of this action.

5. I therefore ask that this Honourable Court may grant the release of DAMON.

Sworn [*etc.*]

This affidavit is filed on behalf of the defendants.

Notice of Motion to Set Aside Writ and Warrant of Arrest on Ground that Ship is Property of Foreign State

[*Heading as in action*]

355 TAKE NOTICE [*continue as in* § 352, *supra*] on behalf of the above-named defendants for an order that the writ of summons and warrant of arrest herein be set aside with costs, on the ground that the motor vessel DAMON is the property of the People's Republic of China, a recognised foreign independent state, and that the said state declines to sanction the institution of these proceedings in this Court.

[*Signature*]

Solicitors for the defendants

To the plaintiffs and to Messrs. C.D. & Co., their solicitors.

Request for Withdrawal of Warrant of Arrest [18]

[*Heading as in action*]

356 We, the undersigned, solicitors for the plaintiffs, request that the warrant of arrest issued by us against the [ship DAMON [19]] may be withdrawn.

Dated the —— day of ——, 19—.

[*Signature*]

Consent to Release [20]

[*Heading as in action*]

357 We the undersigned, solicitors for the plaintiffs and defendants respectively, hereby consent to the release of the [ship DAMON [21]] arrested in this action.

Dated the —— day of ——, 19—.

[*Signatures*]

Praecipe for Issue of Release

[*Heading as in action*]

358 We, A.B. & Co., of [*address*], [solicitors for] the [defendants] in this action against [the ship DAMON [22]] now under arrest by virtue of a warrant issued out of the [Admiralty Registry *or* —— District Registry] request the issue of a release with respect to the said [ship DAMON].

Dated the —— day of ——, 19—.

[*Signature*]

18 This form is used where the arrest has been effected by the plaintiffs and no appearance has been entered.
19 Description of property giving name, if a ship.
20 This form is used where an appearance has been entered.
21 Description of property giving name, if a ship.
22 Description of property giving name, if a ship.

Release

[*Heading as in action*]

359 ELIZABETH THE SECOND [*continue as in* § 250].

To the Admiralty Marshal of Our High Court of Justice, and to all and singular his substitutes, Greeting.

Whereas in this action We did command you to arrest the [ship DAMON [23]] and to keep the same under safe arrest until you should receive further orders from Us.

Now We do hereby command you to release the said [ship DAMON [23]] from the arrest effected by virtue of Our warrant in this action.

Witness [*continue as in* § 250].

Taken out by A.B. & Co., [solicitors for the plaintiffs].

Marshal's indorsement

On —— the —— day of ——, 19—, the [ship DAMON] was released from arrest pursuant to this Instrument.

[*Signature*]

Admiralty Marshal's substitute

Release and Warrant of Possession

[*Heading as in action*]

360 ELIZABETH THE SECOND [*continue as in* § 250, *supra*].

To the Admiralty Marshal of Our High Court of Justice, and to all and singular his substitutes, Greeting.

Whereas in this action the Court has ordered possession of [the ship DAMON, her tackle, apparel and furniture] to be delivered up to ———— or to his solicitor for his use.

We hereby command you to release [the said ship, her tackle, apparel and furniture] from the arrest made by virtue of Our Warrant in that behalf and to deliver possession thereof to the said ———— or to his solicitor for his use.

Witness [*as in* § 250, *supra*].

Taken out by A.B. & Co., [solicitors for the plaintiffs].

[23] Description of property giving name, if a ship

Marshal's indorsement

On the —— day of ——, 19— [the ship DAMON] was released from arrest pursuant to this warrant.

[*Signature*]

Admiralty Marshal's substitute

Receipt

Received from the Admiralty Marshal's substitute on the —— day of ——, 19—, [the ship DAMON and everything on board belonging to her].

[*Signature*]

Memorandum of Particulars in Regard to Release of Property [24]

361 In the High Court of Justice 19—, Folio
Queen's Bench Division
Admiralty Court

Particulars of property to be released:

It is requested that the instrument of release lodged herewith be executed by release of the vessel DAMON lying [in Nelson Dock, Liverpool] [and of the said vessel's cargo [for the freight *or* and freight] mentioned in the release].

An undertaking is hereby given for payment of all the outstanding costs, charges and expenses attending the care and custody of the property whilst under arrest in this action.

Dated the —— day of ——, 19—.

[*Signature of solicitor or his clerk*]

Agreement as to Dismissal of Bail

[*Heading as in action*]

362 We, the undersigned, solicitors for the plaintiffs and defendants respectively, hereby agree that the bail bond given on behalf of the [defendants] by —— of —— in the sum of £—— [and reduced by order of the Court dated the —— day of ——, 19—, to £——] be cancelled and the sureties thereto dismissed from all further observ-

[24] This document will be provided by, and must be completed in, the Admiralty Registry before the release will be effected.

ance of Justice thereunder and that the said bond be taken off the file and handed to Messrs. ——, the [defendants'] solicitors.

[*Signature*]
Solicitors for the plaintiffs
[*Signature*]
Solicitors for the defendants

Notice of Motion to Release Security under Section 5 of the Merchant Shipping (Liability of Shipowners and Others) Act 1958

[*Heading as in action*]

363 TAKE NOTICE that this Honourable Court will be moved on the —— —— day of ——, 19—, or so soon thereafter as counsel can be heard, by counsel on behalf of the defendants for an order pursuant to the provisions of section 5 of the Merchant Shipping (Liability of Shipowners and Others) Act 1958, that the security, given to obtain the release from arrest of the ship DAMON, be released, or alternatively for a declaration that the plaintiffs are not entitled to enforce the letter of undertaking accepted by them as security for their claims as provided by the defendants to obtain the release from arrest of the ship DAMON.

To the plaintiffs [*etc.*[25]].

Affidavit in Support

364 I, H.I.J., of [*residence*], solicitor of the Supreme Court, make oath and say as follows:

1. I am a partner in the firm of Messrs. C.D. & Co., solicitors of [*address*]. I have been instructed by the defendants to represent them and to protect their interest in all matters arising in England in connection with the collision on the —— day of ——, 19—, between PYTHIAS and DAMON.

2. On or about the —— day of ——, 19—, I was informed by Messrs. A.B. & Co. that they had been instructed by the plaintiffs to bring proceedings in England in respect of their loss arising out of the said collision and to arrest DAMON to obtain security for their claim.

3. On the —— day of ——, 19—, the defendants had paid into the Court at Copenhagen the sum of —— Kroner. The said sum is

[25] As in § 352, *supra*.

available to meet all claims arising out of the said collision, including the plaintiffs' claim. I informed Messrs. A.B. & Co. by telephone of the said payment into the Danish court. But by telex message dated the —— day of ——, Messrs. A.B. & Co. informed me that the plaintiffs still intended to arrest DAMON.

4. The defendants' vessel was duly arrested on the —— day of —— in the Port of London. In order to obtain her release from arrest, I procured a letter of undertaking dated the —— day of ——, signed by the University Assurance Company Limited. A copy of the said letter of undertaking, which was accepted by the plaintiffs as security for their claim in lieu of bail, has been produced and shown to me and is exhibited hereto marked "H.I.J.1." On the —— day of ——, DAMON was released.

5. There has been produced and shown to me and is exhibited hereto, marked "H.I.J.2," a certified copy of the particulars of DAMON as registered in Panama. As appears therefrom, her registered tonnage with the addition of engine room space deducted therefrom is —— tons. The multiple of that figure and £—— is £——, which I verily believe would be the amount of her limitation fund in accordance with the Merchant Shipping Acts 1894 to 1970. The equivalent of —— Kroner at the rate of —— Kroner to the pound sterling is £——.

Sworn [*etc.*].

[The next paragraph is 380]

CHAPTER 9

INTERLOCUTORY PROCEEDINGS

1. PRELIMINARY ACTS [1]

Collision in Good Weather, at Night, in Open Sea

380 In the High Court of Justice 19—, Folio ——
Queen's Bench Division
Admiralty Court
Admiralty action in rem against:
The ship DAMON
The owners of the motor vessel PYTHIAS Plaintiffs
and
The owners of the motor vessel DAMON Defendants

PRELIMINARY ACT ON BEHALF OF THE [PLAINTIFFS]

I

The names of the ships which came into collision and their ports of registry.	PYTHIAS: Monrovia. DAMON: Panama.

II

The date and time of the collision.	About 04.30 hours (Ship's time G.M.T.+30 minutes) on March 11, 19—.

III

The place of the collision.	In the English Channel; about 30 miles West-South-West of the Casquets.

IV

The direction and force of the wind.	West-North-West, force 3.

[1] See generally *Admiralty Practice* [B.S.L. 1, §§ 671 *et seq.*].

V

The state of the weather.	The weather was fine and clear. It was a dark night but with good visibility.

VI

The state, direction and force of the tidal or other current.	The tide was setting in a North-Easterly direction at a rate of about 1 knot.

VII

The course steered and speed through the water of the ship when the other ship was first seen or immediately before any measures were taken with reference to her presence, whichever was the earlier.	PYTHIAS was proceeding on a true course of 235° and, with her engines working at full speed ahead, she was making about 19 knots through the water.

VIII

The lights (if any) carried by the ship.	Two white masthead lights, red and green sidelights and a white stern light.

IX

(a) The distance and bearing of the other ship if and when her echo was first observed by radar.	The distance of DAMON was checked on radar when the range was about 1 mile. The echo was then to port of the heading marker.
(b) The distance, bearing and approximate heading of the other ship when first seen.	The two white masthead lights of DAMON were first sighted distant about 10 miles, bearing about 5° on the port bow, and indicating a heading of about 50° (true).

X

What light or combination of lights (if any) of the other ship was first seen.	Two white masthead lights.

XI

What other lights or combinations of lights (if any) of the other ship were subsequently seen before the collision and when.

When DAMON had closed to a range of about 4 to 5 miles, her green sidelight came into view. At the times indicated in article XII (below), her red sidelight opened and her green sidelight closed, whereafter her green sidelight opened and her red sidelight closed.

XII

What alterations (if any) were made to the course and speed of the ship after the earlier of the two times referred to in article VII up to the time of the collision and when, and what measures (if any), other than alterations of course or speed, were taken to avoid the collision and when.

When the two white masthead lights of a vessel that proved to be DAMON were first sighted (as in article IX (b) above) they were carefully watched. When DAMON had closed to a range of about 4 to 5 miles, still bearing about 5° on the port bow, her green sidelight came into view. PYTHIAS maintained her course and speed. Thereafter, when DAMON had closed to a range of about 1 mile (which was checked by radar) and was bearing fine on the port bow, the rudder of PYTHIAS was put 10° to starboard. Very shortly thereafter, the red sidelight of DAMON opened, her masthead lights came into line and her green sidelight closed. It was apparent that she was altering course to starboard. Her bearing began to broaden. Shortly thereafter, when DAMON was distant about 3 cables, bearing about 3 points on the port bow of PYTHIAS, her green sidelight opened suddenly, her masthead lights came into line and began to turn to port, and her red side-

	light closed. It was apparent that she was swinging rapidly to port. PYTHIAS continued to swing under starboard helm.

XIII

The parts of each ship which first came into contact and the approximate angle between the two ships at the moment of contact.	The stem of DAMON struck the port side of PYTHIAS just forward of No. 4 hold; at about a right angle.

XIV

What sound signals (if any) were given, and when.	None.

XV

What sound signals (if any) were heard from the other ship, and when.	None.

Collision in Good Weather, during Day, in Narrow Channel

[*Heading as in* § 380, *supra*]

PRELIMINARY ACT ON BEHALF OF [DEFENDANTS]

I

381 The names of the ships which came into collision and their ports of registry.	DAMON: Panama. PYTHIAS: Monrovia.

II

The date and time of the collision.	About 13.10 hours (B.S.T.) on February 4, 19—.

III

The place of the collision.	In the River Thames, near Blackwall Point, South of mid-channel and abeam of the graving dock upstream of the Weir Wharf.

IV

The direction and force of the wind.	Westerly, force 3.

V

The state of the weather.	Fine and clear.

VI

The state, direction and force of the tidal or other current.	The tide was flooding up-river at a rate of about 2 to 3 knots.

VII

The course steered and speed through the water of the ship when the other ship was first seen or immediately before any measures were taken with reference to her presence, whichever was the earlier.	DAMON had just emerged from the South-West India Dock lock and was manoeuvring onto a down-river heading in a position off the lock entrance just North of the northern edge of the channel, stemming the tide.

VIII

The lights (if any) carried by the ship.	None.

IX

(a) The distance and bearing of the other ship if and when her echo was first observed by radar.	No radar observations.
(b) The distance, bearing and approximate heading of the other ship when first seen.	During the manoeuvre described in article VII (above) PYTHIAS was seen distant about $\frac{3}{4}$ mile proceeding upstream on the North side of the river in the vicinity of Bow Creek.

X

What light or combination of lights (if any) of the other ship was first seen.	None.

XI

What other lights or combinations of lights (if any) of the other ship were subsequently seen before the collision, and when.	None.

XII

What alterations (if any) were made to the course and speed of the ship after the earlier of the two times referred to in article VII up to the time of the collision and when, and what measures (if any), other than alterations of course or speed, were taken to avoid the collision and when.	After DAMON had come onto a down-river heading, her engines were put slow ahead and then full ahead and she began to proceed across the river, heading about 2 points to starboard of a downstream heading. PYTHIAS was carefully watched. DAMON passed a tank barge coming upstream close by starboard to starboard, whereupon her wheel was immediately put to starboard and one short blast was sounded on her whistle. PYTHIAS was seen to be distant about 3 cables bearing about 2 points on the port bow. She was proceeding upstream to the North of mid-channel. DAMON crossed ahead of PYTHIAS, and thereafter when PYTHIAS was distant about 1 to 1½ cables, and bearing about 4 points on the port bow of DAMON, she appeared to begin to alter course to port, whereupon the wheel of DAMON was put hard-a-starboard and another short blast was given on her whistle. Thereafter when PYTHIAS was distant about 400 feet DAMON gave a further short blast on the whistle whereupon PYTHIAS was seen to come rapidly to port, shaping to

	come across the head of DAMON and accordingly the engines of DAMON were put full astern.

XIII

The parts of each ship which first came into contact and the approximate angle between the two ships at the moment of contact.	The stem and port bow of PYTHIAS struck the port bow of DAMON at an angle of about 60° leading aft on DAMON.

XIV

What sound signals (if any) were given, and when.	DAMON sounded one long blast on emerging from the South West India Dock lock. A short blast was sounded on three occasions as described in article XII (above).

XV

What sound signals (if any) were heard from the other ship, and when.	None.

Collated Preliminary Act [1a]: Collision in Fog

[*Heading as in* § 380, *supra*]

	PRELIMINARY ACT ON BEHALF OF THE PLAINTIFFS	PRELIMINARY ACT ON BEHALF OF THE DEFENDANTS
	I	
382 The names of the ships which came into collision and their ports of registry.	PYTHIAS: Monrovia. DAMON: Panama.	DAMON: Panama. PYTHIAS: Monrovia.
	II	
The date and time of the collision.	About 03.57 on October 16, 19—.	About 04.03 hours (G.M.T.+4) on October 16, 19—.

[1a] These forms are adapted from those filed in *The Almizar* [1969] 1 Lloyd's Rep. 1.

	PRELIMINARY ACT ON BEHALF OF THE PLAINTIFFS	PRELIMINARY ACT ON BEHALF OF THE DEFENDANTS
	III	
The place of the collision.	In the Arabian Sea; in a position reckoned to have been latitude 21° 33′ North, longitude 59° 43′ East.	In the Arabian Sea; in a position about latitude 21° 23′ North, longitude 59° 36′ East.
	IV	
The direction and force of the wind.	Westerly, a light breeze.	Little or no wind.
	V	
The state of the weather.	Dense fog.	Fine and clear, but for a bank of fog at the place of collision.
	VI	
The state, direction and force of the tidal or other current.	None of any material force.	No material current.
	VII	
The course steered and speed through the water of the ship when the other ship was first seen or immediately before any measures were taken with reference to her presence, whichever was the earlier.	PYTHIAS was on a course of 203° (true) and, with her engines working at slow speed ahead on stand by (15 nozzles), was making about 6 to 7 knots through the water.	DAMON was proceeding on a course of 23° (true) and, with her engines working at full speed ahead, she was making good a speed of about 16 knots through the water.
	VIII	
The lights (if any) carried by the ship.	Regulation masthead lights, sidelights and stern light.	Two white masthead lights, red and green sidelights, and a fixed

	PRELIMINARY ACT ON BEHALF OF THE PLAINTIFFS	PRELIMINARY ACT ON BEHALF OF THE DEFENDANTS
		white stern light were burning brightly in accordance with the Collision Regulations.
	IX	
(a) The distance and bearing of the other ship if and when her echo was first observed by radar.	Not applicable.	A radar echo was first observed dead ahead of DAMON, distant about 5 miles.
(b) The distance, bearing and approximate heading of the other ship when first seen.	Close to bearing about two points on the starboard bow of PYTHIAS and heading easterly.	The loom of white light was first seen high up, on a bearing between 1 and 2 points on the port bow, distant about 3 ship's lengths. Save that the light appeared to be closing rapidly, no particulars of the heading of the other vessel at this time can be given.
	X	
What light, or combination of lights (if any) of the other ship was first seen.	A single white light.	See IX (b) above.
	XI	
What other lights or combinations of lights (if any) of the other ship were subse-	None.	Very shortly after the loom of a white light had been seen, a green light and bridge

	PRELIMINARY ACT ON BEHALF OF THE PLAINTIFFS	PRELIMINARY ACT ON BEHALF OF THE DEFENDANTS
quently seen before the collision, and when.		lights came into view.

XII

What alterations (if any) were made to the course and speed of the ship after the earlier of the two times referred to in article VII up to the time of the collision, and when, and what measures (if any), other than alterations of course or speed, were taken to avoid the collision, and when.	Prolonged blasts for fog were being sounded on the whistle of PYTHIAS at intervals in accordance with the Regulations. When one prolonged blast was heard from a ship bearing on the starboard bow of PYTHIAS which subsequently proved to be DAMON, the engines of PYTHIAS were immediately stopped and a signal of one prolonged blast was sounded on her whistle in reply. Immediately afterwards her engines were put emergency full speed astern with a double ring and three short blasts were sounded on her whistle. When after a short interval, during which no further signals had been heard from DAMON, PYTHIAS was stopped in the water, her engines were	When the radar echo referred to in article IX (a) was observed those on watch on board DAMON looked carefully ahead but were unable to sight the other vessel. When, shortly thereafter, the radar echo was observed still dead ahead but having closed to a distance of about 3 miles, the course of DAMON was altered by 40° to starboard in two successive steps. Very shortly after DAMON had begun to swing to starboard, the lights of a vessel proceeding in the same direction as DAMON, distant about one mile on the port bow, disappeared from view, whereupon the presence of fog was apprehended, the engine room telegraphs of DAMON were rung to stop and a fog signal of one prolonged blast

PRELIMINARY ACT ON BEHALF OF THE PLAINTIFFS

stopped and a signal of two prolonged blasts was sounded on her whistle. When DAMON replied with one long blast from a much closer position but still on the starboard bow of PYTHIAS a second signal of two prolonged blasts was immediately sounded on the whistle of PYTHIAS. When almost immediately afterwards a single white light became visible over the top of the fog, a series of short blasts were immediately sounded on her whistle as a warning signal to DAMON.

PRELIMINARY ACT ON BEHALF OF THE DEFENDANTS

was sounded upon her whistle. DAMON thereafter continued to sound single prolonged blasts upon her whistle at frequent and diminishing intervals until the collision. Shortly after the engine room watch had shut off the ahead valve and opened the astern valve, the engine room telegraphs were rung to "stand by." When, shortly thereafter, the radar echo from the other vessel had disappeared from the screen of DAMON, the engine room telegraphs were again rung to "stop" but the said order was not carried out by those in the engine room. Those on board DAMON continued to listen carefully for fog signals. The first two signals of one prolonged blast that were heard appeared to come from the port side forward of DAMON's beam, and were

PRELIMINARY ACT ON BEHALF OF THE PLAINTIFFS	PRELIMINARY ACT ON BEHALF OF THE DEFENDANTS
	thought to have been sounded by the vessel proceeding in the same direction as DAMON. Thereafter, two or three more fog signals were heard on the port side, but those on board DAMON were unable to tell which ship had sounded them. DAMON by this time had been steadied up on a course of between 60° and 65°. Very shortly after the radar echo of a vessel bearing about 30° on the port bow had been observed on the screen distant about half a mile, the loom of a white light high up was seen on a bearing between 1 and 2 points on the port bow, distant about 3 ship's lengths and apparently closing rapidly, whereupon the engine room telegraphs of DAMON were at once put " full speed astern " and two signals, each of three short blasts, were sounded upon

	PRELIMINARY ACT ON BEHALF OF THE PLAINTIFFS	PRELIMINARY ACT ON BEHALF OF THE DEFENDANTS
		her whistle in quick succession. The engine room watch, which had only just opened the ahead valve, in response to the order "stand-by," promptly executed the order "full speed astern."

XIII

The parts of each ship which first came into contact and the approximate angle between the two ships at the moment of contact.	Starboard side of PYTHIAS about 70 feet abaft her stem, and stem and starboard bow of DAMON at an angle of 50°–60° leading aft on PYTHIAS.	The starboard side of PYTHIAS in way of Nos. 1 and 2 wing tanks struck the stem and starboard bow of DAMON at an angle of about 70°–80° leading aft on PYTHIAS.

XIV

What sound signals (if any) were given, and when.	As stated in article XII.	See article XII (above).

XV

What sound signals (if any) were heard from the other ship, and when.	As stated in article XII.	See article XII (above).

Filed this —— day of ——, 19—, by A.B. & Co. of [*address*], solicitors for the plaintiffs.

Filed this —— day of ——, 19—, by C.D. & Co. of [*address*], solicitors for the defendants.

Consent to Open and Collate Preliminary Acts

[*Heading as in action*]

383 We, the solicitors for the plaintiffs and defendants, respectively, hereby consent to the preliminary acts filed in this action being opened and collated.

Dated the —— day of ——, 19—.

[*Signature*]

Solicitors for the plaintiffs

[*Signature*]

Solicitors for the defendants

[The next paragraph is 388]

2. Summonses and Notices

Notice of Intention to Rely on Defence of Compulsory Pilotage

388 Dear Sirs,

Please accept this as notice, pursuant to R.S.C., Ord. 75, r. 18 (3), that the defendants in this action intend to rely on the defence of compulsory pilotage with respect to the navigation of DAMON.

Summons to Dispense with Preliminary Acts

[*Heading as in action*]

389 Let all parties concerned, their solicitors or agents, attend before the [Admiralty Registrar in Room 730, Royal Courts of Justice, Strand, London WC2A 2LL *or* District Registrar in Chambers at the office of the —— District Registry at [*address*],] at —— o'clock in the ——noon, on ——day, the —— day of ——, 19—, on the hearing of an application on behalf of the [plaintiffs *or* defendants] for an order that the filing of preliminary acts in this action be dispensed with and that the costs of this application be costs in the cause.

Dated this —— day of ——, 19—.

This summons was taken out by A.B. & Co., of [*address*], solicitors for the [plaintiffs *or* defendants].

To Messrs. C.D. & Co., of [*address*], solicitors for the [plaintiffs *or* defendants].

Summons for Leave to Serve a Reply and Defence to Counterclaim

[*Heading as in action*]

390 LET ALL PARTIES concerned, their solicitors or agents, attend before the [Admiralty Registrar in Room 730, Royal Courts of Justice, Strand, London, WC2A 2LL *or* District Registrar in Chambers at the office of the —— District Registry at [*address*],] at —— o'clock in the ——noon, on ——day, the —— day of ——, 19—, on the hearing of an application on behalf of the plaintiffs for an order that they be at liberty to serve a Reply and Defence to Counterclaim in the terms attached hereto and that the costs of this application be costs in the cause.

Dated this —— day of ——, 19—.

This summons was taken out by A.B. & Co., of [*address*], solicitors for the plaintiffs.

To Messrs. C.D. & Co., of [*address*], solicitors for the defendants.

Summons to Consolidate Actions

[*Heading as in action*]

391 LET ALL PARTIES concerned, their solicitors or agents, attend before the [Admiralty Registrar in Room 730, Royal Courts of Justice, Strand, London, WC2A 2LL *or* District Registrar in Chambers at the office of the —— District Registry at [*address*],] at —— o'clock in the ——noon, on ——day, the —— day of ——, 19—, on the hearing of an application on behalf of the [plaintiffs *or* defendants] for an order that this action be consolidated with action 19—, Folio —— [and that the conduct of the consolidated actions be given to the plaintiffs herein] and that the costs of this application be costs in the cause.

Dated the —— day of ——, 19—.

This summons was taken out by A.B. & Co., of [*address*], solicitors for the [plaintiffs *or* defendants].

To Messrs. C.D. & Co., of [*address*], solicitors for the [plaintiffs *or* defendants].

Summons to Stay Action [1b] for Loss of Life, Personal Injury, Damage to Cargo, etc., Pending the Result of a Collision Action

[*Heading as in action*]

392 LET ALL PARTIES concerned, their solicitors or agents, attend before the [Admiralty Registrar in Room 730, Royal Courts of Justice, Strand, London, WC2A 2LL *or* District Registrar in Chambers at the office of the —— District Registry at [*address*],] at —— o'clock in the ——noon, on ——day, the —— day of ——, 19—, on the hearing of an application on behalf of the [plaintiffs *or* defendants] for an order that all proceedings in this action be stayed pending the result of action 19—, Folio ——, and that the cost of this application be costs in the cause.

Dated the —— day of ——, 19—.

This summons was taken out by A.B. & Co., of [*address*], solicitors for the [plaintiffs *or* defendants].

To Messrs. C.D. & Co., of [*address*], solicitors for the [plaintiffs *or* defendants].

Summons for Payment out of Money in Court

[*Heading as in action*]

393 LET ALL PARTIES concerned, their solicitors or agents, attend before the [Judge in Chambers *or* Admiralty Registrar in Room 730, Royal Courts of Justice, Strand, London WC2A 2LL *or* District Registrar in Chambers at the office of the —— District Registry at [*address*],] at —— o'clock in the —— noon, on —— day, the —— day of ——, 19—, on the hearing of an application on behalf of the plaintiffs that [*specify order sought, e.g.*].

[[by consent] the sum of £——, paid into Court by the defendants on the —— day of ——, 19—, be paid out to the plaintiffs' solicitors in [part] satisfaction of the plaintiffs' claim herein and that the defendants do pay the plaintiffs' costs of this action, up to and including the —— day of ——, 19—,[2] and that the plaintiffs do pay the defendants' costs thereafter and that the costs of this application be paid by the defendants.]

or:

[[by consent of all persons interested in the fund in Court] the sum of £—— be paid out to the plaintiffs' solicitors in satisfaction of

1b For Notice of Motion to Stay Action pursuant to section 4 of the Arbitration Act 1950, see *infra*, §§ 498 *et seq.*

2 This date is usually 14 days from receipt of the notice of payment into court, giving time for consideration of the payment in.

the judgment of the Honourable Mr. Justice —— dated the —— day of ——, 19—, together with interest thereon and costs.]

[The plaintiffs are resident outside the scheduled territories as defined by the Exchange Control Act 1947.]

[Treasury permission authorising payment of the above sums has been given [unconditionally *or* on condition that [*state conditions*] and these conditions have been complied with [3]].]

Dated the —— day of ——, 19—.

This summons was taken out by A.B. & Co., solicitors for the plaintiffs.

To Messrs. C.D. & Co., solicitors for the defendants.

Summons for Directions on Collision Action

394 LET ALL PARTIES concerned, their solicitors or agents, attend before the Judge in Chambers on Monday, the —— day of ——, 19—, at —— o'clock in the ——noon, on the hearing of an application on behalf of the plaintiffs herein for the following directions:

1. That the plaintiffs be given leave to amend article XII of their Preliminary Act and paragraph 3 of their Statement of Claim in the following respects:

[*Set out the proposed amendments.*]

2. That the defendants be ordered within 14 days to give the following further and better particulars of the Defence herein:

[*Set out the particulars required.*]

3. That the plaintiffs be at liberty to call the following witnesses to give oral evidence at the trial:

(a) ——, master,
(b) ——, pilot,
(c) ——, chief officer,
(d) ——, chief engineer,

together with any other witness whose attendance is required pursuant to the provisions of R.S.C., Ord. 38, rr. 26 and 27.

4. That a written interpretation of the gyro course records of each vessel be agreed (if possible); failing agreement, each party to be at liberty to call one expert witness.

5. That the report on the speed of the vessels at the time of collision and angle of blow prepared by Messrs. Universal Surveyors be agreed (if possible); failing agreement, the plaintiffs to be at liberty to call the maker of the said documents.

[3] If such permission has been given the permission must be attached to the summons.

6. That translations of the documents disclosed by both parties be agreed (if possible).

7. That Admiralty chart no. 3333 be available for use at the trial.

8. That a bundle of photographs illustrative of the damage to both vessels be agreed (if possible).

9. That two Elder Brethren of Trinity House be appointed as assessors to the Court for the trial of this action.

10. That a date for trial be appointed; the hearing is expected to last about 4 days.

11. That the costs of this application be costs in the cause.

Dated the —— day of ——, 19—.

This summons was taken out by Messrs. A.B. & Co. of [*address*], the plaintiffs' solicitors.

To the defendants and to Messrs. C.D. & Co. of [*address*], the defendants' solicitors.

Counternotice on Summons for Directions on Collision Action

395 TAKE NOTICE that upon the hearing of the plaintiffs' summons for directions herein, the defendants intend to apply for the following directions:

[*Alternatively*]

Dear Sirs,

Please accept this letter as notice, pursuant to R.S.C., Ord. 25, r. 7 (i), that the defendants intend to apply for the following directions at the hearing of the Summons for Directions:

1. That they be at liberty to call the following witnesses to give oral evidence at the trial:

(a) ——, master,

(b) ——, third officer.

2. That ——, pilot of DAMON, be examined on oath before a Judge sitting in Court as if for the trial of this action without the action having been set down for trial or called on for trial.

Notice Pursuant to R.S.C. Order 38, rules 21, 22 and 24, and Order 75, rule 32 (4) in Collision Action [3a]

396 TAKE NOTICE that pursuant to the provisions of the Civil Evidence Act

[3a] See the Practice Direction as to the evidence of expert witnesses in Admiralty actions [1968] 1 W.L.R. 312. See also the provisions of the Civil Evidence Act 1972, part of which came into force on January 1, 1973.

1968, and the Rules of the Supreme Court made thereunder, the plaintiffs desire to give in evidence at the trial of this action the following statements:

1. The signed statements in writing made to a representative of the plaintiffs' solicitors at Southampton on or about the —— day of ——, 19—, in the course of their investigation of the collision, by the following persons:

(a) ——, second officer,
(b) ——, helmsman,
(c) ——, third engineer,
(d) ——, able seaman.

The plaintiffs contend that the same are admissible by virtue of section 2 of the Act. Further, the said persons should not be called as witnesses at the trial because they are or are likely to be beyond the seas.

2. The statements in writing contained in the following documents kept on board PYTHIAS referable to the morning of —— day of ——, 19—, which were made contemporaneously, or shortly afterwards, in the course of their duties by the persons named:

(a) deck scrap log made by ——;
(b) engine room movement book made by ——.

The plaintiffs contend that the same are admissible by virtue of section 2 of the Act.

3. The statement in writing contained in the deck fair log and the engine fair log referable to the morning of the —— day of ——, being part of the record compiled by responsible officers on board PYTHIAS in the course of their duties on or about the same day, who have set out therein information of which they had knowledge, or information which they had received from the deck scrap log and the engine room movement book, referred to in paragraph 2 above. The nature of the records are apparent on their face. The plaintiffs contend that the same are admissible by virtue of sections 2 and/or 4 of the Act.

4. The statements referable to the morning of the —— day of ——, contained in the document produced by the gyro course recorder installed on board PYTHIAS, which at all material times and for all relevant activities was under the management of the master. Information was supplied to the said device directly by the manipulation of the helm which was under the management of the master and/or helmsman and/or automatic steering mechanism. The said device was, so far as is known, operating properly at the material time. The helmsman should not be called as a witness at the trial as he is or is likely to be beyond the seas. The defendants contend that the said statements are admissible by virtue of section 5 of the Act.

5. The statements contained in the sea protest, dated the —— day of ——, made at Southampton by the master of PYTHIAS, and the report in the form of a letter dated the —— day of —— from the said master to the defendants. The defendants contend that the same are admissible by virtue of section 2 of the Act.

6. The statements made orally or in writing to a Liberian board of inquiry which investigated the collision between PYTHIAS and DAMON by the master, and the chief officer, of PYTHIAS. The defendants contend that the same are admissible by virtue of section 2 of the Act.

7. The statements contained in the documents which have been disclosed and produced for inspection by the defendants and which are set out in their list of documents (schedule 1, part 1). The plaintiffs cannot give particulars of the makers of the said statements or of the circumstances in which they were made, but will apply (if necessary) at the trial under R.S.C., Ord. 38, r. 29, for leave to give the statements in evidence.

Summons for Trial as an Admiralty Short Cause

[*Heading as in action*]

397 LET ALL PARTIES concerned, their solicitors or agents, attend before the [Admiralty Registrar in Room 730, Royal Courts of Justice, Strand, London, WC2A 2LL, *or* District Registrar in Chambers at the office of the —— District Registry at [*address*],] at —— o'clock in the ——noon, on ——day, the —— day of ——, 19—, on the hearing of an application on behalf of the [plaintiffs *or* defendants] for an order that:

1. This action be tried as an Admiralty short cause;

2. This action be tried without [further] pleadings;

3. The parties prepare a statement of the issues in dispute in this action;

4. The parties respectively do, within —— days, file and serve a statement of the grounds on which they charge the other party with negligence in connection with the collision the subject of this action;

5. The parties be ordered to lodge their respective preliminary acts within —— days;

6. The parties do within —— days make mutual discovery of documents;

7. If the parties so agree, the evidence in support of their respective causes be given in whole or in part by the production of documents or entries in books;

8. A date be fixed for the trial of this action which is expected to last for —— days;

9. The Court be assisted by [2] Elder Brethren of Trinity House;

10. [*Specify such other directions sought as could be given on a summons for directions in the action.*]

11. The parties be at liberty to apply;

12. The costs of this application be costs in the cause.

Dated the —— day of ——, 19—.

This summons was taken out by A.B. & Co., of [*address*], solicitors for the [plaintiffs *or* defendants].

To Messrs. C.D. & Co., of [*address*], solicitors for the [plaintiffs *or* defendants].

Notice of Trial

[*Heading as in action*]

398 Take notice of trial of [this action *or* the issues in this action ordered to be tried] by a Judge [alone *or* with Trinity Masters] for the —— day of ——, 19—.

Dated the —— day of ——, 19—.

[*Signature*]

Solicitors for the [plaintiffs *or* defendants]

To Messrs. A.B. & Co., solicitors for the [plaintiffs *or* defendants].

Praecipe for the Attendance of Trinity Masters or Nautical Assessors [4]

[*Heading as in action*]

399 The solicitors for the [plaintiffs *or* defendants] pray that the attendance of [a *or* two] [Trinity Master(s) *or* Nautical Assessor(s)] may be requested at the hearing of this action.

Dated the —— day of ——, 19—.

[*Signature of solicitor or his clerk on his behalf*]

[4] Suitably adapted, this form may also be used for an appeal with nautical and other assessors.

Letter Offering Settlement of Liability in Collision Action

400 Dear Sirs,

THE DAMON

Please accept this letter as an offer on behalf of the defendants to settle this action on the basis that DAMON was three-fifths (60 per cent.) to blame for the collision and that PYTHIAS was two-fifths (40 per cent.) to blame.

We hope to receive your acceptance of this offer. If the offer is not accepted, we reserve the right to bring this letter to the attention of the Court for the purpose of assessing liability to pay the costs of the action.

Yours faithfully,

[*Signature*]

[The next paragraph is 410]

3. Limitation of Actions (Time) [5]

Notice of Motion under Proviso to Section 8 of the Maritime Conventions Act 1911 to Extend Time [6]

[*Heading as in action*]

410 TAKE NOTICE that this Honourable Court will be moved on Monday the —— day of —— 19—, at —— o'clock or so soon thereafter as counsel can be heard, by counsel on behalf of the plaintiffs that the Court may grant them leave pursuant to and for the purposes of the proviso to section 8 of the Maritime Conventions Act 1911, in respect of the above-mentioned action being a claim in respect of damage arising out of a collision between the plantiffs' ship PYTHIAS and the defendants' ship DAMON, in the English Channel on or about the —— day of ——, 19—, which was caused by the negligence of the defendants, their servants or agents. And that the costs of this application be costs in the cause.

5 See generally *Admiralty Practice* [B.S.L. 1, §§ 31 *et seq.*]. Contrast Limitation of Action (Liability), §§ 460, 469, *infra*.

6 See *Admiralty Practice* [B.S.L. 1, § 36].

Affidavit in support of Motion for Leave to Maintain Action Outside Limitation Period

411 I, P.Q., of [*residence*], solicitor of the Supreme Court of Judicature, make oath and say as follows:

1. I am a partner in the firm of Messrs. A.B. & Co. of ——. I have the conduct of this action on behalf of the plaintiffs. I have been fully instructed by the plaintiffs in this matter. I have made all necessary inquiries of them and I have considered documents which they have placed before me. The matters to which I depose hereafter are in accordance with my instructions and are true to the best of my knowledge, information and belief.

2. On the —— day of ——, 19—, a collision occurred in the English Channel between the plaintiffs' motor vessel PYTHIAS and the defendants' motor vessel DAMON as a consequence of which both vessels sustained damage.

3. At the time of the said collision, DAMON was, according to Lloyd's Register of Shipping, owned by Universal Steam Ships Company Limited. Negotiations were accordingly entered into between the plaintiffs and the said company. It was expressly agreed that the issue of any writ should be deferred pending the outcome of the said negotiations. A bundle of correspondence relating to the said negotiations has been produced and shown to me, marked " P.Q.1," and is exhibited hereto.

4. On the —— day of ——, 19—, after making inquiries of responsible persons at Messrs. C.D. & Co. Solicitors for the said company and at Lloyd's Register of Shipping, I was informed that DAMON had been sold and/or transferred sometime after the —— day of ——, 19—, to International Steam Ships Company Limited.

5. By a letter dated the —— day of ——, 19—, C.D. & Co. informed me that they were unable to continue the negotiations since their clients were no longer owners of DAMON.

6. Immediately I received that letter I issued the writ of summons in this action. DAMON arrived in an English port on the —— day of ——, 19—. I verily believe that the said vessel had not been into an English port since the collision until that date, save for the —— day of ——, 19—, when negotiations were in progress as aforesaid and I was abroad.

7. In the premises, I respectfully ask this Court to give leave to the plaintiffs to maintain this action notwithstanding that the action was not commenced within 2 years from the date of the said collision.

Sworn (*etc.*]

Notice of Motion to Stay [6a] Collision Action on Grounds that not Commenced within two years of Collision

[*Heading as in action*]

412 TAKE NOTICE [etc.] [7] on behalf of the above-named defendants for an order that this action is not maintainable and that all further proceedings herein be stayed on the ground that the action was not commenced within two years from the date of the alleged collision between the motor vessel PYTHIAS and the defendants' motor vessel DAMON on the —— day of ——, 19—, as required by section 8 of the Maritime Conventions Act 1911.

To the plaintiffs [*etc.*[7]]

[*Signature*]

Solicitors for the defendants

[The next paragraph is 420]

[6a] For Notice of Motion to Stay Action pursuant to section 4 of the Arbitration Act 1950, see *infra*, §§ 498 *et seq.*

[7] See § 352, *supra*.

CHAPTER 10

JUDGMENT IN DEFAULT

Notice of Motion for Judgment by Reason of Failure to File Preliminary Act

420 TAKE NOTICE that this Honourable Court will be moved on Monday, the —— day of ——, 19—, at —— o'clock, or so soon thereafter as counsel can be heard, by counsel on behalf of the plaintiffs for an order that, by reason of the defendants' failure to file a preliminary act in accordance with the terms of the order of the Admiralty Registrar dated the —— day of ——, 19—, judgment be entered for the claim of the above-named plaintiffs against the defendants and for their bail, and that their costs in this action, including the costs of this motion, be taxed, and for an order that the said claim be referred to the Registrar for his assessment.

Notice of Motion for Judgment in Default of Appearance to a Writ of Summons in Rem

421 TAKE NOTICE that this Honourable Court will be moved on ——, the ——day of ——, 19—, at —— o'clock, or so soon thereafter as counsel can be heard, by counsel on behalf of the plaintiffs that judgment in default of appearance be given for the plaintiffs in the sum of £—— with interest thereon, and for the costs of this action, including the costs of the motion, to be taxed, and for an order that the ship DAMON be appraised and sold by the Marshal.

Affidavit of Service of Writ in Action in Personam [1]

[*Heading as in action*]

422 I, A.B., of [*residence and description*] make oath and say as follows:

1. I did on [Monday], the —— day of ——, 19—, at [*state where*] personally serve C.D., [the above-named defendant, *or* one of the above-named defendants,] with a true copy of the writ of summons in this action, which appeared to me to have been regularly issued

[1] See *Admiralty Practice* [B.S.L. 1, §§ 552 *et seq.*].

out of the [Admiralty Registry *or* —— District Registry] of the High Court of Justice against the above-named [defendant *or* defendants] at the suit of the above-named [plaintiff *or* plaintiffs] and which was dated the —— day of ——, 19—.

2. At the time of the said service, the said writ and the copy thereof were subscribed [and indorsed] in the manner and form prescribed by the Rules of the Supreme Court.

3. I did on the —— day of ——, 19—, indorse on the said writ the day of the month and the week of the said service on the said [defendant *or* defendants].

Sworn [*etc.*].

This affidavit is filed on behalf of the [plaintiff *or* plaintiffs].

Affidavit of Service of Writ in Action In Rem

[*Heading as in action*]

423 I, A.B. of [*residence*], [*description, or* Admiralty Marshal's Officer, Royal Courts of Justice, Strand, London, WC2A 2LL, *or* Preventive Officer, H.M. Customs and Excise, Customs House, Newhaven, Sussex, *or as may be*] make oath and say as follows:

1. I did on [Monday], the —— day of ——, 19—, serve the ship DAMON with a true copy of the writ of summons in this action, which appeared to me to have been regularly issued out of the [Admiralty Registry *or* —— District Registry] of the High Court of Justice, against the above-named defendants at the suit of the above-named plaintiffs, and which was dated the —— day of ——, 19—, by placing the original writ for a short time on the [mainmast] of the ship DAMON lying at [The Quay, Newhaven, Sussex], and on removing the process leaving a copy thereof [on the inside of the wheel-house] of the said ship.

2. At the time of the said service, the said writ and the copy thereof were subscribed and indorsed in the manner and form prescribed by the Rules of the Supreme Court.

3. I did, on the —— day of ——, 19—, indorse on the said writ the day of the month and the week of the said service on the said ship DAMON.

Sworn [*etc.*].

This affidavit is filed on behalf of the plaintiffs.

Affidavit Verifying Statement of Claim in Claim for Repairs

424 I, C.D., of [*residence*], make oath and say as follows:

1. I am a director of the Universal Ship Repair Company Limited

and I have been authorised to make this affidavit on their behalf. Save as is otherwise stated, the matters to which I depose hereafter are within my own knowledge and are true.

2. On the —— day of ——, 19—, I received a letter, dated the —— day of —— from Messrs. ——, which stated that they were the defendants' managing agents. They requested that the plaintiffs carry out certain work on DAMON. By letter dated the —— day of ——, I replied stating the plaintiffs would undertake the work. The said letters have been produced and shown to me, and are exhibited hereto marked " C.D.1."

3. On the —— day of ——, DAMON arrived at the plaintiffs' yard and the work was commenced immediately. The work was completed on the —— day of ——. The plaintiffs' account was drawn up and sent under cover of a letter dated the —— day of —— to the defendants and to their managing agents. The account has not been paid. The said letter and account have been produced and shown to me, and are exhibited hereto marked " C.D.2."

4. I have had the opportunity of considering the contents of this my affidavit carefully, and to refer to the exhibits herein mentioned, before swearing it. I am satisfied that it is in all respects true and accurate.

Sworn [*etc.*].

Affidavit Verifying Statement of Claim in Mortgage Action

425 I, E.F., of [*residence*], [*occupation*] make oath and say as follows:

1. I am authorised by the plaintiffs to make this affidavit on their behalf.

2. The facts deposed to herein are (save where specifically stated to be otherwise) within my own knowledge. Those facts deposed to herein which are not within my own knowledge are true to the best of my information and belief.

3. The plaintiffs are a corporation which offers loans to shipowners against ship mortgages.

4. The plaintiffs' claim arises under a first priority ship's mortgage dated the —— day of ——, 19—, registered against DAMON. A copy of the said mortgage has been produced and shown to me and is exhibited hereto marked " E.F.1."

5. It is provided in the said mortgage that instalments thereunder are to be paid in equal amounts on the —— day of —— and the —— day of —— in each year, the first instalment on the —— day of ——, 19—, and the last instalment on the —— day of ——, 19—. It

follows therefore that [19] instalments were payable, each of N.Kr. ——, totalling the principal sum of N.Kr. ——.

6. By the —— day of ——, 19—, [18] instalments had been paid and leaving a balance of N.Kr. —— outstanding. On that date, DAMON was sold by the then mortgagor to the defendants subject to the said mortgage which thereby became binding on the defendants.

7. The defendants have failed to pay the final instalment together with interest thereon due on the —— day of ——, 19—, and the said sums are still outstanding and unpaid.

8. I therefore ask this Honourable Court for an order in the terms of the motion or in such terms as it shall think fit.

Sworn [*etc.*].

This affidavit is filed on behalf of the plaintiffs.

Affidavit of Foreign Law in Mortgage Action

[*Headings as in action*]

426 I, G.H., of [*residence*], make oath and say as follows:

1. I am an advocate of the Supreme Court of Norway and practise before the courts of Norway. I am conversant with the law and constitution of Norway.

2. At the request of the plaintiffs in this action, I have examined the original of the ship's mortgage bond, dated at Bergen on the —— day of ——, 19—, with a view to determining the validity of the said mortgage under the law of Norway. A copy of the said mortgage and translations thereof are exhibited hereto marked " G.H.1."

3. I have considered the relevant provisions of Norwegian law relating to ship's mortgages, and I hereby declare:

(a) That the said mortgage became binding on the defendants on their taking delivery of DAMON.

(b) That the said mortgage has been duly executed in the standard form presented for ship's mortgages and duly registered with the Bergen Registry on the —— day of——, 19—.

(c) That the said mortgage is, according to Norwegian law, proper and sufficient evidence that a valid mortgage on DAMON has been validly executed in favour of the plaintiffs and the burden thereof transferred to the defendants, and the courts of Norway would accept these documents as evidence of the execution of a valid and properly registered mortgage in favour of the plaintiffs.

Sworn [*etc.*].

Praecipe for Commission for Appraisement

[*Heading as in action*]

427 We, A.B. & Co., of [*address*], [solicitors for] the [plaintiffs] request a commission for the appraisement of [the ship DAMON] which was ordered by the Court on the —— day of ——, 19—.

Dated the —— day of ——, 19—.

[*Signature*]

Praecipe for Commission for Appraisement and Sale

[*Heading as in action*]

428 We, A.B. & Co., of [*address*], [solicitors for] the [plaintiffs] request a commission for the appraisement and sale of [the ship DAMON] which was ordered by the Court on the —— day of ——, 19—.

Dated the —— day of ——, 19—.

[*Signature*]

Commission for Appraisement and Sale

[*Heading as in action*] [2]

429 ELIZABETH THE SECOND [*continue as in* § 250, *supra*].

To the Admiralty Marshal of Our High Court of Justice, and to all and singular his substitutes, Greeting:

Whereas in this action the Court has ordered [the ship DAMON] to be appraised and sold.

We hereby authorise and command you to choose one or more experienced persons and to swear him or them to appraise the said [ship DAMON] according to the true value thereof, and, such value having been certified in writing by him or them, to cause the said [ship DAMON] to be sold by [private treaty *or* public auction] for the highest price that can be obtained for it, but not for less than the appraised value unless the Court on your application allows it to be sold for less.

And We further command you, immediately upon the sale being completed, to pay the proceeds thereof into Court and to file the certificate of appraisement signed by you and the appraiser or appraisers, and an account of the sale signed by you, together with this commission.

Witness [*as in* § 250, *supra*].

Taken out by A.B. & Co., [solicitors for] the [plaintiffs].

[2] As to valuation fees, see *Admiralty Practice* [B.S.L. 1, § 390].

Appraisement [3]

[*Heading as in action*]

430 I, P.V.G., Marshal of the Admiralty Court of the High Court of Justice, do certify that, by virtue of a commission of appraisement dated the —— day of ——, 19—, and issued in this action, I have chosen B.C., of [*address*], an experienced person, and have sworn him to appraise the steamship DAMON according to the true value thereof, as on the —— day of ——, 19—, lying at [Wellington Dock, Dover, Kent].

And I, the said B.C., whose name is hereunto subscribed, do certify that, having appointed D.E., of [*address*], marine surveyor, to make an examination of the said steamship, and having carefully perused his report thereon, by virtue of my said oath, I have faithfully and justly appraised the DAMON at the date aforesaid at the sum of £——.

In Witness whereof we have hereunto respectively set our hands this —— day of ——, 19—.

[*Signature*]
Admiralty Marshal
[*Signature of B.C.*]

Admiralty Marshal's Delivery Order [4] **with Purchaser's Receipt**

DELIVERY ORDER

Admiralty Marshal's Office,
Royal Courts of Justice.
January 1, 19—.

431 Name of ship: the DAMON.

Please deliver to P.Q., or to his written order, the ship DAMON and everything on board belonging to her, taking a receipt therefor. The purchaser is entitled to delivery of the ship, free of all charges up to [noon], the —— day of ——, 19—, after which, if delivery be not taken, all charges must be claimed from the purchaser. Please forward to me all outstanding accounts against the ship up to [noon], the —— day of ——, 19—.

[*Signature*]
Admiralty Marshal

To The Collector,
H.M. Customs and Excise,
[*address*]

[3] See *Admiralty Practice* [B.S.L. 1, §§ 356 *et seq*.].
[4] For delivery fee, see *Admiralty Practice* [B.S.L. 1, § 391].

Purchaser's receipt

Received of the Collector of Customs at [*address*] the ship DAMON and everything on board belonging to her.

Dated this —— day of ——, 19—.

[*Signature*]

[*Description*]

Admiralty Marshal's Bill of Sale

432 Official Number if registered
Name of Ship
No., Date, and Port of Registry, if registered
Whether a Sailing, Steam or Motor Ship
Horse Power of Engines, if any
Length from forepart of stem to the aft side of the head of the stern post about
Main breadth to outside of plank about
Depth from top of deck at side amidships to bottom of keel about

NUMBER OF TONS

Gross about Registered about

and as may be described in more detail in the Register Book
I, [*name*], Marshal of the Admiralty Court of the High Court of Justice acting under a Commission of the said Court dated —— in consideration of the sum of —— pounds paid by A.B., receipt of which is hereby acknowledged transfer all the shares in the Ship above described and in everything on board belonging to her except any equipment on hire to the said A.B.

FURTHER I, the said [*name*], Marshal of the Admiralty Court of the said High Court of Justice covenant with the said A.B. and his/her/their/its assigns that I have power to make the above transfer and I hereby certify that the effect in English Law of this judicial sale is that the Ship above particularly described has been freed from all liens encumbrances and debts whatsoever up to the —— day of —— One Thousand Nine Hundred and ——.

IN WITNESS whereof I have hereunto set my Hand and Seal
the —— day of —— One Thousand Nine Hundred and ——.
Signed, Sealed and Delivered by the said
in the presence of

[*Signature*]

Admiralty Marshal

Affidavit in Support of Summons for Leave to Intervene [5] in Action

[*Heading as in action*]

433 I, A.B.C., of [*residence*], solicitor of the Supreme Court and a member of the firm of Messrs. R.S. & Co., of [*address*], make oath and say as follows:

1. I have been instructed by one Robert Brown and one Francis Smith to represent them and to protect their interests in respect of certain claims they have against the owners of the proceeds of sale of the ship DAMON. The facts and matters to which I depose are based on information and documents supplied by the said persons, by the French Consul-General and by members of the firm of Messrs. K.L. & Co.

2. The said persons were at all material times the master and chief officer of the ship DAMON. Pursuant to agreements between the said persons and the defendants, certain outstanding sums are due and owing to the said persons as wages in respect of their service upon DAMON.

3. Further, pursuant to agreements between the crew of DAMON and the defendants and the Etablissement National des Invalides de la Marine (a department of the French Government having civil personality), contributions from the said persons were due to be paid to the said department. The said contributions were duly deducted from wages which were paid to the said persons and held by the defendants for payment to the said department. This the defendants failed to do.

4. The total of the claims of the said Brown and Smith is £3,500. I am informed by Messrs. Universal Ship Valuers & Co. that the value of DAMON in her present condition is about £10,000. Accordingly, her value may be insufficient to cover the amount of this claim together with the claim of Universal Salvors Ltd. The claim of the salvors, the plaintiffs in this action, will probably rank prior to claims of my clients.

5. In the circumstances I humbly request that the said persons be granted leave to intervene in this action.

Sworn [*etc.*].

Notice of Motion for Determination of Priorities [6] and Payment Out [7]

434 TAKE NOTICE [*etc.*[8]] on behalf of the plaintiffs for an order determin-

[5] See *Admiralty Practice* [B.S.L. 1, §§ 294 *et seq*., §§ 310 *et seq*.].
[6] See *Admiralty Practice* [B.S.L. 1, §§ 380 *et seq*.].
[7] See *Admiralty Practice* [B.S.L. 1, §§ 395 *et seq*.].
[8] As in § 352, *supra*.

ing the priority of payments to the several claimants against the proceeds of sale of DAMON and for payment out of the amounts found due to the said claimants.
To the plaintiffs [*etc.*[8]].

Dated this —— day of——, 19—.

[*Signature*]

[The next paragraph is 441]

CHAPTER 11

REFERENCE TO REGISTRAR [1]

Admission of Liability and Consent to Reference to the Admiralty Registrar

[*Heading as in action*]

441 We, the solicitors for the [defendants], hereby admit liability for the [collision *or* damage *or as may be*] the subject of this action, and we, the solicitors for the said defendants and the plaintiffs hereby consent to the [plaintiffs'] claim being referred to the Admiralty Registrar, assisted if necessary by merchants, for assessment.

Dated the —— day of ——, 19—.

[*Signature*]

Solicitors for the plaintiffs

[*Signature*]

Solicitors for the defendants

Agreement of Settlement of Liability

[*Heading as in action*]

442 We, the undersigned solicitors for the plaintiffs and defendants respectively, hereby agree to the settlement of the question of liability for the collision, the subject of this action, upon the following terms:

1. That the plaintiffs be 60 per cent., and the defendants 40 per cent. to blame for the said collision.

2. That the plaintiffs shall pay to the defendants two-fifths of their costs of determining liability as taxed or agreed.

3. That the damages occasioned to the respective parties by reason of the said collision shall, failing agreement, be referred to

[1] Or District Registrar, see generally *Admiralty Practice* [B.S.L. 1, §§ 1261 *et seq.*].

the Admiralty Registrar, assisted, if necessary, by merchants, for assessment.

Dated this —— day of ——, 19—.

[*Signature*]

Solicitors for the plaintiffs

[*Signature*]

Solicitors for the defendants

Agreement in Settlement of Liability and Consent to Reference [2]

443 AN AGREEMENT made this —— day of ——, 19—, BY and BETWEEN the owners of the Panamanian motor vessel PYTHIAS (hereinafter called " the ship-claimants "), and the owners of the cargo lately laden on board PYTHIAS (hereinafter called " the cargo-claimants ") and the owners of the Liberian motor vessel DAMON (hereinafter called " the respondents ").

WITNESSETH:

WHEREAS on the —— day of ——, 19—, a collision took place in the English Channel between PYTHIAS and DAMON

AND WHEREAS PYTHIAS, the cargo laden on board her and DAMON were severally damaged as a consequence of the said collision

AND WHEREAS the ship-claimants and the cargo-claimants commenced the following legal proceedings to recover the loss, damage and expense sustained by them as a result of the collision, *viz.*:

19—, Folio ——

19—, Folio ——

19—, Folio ——

AND WHEREAS the respondents commenced the following legal proceedings to recover the loss, damage and expense sustained by them as a result of the collision, *viz.*:

19—, Folio ——

AND WHEREAS the respondents have furnished security by way of the following guarantees in writing in relation to the claims of the ship and cargo claimants, *viz.*:

(i) guarantee of the General Protection and Indemnity Club dated the —— day of ——, 19—;

(ii) letter of undertaking of the Universal Bank Limited dated the —— day of ——, 19—.

2 See *Admiralty Practice* [B.S.L. 1, §§ 1263 *et seq.*].

NOW THEREFORE, in consideration of the premises and the covenants herein contained, the parties do hereby mutually agree as follows:

1. The respondents shall and hereby agree to withdraw, terminate and discontinue all legal proceedings brought by them against the ship-claimants whether by way of claim counterclaim or otherwise.

2. Subject to clause 1 hereof and the terms and conditions hereinafter set forth, the respondents hereby admit, and the parties hereto agree, by way of settlement of all proceedings herein recited that the respondents are liable for the damage, loss and expense sustained by the ship and cargo claimants as a result of the collision.

3. The respondents shall, and hereby agree to, pay one half (50 per cent.) of the just claims of the ship and cargo claimants made in the legal proceedings recited herein, and the ship and cargo claimants shall, and hereby agree to, accept the same in full and final settlement of all the said claims made therein.

4. The parties hereto agree that, in default of agreement, the value of the said claims made in the legal proceedings recited herein shall be determined by way of reference to the Admiralty Registrar in London, assisted, if necessary, by merchants.

5. The respondents agree to pay interest on the claims of the ship and cargo claimants as proved or agreed, from the —— day of ——, 19—. The rate of interest shall be the rate of interest allowed by the English High Court on money which is placed on short term investment account pursuant to the Supreme Court Fund Rules taken as an average from the said —— day of ——, 19—, to the date of payment, unless some other period or rate are otherwise ordered by the Admiralty Registrar on the hearing of the reference.

6. The respondents agree to pay all the costs of the ship and cargo claimants incurred by them in contesting liability and in proving their claims, save in so far as the Court may otherwise order. The said costs shall be paid on a party and party basis as taxed or agreed.

7. The parties hereto agree to do all such things and to take all such steps as may be necessary to make the terms of clauses 1 to 6 inclusive hereof an order of the English High Court pursuant to Order 75 rule 35 of the Rules of the Supreme Court.

8. The ship and cargo claimants jointly and severally represent and warrant that no other person or body owned or was bailee of PYTHIAS or the cargo laden on board her at the time of the collision, or any part or share of the said ship or cargo.

9. Subject to the due performance of the terms and conditions herein contained, the respondents undertake and warrant not to obtain the benefit of any enactment limiting their liability for the said collision or take any steps to bring proceedings to limit their liability for the said collision, pursuant to the Merchant Shipping Acts 1894 to 1970 or pursuant to the International Convention for the Unification of Certain Rules relating to the Limitation of the Liability of Owners of Sea-Going Vessels, signed at Brussels in 1924, or pursuant to the International Convention relating to the Limitation of the Liability of Owners of Sea-Going Ships done at Brussels in 1957, or any national statute or enactment made thereunder or to the same effect:

PROVIDED THAT the respondents shall be entitled to take any such steps as aforesaid if the same appear to be necessary or desirable for the purpose of enabling liability to be limited in relation to any claim or claims made or prosecuted against them and in respect of which no settlement is accorded hereby.

10. The respondents shall and hereby agree to substitute for the guarantees referred to in the recital hereto, and the ship and cargo claimants hereby agree to accept in substitution therefor, a guarantee in writing whereby the Universal Protection and Indemnity Association Limited shall guarantee the obligations assumed by the respondents under clauses 3, 5 and 6 of their agreement.

11. This agreement shall be construed in accordance with English Law.

Agreement of Settlement of Quantum

[*Heading as in action*]

444 We, the undersigned solicitors of the plaintiffs and defendants respectively, hereby agree to a settlement of this action upon the following terms:

1. That the plaintiffs' claim is agreed at the sum of £—— [of which 40 per cent. is payable by the defendants pursuant to the agreement dated the —— day ——, 19—,] together with interest thereon at — per cent. per annum from the —— day of ——, 19—, to the date of payment.

2. That the defendants do pay the plaintiffs' taxed or agreed costs of proving their claim.

3. That the defendants' claim is agreed at the sum of £—— [of which 60 per cent. is payable by the plaintiffs pursuant to the agreement above mentioned] together with interest thereon at — per cent. per annum, from the —— day of ——, 19—, to the date of payment.

4. That the plaintiffs do pay the defendants' taxed or agreed costs of proving their claim.

Dated this —— day of ——, 19—.

[*Signature*]

Solicitors for the plaintiffs

[*Signature*]

Solicitors for the defendants

Claim on Reference to Registrar

[*Heading as in action*]

REFERENCE TO REGISTRAR

445 The plaintiffs' claim is for damages arising out of a collision which occurred at about 01.63 hours (GMT) on the —— day of ——, 19—, between their ship PYTHIAS and the defendants' ship DAMON in the English Channel.

The PYTHIAS, a ship of 12,351 tons gross, was at the time bound from Monrovia to Nordenham, West Germany, laden with a cargo of iron ore.

As a result of the collision, the PYTHIAS sustained damage to her stem and starboard bow. After the collision, the PYTHIAS proceeded to her destination, discharged her cargo, and proceeded to Newcastle for permanent repairs.

On the —— day of ——, 19—, liability for the collision was agreed between the parties on the basis of the plaintiffs being 40 per cent. to blame and the defendants being 60 per cent. to blame.

Item	*Particulars*		*Claimed*
1	At Nordenham		
	Lloyd's Register of Shipping, services		
	of Bremen Surveyors	£25	
	expenses	10	
		——	£35
2	Superintendence,		
	5 days at £12 per day	60	
	expenses (Travelling)	30	
		——	90
3	Tyne Pilotage Authority,		
	piloting ship from sea to dry dock		25
	Piloting ship from Smith's Dry Dock		
	to quay		18
4	Tyne Tugs Limited		
	Towage		150
5	H. Brown & Co.		
	Riggers assisting at undocking	22	
	Riggers attending moorings		
	April 22, 23, 24, 19—	30	
		——	52
6	Lloyd's Register of Shipping,		
	Newcastle-upon-Tyne		
	Damage survey fee		27
7	Smith's Dock Company Limited		
	Docking and undocking ship,		
	including 4 days dock rent and		
	shore electric current for 10 days	287	
	Shoring	40	
	Ballasting for undocking	112	
		——	439
8	Smith's Dock Company Limited		
	Permanent repairs of collision		
	damage		4,040
9	Superintendence,		
	12 days at £12		144
10	Claim for loss of use of ship		

	Days	hrs.	mins.
Delay at time of collision	—	2	16
At Nordenham for repairs	5	—	—
At Newcastle-upon-Tyne for repairs	12	1	44
Total detention	17	4	—

Item	*Particulars*			*Claimed*
	Detention rate: Rate of hire as per charter party per month £30,000 17 days 4 hours at £30,000 per month equals	£17,166		
	Less savings Crew's wages	2,166		
			£15,000	
	Deck and engine stores		50	
				14,950
11	Agency			285
				£20,255

The plaintiffs claim 60 per cent. of the sum of £20,255 plus interest.

Served this —— day of ——, 19—.

[*Signature*]

[*address*]

Solicitors for the plaintiffs

Claim under the Fatal Accidents Acts 1846 to 1959 and under the Law Reform (Miscellaneous Provisions) Act 1934

[*Heading as in action*]

446 1. The claimant is the widow and [executrix *or* administratrix] of the estate of John Bloggs deceased (hereinafter called the deceased). The claimant is also the lawful mother of Peter Bloggs infant.

2. The claimant as [executrix *or* administratrix] of the estate of the deceased under the Fatal Accidents Acts 1846 to 1959 and under the Law Reform (Miscellaneous Provisions) Act 1934 claims damages for negligence on the part of the defendants, their servants or agents in consequence of which the deceased lost his life in, or in consequence of, a fire on board the defendants' trawler DAMON on January 1, 19—.

3. By an Agreement of Settlement dated the —— day of ——, 19—, it was agreed between the parties herein that the defendants do pay to the plaintiff 85 per cent. of her proved or agreed damages.

4. The deceased was born on the —— day of ——, 19—.

5. The claimant was born on the —— day of ——, 19—.

6. The deceased was lawfully married to the claimant on the —— day of ——, 19—, at St. Magnus Church, Nottingham.

7. The said marriage had issue of one child, Peter Bloggs born on the —— day of ——, 19—.

8. Prior to his death, the deceased was a happy and healthy man and was employed as spare hand on board the DAMON with prospects of promotion and increased earnings.

9. The gross earnings of the deceased for the year prior to his death were £—— from which the defendants deducted £—— in respect of Income Tax and £—— in respect of National Insurance Contributions.

10. During the last year of his life, the deceased made an allotment to the claimant of £—— per week which was paid by the defendants to her. In addition, the deceased gave the claimant varying amounts on each occasion when he returned home from sea. In a full year, the total amount so given to the claimant amounted to about £——. In addition the deceased paid the rent of the family house amounting to £—— per annum.

11. The deceased, when not at sea, lived at the family home and the claimant spent an estimated £—— per annum for food for the deceased when at home. The remainder of the said money received from the deceased was used by the claimant for the support of herself and her son.

12. As a result of the said fire on board the DAMON, the deceased lost the following personal effects:

[*list the effects lost with values*]

[*Signature*]

Solicitors for the claimant

To Messrs. C.D. & Co.,

Solicitors for the defendants.

[The next paragraph is 448]

Letter Asking which Items of Claim are Admitted

448 Dear Sirs,

The PYTHIAS and DAMON

We enclose herewith a copy of the plaintiffs' claim together with copies of supporting vouchers.

We shall be obliged if you will let us know what items are admitted and whether you have any proposals to put forward with regard to any items not admitted.

Yours faithfully,

[*Signature*]

Letter with Observations on Claim

WITHOUT PREJUDICE

449 Dear Sirs,

The PYTHIAS and DAMON

We have been instructed by our clients to make the following observations on your clients' claim:

(a) Items 1, 3, 4, 5, 6 and 8 are admitted as claimed.

(b) We are prepared to agree item 2 at £— per day plus expenses, making a total of £—, and item 11 at £—.

(c) With regard to item 7, we contend that the damage to your clients' ship did not necessitate dry-docking.

(d) On items 9 and 10 for superintendence and loss of profit, we contend that other urgent repairs arising out of a previous casualty to your ship were carried out at the same time as the collision damage repairs and that therefore we must repudiate any liability for the detention of your clients' ship.

We shall be obliged if you will obtain your clients' instructions on the above observations and we await to hear from you in due course.

Yours faithfully,

[*Signature*]

Messrs. C.D. & Co.,

[*address*]

List of Undisputed Items of Claim

[*Heading as in action*]

LIST OF UNDISPUTED ITEMS

450

Item	*Claimed*	*Agreed*
1	£35	£25
2	90	80
3	25	25
	18	18
4	150	150
5	52	Withdrawn
6	27	27
8	4,040	3,050
11	285	225

Dated the —— day of ——, 19—.

[*Signature*]
Solicitors for the plaintiffs
[*Signature*]
Solicitors for the defendants

Praecipe to Place Reference on List for Hearing

[*Heading as in action*]

451 We, A.B. & Co., solicitors for the [plaintiffs *or* defendants] pray that the reference on the [plaintiffs' *or* defendants'] claim in this action may be placed on the list for hearing.

We undertake to pay when called upon the fees of any merchants or assessors assisting the Registrar at the reference.

Dated the —— day of ——, 19—.

[*Signature of solicitor or his clerk on his behalf*]

Notice of Motion in Objection to Registrar's Decision on Reference [3]

452 TAKE NOTICE [*etc.*], on behalf of the above-named plaintiffs, that the decision of the Admiralty Registrar herein dated the —— day of ——, 19—, upon the plaintiffs' claim herein be varied as follows and for the following reasons:

1. That the amount claimed under item 6 ought to be allowed. The said expenses in the form of port dues payable at Rotterdam, were consequential upon the entry of PYTHIAS for repairs in that port.

[3] See *Admiralty Practice* [B.S.L. 1, § 1279].

2. That the amount allowed under item 18 ought to be increased by the equivalent of 2 days loss of use on account of the time required to fair the bottom-plating in way No. 3 double bottom tank; the said repairs should be included in assessing damages for detention because:

(a) They were included in the cost of collision repairs paid by the defendants;

(b) They were incurred as a consequence of the collision and not as a consequence of PYTHIAS stranding on September 10 prior to the collision.

3. That the defendants be ordered to pay interest on the above sums.

AND FURTHER TAKE NOTICE that this Court will be moved to order that the costs of this motion be paid by the defendants.

[The next paragraph is 460]

CHAPTER 12

LIMITATION OF LIABILITY [1]

Writ of Summons for Limitation of Liability for Damage Arising out of a Collision [2]

460 In the High Court of Justice 19—, Folio ——
Queen's Bench Division
Admiralty Court
Between

A.B. Steamship Company Plaintiffs

and

C.D. Limited, the owners of the ship DAMON, and all other persons claiming or being entitled to claim damages by reason of, or arising out of, the collision between the ship PYTHIAS and the ship DAMON which occurred off Gibraltar on the —— day of ——, 19—. Defendants [3]

ELIZABETH THE SECOND [*continue as in* § 260].

To C.D. Limited of [*address*], and all other persons claiming to have sustained damage by reason of, or arising out of, the collision between the ship PYTHIAS and the ship DAMON which occurred off Gibraltar on the —— day of ——, 19—.

We command you [*continue as in* § 260].

Indorsement of claim [4]

The plaintiffs, as owners of the ship PYTHIAS of the Port of London, claim to have their liability limited in respect of damage resulting from the collision between the ship PYTHIAS and the ship DAMON which occurred off Gibraltar on the —— day of ——, 19—, pursuant to the provisions of the Merchant Shipping Acts 1894 to 1970, and that all proper directions may be given for the purpose of ascertaining and distributing the amount of the plaintiffs' said liability between the parties entitled thereto.

1 Defined as meaning "an action by shipowners or other persons under the Merchant Shipping Acts 1894 to 1970, for the limitation of the amount of their liability in connection with a ship or other property." See R.S.C., Ord. 75, r. 1.
2 See *Admiralty Practice* [B.S.L. 1, §§ 450 and 520].
3 As to whom should be made defendant, see R.S.C., Ord. 75, r. 37.
4 For alternative form of indorsement, see § 461, *infra*.

Indorsement on Writ of Summons for Limitation of Liability for Damage Arising out of a Collision [5]

[*Heading and formal parts as in* § 460, *supra*]

461 The plaintiffs as owners of the ship PYTHIAS of the Port of London claim:

1. A declaration that, by reason of the provisions of the Merchant Shipping Acts 1894 to 1970, they are not answerable in damages beyond the aggregate amount of £—— for each ton of the tonnage of the PYTHIAS, ascertained in accordance with the said provisions, in respect of damage or loss caused to any goods, merchandise, or other things whatsoever on board the ship PYTHIAS, and/or in respect of loss or damage caused to any other property or the infringement of any rights through their act or omission or through the act or omission of any person on board the PYTHIAS in the navigation or management of the PYTHIAS when the said ship PYTHIAS came into collision with the ship DAMON off Gibraltar on the —— day of ——, 19—.

2. A declaration that the tonnage of the PYTHIAS ascertained in accordance with the provisions of the Merchant Shipping Acts 1894 to 1970 is —— tons and that the liability of the plaintiffs, as aforesaid, is limited to £——, together with interest, and no more.

3. An order that, upon the plaintiffs paying into Court the said sum of £—— with interest as aforesaid, all further proceedings in any action or arbitration arising out of the said collision (other than claims for loss of life or personal injury) be stayed, except for the purpose of taxation and payment of costs, and that it may be declared that the plaintiffs are entitled to relief under the Merchant Shipping Acts 1894 to 1970 and the Judicature Acts against any action or actions in respect of the said collision (other than claims for loss of life or personal injury) in the High Court of Justice, and that the above-named defendants, and all or any other person or persons whatsoever interested in the ship PYTHIAS or other things on board, or having any right, title or interest whatsoever with reference to, or arising out of, the said collision, be restrained from bringing any action or actions against the plaintiffs or the ship PYTHIAS in respect of the same, in any other court other than the High Court of Justice.

4. That all proper directions may be given by this Court for ascertaining the persons who may have any just claim for loss or damage arising out of or caused by the said collision.

[5] Where liability for loss of life and personal injury claims are sought to be included, the form must be suitably amended. For the relevant rates, which may be changed from time to time, see R.S.C., Ord. 75, r. 37. For alternative form of indorsement, see § 460, *supra*.

5. That the said sum may be rateably distributed among the several persons who may make out their claims thereto and that proper directions may be given for the exclusion of such claimants as shall fail in their claims within a certain time to be fixed for such purpose.

Summons for Decree of Limitation of Liability: Short Form

[*Heading as in action*]

462 LET ALL PARTIES concerned, their solicitors or agents, attend before the [Admiralty Registrar in Room 730, Royal Courts of Justice, Strand, London, WC2A 2LL, *or* District Registrar in Chambers at the office of the —— District Registry at [*address*],] at —— o'clock in the ——noon, on ——day, the —— day of ——, 19—, on an application by the plaintiffs for a decree under section 503 of the Merchant Shipping Acts 1894 to 1970, limiting the plaintiffs' liability for damages resulting from the collision between their ship PYTHIAS and the ship DAMON which occurred in the English Channel on the —— day of ——, 19—, or in default of such decree, for directions for the further conduct of these proceedings as to the court may seem just.

Dated the —— day of ——, 19—.

This summons was taken out by A.B. & Co., of [*address*], solicitors for the plaintiffs.

To Messrs. C.D. & Co., of [*address*], and to Messrs. E.F. & Co., of [*address*], solicitors for the defendants.

Affidavit in Support of Summons for Decree of Limitation [6]

[*Heading as in* § 460, *supra*]

463 I, John Smith, of the River House, River Street, London, E.C.10 make oath and say as follows:

1. I am the managing director of the Universal Towage Company Limited, the plaintiffs in this action. The plaintiffs own the tug DAMON and have their principal place of business at The Wharf, London. I am duly authorised to make this affidavit on their behalf.

2. On the —— day of ——, 19—, on the River Thames, DAMON was towing the barge BOXER laden with cargo, when the barge collided with the motor vessel PYTHIAS. Shortly afterwards, BOXER filled with water and sank. In consequence of the collision, Philip Jones and

[6] See *Admiralty Practice* [B.S.L. 1, §§ 705, 1218 and 1225].

David Clark lost their lives and James Brown sustained personal injuries. Furthermore, PYTHIAS suffered damage, and the Port of London Authority were put to expense in raising the wreck of BOXER.

3. On the —— day of ——, 19—, an action (19—, Folio —) was commenced in this Court by the owners of the barge against the owners of PYTHIAS in respect of the damage sustained by them as a result of the collision, and the owners of PYTHIAS, by their defence, counterclaimed against the owners of BOXER and the present plaintiffs as owners of DAMON. On the —— day of ——, 19—, this Court found both PYTHIAS and DAMON equally to blame for the collision and pronounced judgment for the owners of PYTHIAS against the owners of DAMON for one half of the damage sustained by the owners of PYTHIAS by reason of the collision.

4. The only allegations made against the present plaintiffs in the course of the said proceedings were that those on board DAMON were negligent in the navigation of the tug. This Court found that they were negligent in the following respects:

(i) They failed to keep a good look-out.
(ii) They altered course to port at an improper time.
(iii) They failed to keep to that side of the fairway which lay on their starboard side.
(iv) They failed to comply with Rules 25 and 29 of the Collision Regulations.

5. Accordingly, the collision and the consequential damage were caused partly by the negligent navigation of DAMON by those on board her, and partly by the negligent navigation of PYTHIAS by those on board her. The collision was not caused by the negligence of any other person. The collision, therefore, occurred without the actual fault or privity of the plaintiff company and the present plaintiffs are entitled to limit their liability under the provisions of the Merchant Shipping Acts 1894 to 1970.

6. Other claims are likely to be brought against the plaintiffs by the dependants of Philip Jones deceased, by James Brown, by the Port of London Authority and the owners of BOXER and her cargo.

7. There is now produced and shown to me and exhibited hereto marked "J.S.1.," a certified copy of the certificate of registry of DAMON. As appears therefrom, the registered tonnage of DAMON with the addition of the engine room space is 200 tons and no more.

8. The amount of the claims for which the plaintiff may become liable in respect of the loss of life, personal injuries and damage sustained as a result of the collision, apart from limitation, would exceed the aggregate amount of £——, being the sum of £——[6a]

[6a] For the relevant rates, which may be changed from time to time, see the notes to R.S.C., Ord. 75, r. 37.

multiplied by 300, in accordance with the provisions of the Merchant Shipping Acts 1894 to 1970. The claims in respect of damage other than loss of life and personal injury, would apart from limitation exceed the aggregate of £——, being the sum of £—— [6a] multiplied by 200 tons, in accordance with said provisions.

9. On the —— day of ——, 19—, Messrs. A.B. & Co., solicitors acting on behalf of the second-named defendants, accepted service of the writ in this action on their behalf.

10. The contents of paragraphs 1, 2, 3, 4, 5, 6 and 7 of this my affidavit are within my own knowledge and are true. The contents of paragraphs 8 and 9 are true to the best of my knowledge, information and belief.

Sworn [*etc.*].

Statement of Claim in Limitation Action

[*Heading as in* § 460, *supra*]

STATEMENT OF CLAIM

464 1. The plaintiffs have at all material times been the owners of the Panamanian motor vessel DAMON.

2. On the —— day of ——, 19—, DAMON was in the Port of Lagos and was completing loading her cargo for a voyage to Accra. Shortly before 23.15 hours (local time) on the said date, the vessel became unstable and, despite the jettisoning of some of her cargo, capsized and sank.

3. As a result of the said sinking, loss and damage were caused to the cargo and other property on board the vessel and the vessel became an obstruction in the harbour obstructing the Port of Lagos and infringing rights.

4. On the —— day of ——, 19—, an action was commenced in the High Court (19—, Folio —), by persons describing themselves as " the owners and persons entitled to possession of the cargo lately laden on board the motor vessel DAMON," claiming compensation for the loss and damage allegedly suffered by them by reason of the breach of contract and/or breach of duty and/or negligence of the plaintiffs, their servants or agents.

5. The plaintiffs admit that the said sinking was caused by the breach of the contracts of carriage covering the said cargo. The plaintiffs do not admit that the persons described in paragraph 4 hereof are entitled to sue in respect of such breaches of contract or in respect of any torts which may have been committed in the course of the said incident; nor do the plaintiffs admit the said persons' alleged loss or damage.

6. As a result of the said sinking and the vessel's becoming an obstruction and infringing rights as aforesaid, the plaintiffs incurred obligations and/or liabilities under the laws of Nigeria which arose in connection with the raising, removal and/or destruction of the vessel and the cargo and other property on board her. The plaintiffs have discharged their obligations and liabilities in connection therewith at a cost of £——. Particulars of the said cost will be given on discovery.

7. The said sinking and the loss, damage and infringement caused thereby occurred without the actual fault or privity of the plaintiffs.

Particulars

(i) The vessel was built in England in 19—, to Lloyd's Register classification rules and remained fully classed 100 A1 thereafter.

(ii) The plaintiffs purchased the vessel in 19— and traded the vessel until the date of the sinking. At all times the vessel performed satisfactorily in all respects regarding her stability.

(iii) The vessel was furnished with the appropriate stability data, including the following documents:

(a) details of an inclining experiment prepared by the builders dated May —, 19—;

(b) trim and stability booklet prepared by the builders dated June, 19—;

(c) T.P.I. and deadweight scale prepared by the builders, dated June, 19—.

(iv) At the time of the sinking, the vessel was manned by a crew of 25 hands all told. She was under the command of Captain —— and had a chief officer, a second officer and a third officer, who were all duly certificated and had been in the service of the plaintiffs for at least 5 years.

(v) During their said period of service, the master and officers had regularly been employed on voyages to and from West African ports (including voyages on DAMON), carrying cargoes similar to that laden on the vessel for the intended voyage, the subject matter of this action, and had shown themselves to be in all respects fully competent and qualified to hold the positions and discharge the duties entrusted to them.

(vi) Loading commenced on the —— day of ——, 19—, in accordance with the instructions of the master and under the supervision of the chief officer. During loading, the vessel's double bottom tanks and fore and aft peak tanks were all slack.

(vii) During the afternoon of the —— day of ——, 19—, the vessel developed a heavy starboard list. With a view to correcting this, the chief officer stopped the loading and began ballasting but the master countermanded this and ordered loading to continue on the port side. Shortly afterwards the vessel swung over to port. The master then ordered cargo to be loaded on the starboard side. Shortly afterwards the vessel swung over to starboard so heavily that water began to enter the shelter deck. The master then ordered the resumption of ballasting and for loading to be continued on the port side.

(viii) Under the influence of the Easterly wind, the vessel shortly afterwards swung heavily over to port and the shelter deck continued to flood. Thereafter, despite jettisoning of some of the cargo, the vessel listed further and further to port, finally capsizing and sinking at about 23.15 hours on the —— day of ——, 19.

8. The casualty was caused as aforesaid by the acts and omissions of the master in the navigation and/or management of the vessel and/or in the loading and/or carriage of the cargo.

9. The net registered tonnage of DAMON, after addition of space required for propelling power, is —— tons. The product of this figure at the rate of £—— is £——. In the premises, the plaintiffs are entitled to limit their liability to that sum.

10. The claim made against the plaintiffs and the liabilities and obligations discharged by the plaintiffs referred to in paragraph 6 hereof, exceed the said sum of £——.

11. Subject to paragraph 10, the plaintiffs are willing and hereby offer to pay into court the said sum of £——, together with interest thereon at —— per cent. per annum from the date of the said sinking until payment.

Defence in Limitation Action

DEFENCE OF FIRST-NAMED DEFENDANTS

465 1. Paragraphs 1, 2, 3, and 4 of the Statement of Claim are admitted.

2. Save in so far as they are admissions, these defendants join issue with the plaintiffs upon the matters alleged in paragraph 5 of the Statement of Claim.

3. Paragraph 6 of the Statement of Claim is not admitted.

4. The allegation contained in paragraph 7 of the Statement of Claim is denied. These defendants do not admit, and put the plaintiffs to proof of, the particular facts and matters therein set out.

5. Further, the said sinking was caused, or contributed to, by actual fault on the part of the plaintiffs, or alternatively occurred with their privity, in one or more of the following particular respects:

(a) They failed to prohibit stowage of cargo on the spar deck or awning deck.

(b) They failed to ensure that no cargo was worked during ballasting.

(c) They failed to provide on board adequate plans and stability data in a form and in a language which the master and officers of DAMON could readily read, understand and apply.

(d) They failed to appoint and properly to instruct competent persons ashore and on board to supervise the reception, loading and stowing of cargo.

(e) They failed to appoint competent and adequately trained and experienced master and officers to serve on board DAMON; these defendants will rely on the facts alleged in paragraph 7 of the Statement of Claim and also upon the following facts:

(i) that cargo had been laden on the spar deck and the awning deck;

(ii) that the heaviest cargo had not been stowed in the lowest part of the holds;

(iii) that there were unnecessary free surfaces in the ship;

(iv) that no proper calculations were made at any time to determine the stability of DAMON.

(f) They failed to exercise due diligence to make the vessel seaworthy and to make the holds and all other parts of the ship, in which the said cargo was carried, fit and safe for their reception, carriage and preservation, and to man, equip and supply the vessel properly; these defendants will rely upon the fact that DAMON capsized for no apparent external reason and upon all other matters hereinbefore set out.

6. Paragraph 8 of the Statement of Claim is denied.

7. No admissions are made as to the allegations contained in paragraphs 9 and 11 of the Statement of Claim.

8. Paragraph 10 of the Statement of Claim is admitted.

Summons to Set Aside Decree of Limitation of Liability [7]

[*Heading as in action*]

466 LET ALL PARTIES concerned, their solicitors or agents, attend before the [Admiralty Registrar in Room 730, Royal Courts of Justice,

[7] See *Admiralty Practice* [B.S.L. 1, § 1225].

Strand, London, WC2A 2LL, *or* District Registrar of the —— District Registry at [*address*],] at —— o'clock in the ——noon, on ——day, the —— day of ——, 19—, on the hearing of an application by the defendants [the owners of part of the cargo lately laden on board the ship DAMON] that the decree of limitation granted to the plaintiffs herein by the [Admiralty Registrar *or* District Registrar] on the —— day of ——, 19—, be set aside and that such directions be given, as to the further proceedings in the action as appear to the Registrar to be appropriate, and in particular [*specify any particular direction sought*, e.g. *discovery of documents, pleadings, summons for directions*]. And that the costs of this application be costs in the cause.

Dated the —— day of ——, 19—.

This summons was taken out by A.B. & Co., of [*address*], solicitors for the defendants [the owners of part of the cargo lately laden on board the ship DAMON].

To Messrs. C.D. & Co., solicitors for the plaintiffs.

And to Messrs. E.F. & Co., solicitors for the defendants [the owners of the ship PYTHIAS].

Affidavit Supporting Summons to Set Aside Decree of Limitation

467 I, A.B., of —— make oath and say as follows:

1. I am the managing director of the General Products Company Limited. I am duly authorised to make this affidavit on their behalf.

2. By a decree dated the —— day of ——, 19—, the Admiralty Registrar pronounced that the Universal Shipping Company Limited the plaintiffs in this action, were entitled to limit their liability in respect of a collision which occurred between the plaintiffs' ship DAMON and the ship PYTHIAS in the English Channel on the —— day of ——, 19—. He further ordered that any persons wishing to take out a summons to set aside the decree must enter an appearance on or before the —— day of ——, 19—. The General Products Company Limited entered an appearance on the —— day of ——, 19—, within the said time limit.

3. The General Products Company Limited were not named as defendants in the writ of summons in this action and the writ was not served on them.

4. At the time of the collision, the said company were the owners of part of the cargo laden on board DAMON. By reason of the collision, the cargo suffered damage and thereby the General Products Company Limited have sustained loss, damage and expense estimated to amount to £——.

5. The said company admit that the collision was in part caused

by the negligent navigation of those on board DAMON in the respects alleged in the affidavit of P.Q. filed herein on behalf of the plaintiffs but they deny that the said collision was caused without the actual fault or privity of the plaintiffs.

6. I have reason to believe that not only was the master of DAMON navigating his vessel in fog at an excessive speed, at the time of collision, as is admitted by the plaintiffs, but also the said master navigated his vessel in the same fashion on numerous occasions prior to the collision. The grounds for my belief stem from an examination of the entries in the deck log of DAMON between the —— day of ——, 19—, and the date of the collision.

7. I therefore ask that the said decree be set aside and that the General Products Company Limited be allowed to defend this action. Sworn [*etc.*].

Notice of Advertisement of Limitation Decree [8]

NOTICE

468 In the High Court of Justice 19—, Folio ——
Queen's Bench Division
Admiralty Court

Ships: The PYTHIAS and the DAMON.

NOTICE is hereby given to all persons with claims against A.B. Line Limited, the owners of the ship PYTHIAS, in respect of the collision between the PYTHIAS and the ship DAMON which occurred on the —— day of ——, 19—, that, in the Admiralty action in the High Court of Justice, 19—, Folio ——, between the said A.B. Line Limited, plaintiffs, and the owners of the ship DAMON and others, defendants, a decree was made on the —— day of ——, 19—:

(a) Limiting the liability of the plaintiffs to damages in respect of the said collision as regards claims in respect of:

(i) any damage or loss caused to any goods, merchandise or other things whatsoever on board the PYTHIAS;

(ii) any loss or damage caused to any other property or any rights infringed through the act or omission of any person (whether on board the PYTHIAS or not) in the navigation or management of the PYTHIAS, or in the loading, carriage or discharge of its cargo, or in the embarkation, carriage or disembarkation of its passengers, or through any other act or omission of any person on board the PYTHIAS, to £—— with

[8] This form is prepared by the Admiralty Registry or District Registry. See *Admiralty Practice* [B.S.L. 1, § 1218, n. 17, and § 1219].

interest; and in respect of such loss, damage or infringement as aforesaid, together with:

(iii) any loss of life or personal injury caused to any person being carried in the PYTHIAS;

(iv) any loss of life or personal injury caused to any person not carried in the PYTHIAS, through the act or omission of any person (whether on board the PYTHIAS or not) in the navigation or management of the PYTHIAS or in the loading, carriage or discharge of its cargo or in the embarkation, carriage or disembarkation of its passengers, or through any other act or omission of any person on board the PYTHIAS, to £—— with interest [9];

(b) Allowing until the —— day of ——, 19—, for the entry of appearances, the filing of claims and the taking out of summonses to set the decree aside.

C.D. & Co.,

[*address*],

Solicitors for the said A.B. Line Limited

Notice by Defendants that They no Longer Dispute Plaintiffs' Right to Limit

469 TAKE NOTICE that, pursuant to R.S.C., Ord. 75, rule 38 (8), the second-named defendants hereby cease to dispute the plaintiffs' right to limit their liability in accordance with the provisions of the Merchant Shipping Acts 1894 to 1970.

[*Signature*]

Solicitors for A.B. & Co.

[The next paragraph is 480]

[9] If a decree has not been granted in respect of claims for loss of life or personal injury, paras. (iii) and (iv) will not be included.

CHAPTER 13

APPEAL

Notice of Appeal from Judge's Order Allowing Objection to Registrar's Decision

480 In Her Majesty's Court of Appeal 19—, Folio ——

On appeal from the High Court of Justice

Queen's Bench Division

Admiralty Court

Action in rem against:

The Ship DAMON

The owners of the ship PYTHIAS Plaintiffs

and

The owners of the ship DAMON Defendants

NOTICE OF APPEAL

TAKE NOTICE that the Court of Appeal will be moved, so soon as counsel can be heard, by counsel on behalf of the appellants (defendants), on appeal from part of the Judgment [or Order] of the Honourable Mr. Justice ——, made on the —— day of ——, 19—, and perfected on the —— day of ——, 19—, whereby he allowed the respondents' (plaintiffs') appeal from the decision of the Registrar, dated the —— day of ——, 19—, and pronounced in favour of item 6 and the whole of item 18 of the plaintiffs' claim, and condemned the defendants in the costs of the reference to the Registrar and in the costs of and incidental to the motion in objection to the Registrar's decision, FOR AN ORDER that the said Judgment may be reversed or varied, and that the plaintiffs' objections to the said decision may be disallowed, and that the said decision may be confirmed, and that the plaintiffs may be ordered to pay the costs of this appeal and the costs of and incidental to the motion in objection to the said decision, or for such other order as to the Court may seem just.

AND FURTHER TAKE NOTICE that the grounds of this appeal are:

1. That the learned Judge was wrong in law and/or misapprehended the facts in holding that item 6 of the plaintiffs' claim was a consequence of the collision.

2. That the learned Judge ought to have found that the damage

claimed in item 18 of the plaintiffs' claim was caused when the plaintiffs' ship PYTHIAS went aground on the —— day of ——, 19—.

3. That the learned Judge was wrong in holding that the plaintiffs suffered loss of profit by reason of the same damage as included in item 18.

AND FURTHER TAKE NOTICE that the appellants propose to apply to set down this appeal in the Admiralty (Final List) [with assessors].

Dated the —— day of ——, 19—.

C.D. & Co.

of [*address*],

Solicitors for the appellants [defendants]

To A.B. & Co., of [*address*],

Solicitors for the respondents [plaintiffs]

Note: No notice as to the date on which this Appeal will be in the list for hearing will be given: it is the duty of the solicitors to keep themselves informed as to the state of the list. A respondent intending to appear in person should inform the Appeal Clerk, Room 136, Royal Courts of Justice, Strand, London, WC2A 2LL, of that fact and give his address. If he does so he will be notified by telegram to the address he has given of the date when this appeal is expected to be heard.

Notice of Appeal [1] in Collision Action

[*Heading as in* § 480, *supra*]

NOTICE OF APPEAL

481 TAKE NOTICE that the Court of Appeal will be moved, so soon as counsel can be heard on behalf of the above-named defendants, on appeal from the order or decree herein of the Honourable Mr. Justice ——, dated the —— day of ——, 19—, and perfected the —— day of ——, 19—, whereby he pronounced that the collision in question in this action was occasioned by the fault or default of the owners, master and crew of the steam tanker PYTHIAS or some or one of them and by the fault or default of the owners, master and crew of the steam tanker DAMON or some or one of them, and ordered that the damages arising therefrom be borne, as to two-fifths, by the owners of the steam tanker PYTHIAS and, as to three-fifths, by the owners of the steam tanker DAMON, and condemned the above-named

[1] This form is adapted from that entered in *The Almizar* [1970] 1 Lloyd's Rep. 67 (C.A.). For the cross-appeal, see § 482, *infra*.

plaintiffs in two-fifths of the defendants' counterclaim, and condemned the defendants' in three-fifths of the plaintiffs' claim for damages, proceeded for in this action, and made no order as to costs FOR AN ORDER that the said Judgment may be reversed or varied and that it be ordered that the damages arising from the collision in question in this action be borne in such proportions more favourable to the defendants and less favourable to the plaintiffs as to this Honourable Court may seem just and condemning the plaintiffs for the costs of the action and of this appeal or for such further order as to the costs of the action and of this appeal as to this Honourable Court may seem just.

AND FURTHER TAKE NOTICE that the grounds of this appeal are:

1. That the learned Judge was wrong in law, and/or misapprehended the facts, in holding that the navigation of the defendants' vessel was at fault to a greater degree than the navigation of the plaintiffs' vessel.

2. That the learned Judge was wrong to hold that the most important error committed by either vessel was that of DAMON in altering to starboard when she did.

(a) In the circumstances in which she found herself, it was the appropriate action for her to take to avoid collision.

(b) Alternatively, if wrong, it was no more than an error of judgment.

(c) Alternatively, if it was a fault, it would not have contributed to the collision if PYTHIAS had not, at or about the same time, improperly altered course to port.

(d) In any event, it was far less potent a cause of the collision, and/or far less blameworthy, than the immoderate speed in fog of PYTHIAS.

3. That the learned Judge was wrong to hold that the second officer of DAMON failed to keep a proper look-out. Alternatively, any inadequacies in his appreciation of the approach of PYTHIAS did not cause or contribute to the collision.

4. That he failed sufficiently, or at all, in assessing the blameworthiness of the faults found against the vessels respectively, to give any or any adequate weight to the fact that PYTHIAS had long been in fog whereas DAMON had entered fog only shortly before the collision.

5. That he failed to find that PYTHIAS was in breach of Rule 16 (b) of the Collision Regulations in failing to stop engines on hearing a fog signal forward of her beam.

6. That he failed to give proper weight, in apportioning blame for

the collision, to the gravity of two faults found against the plaintiffs, namely:

(a) the excessive speed maintained in fog by PYTHIAS; and

(b) her improper alteration of course to port in fog.

AND FURTHER TAKE NOTICE that the defendants purpose to apply to set down this appeal in the Admiralty (Final List) with assessors.

Dated the —— day of ——, 19—.

C.D. & Co., of [*address*].

Solicitors for the above-named appellants [defendants]

To the owners of the steam tanker PYTHIAS and to Messrs. ——, of ——, their solicitors.

No notice as to the date on which this appeal will be in the list for hearing will be given: it is the duty of solicitors to keep themselves informed as to the state of the lists.

A respondent intending to appear in person should inform the Appeal Clerk, Room 136, Royal Courts of Justice, London, WC2A 2LL, of that fact and give his address; if he does so, he will be notified by telegram, to the address he has given, of the date when the appeal is expected to be heard.

Notice of Cross Appeal in Collision Action [1]

[*Heading as in* § 480, *supra*]

CROSS-NOTICE OF APPEAL

482 TAKE NOTICE that, on the hearing of the defendants' appeal (or, if abandoned, at the expiration of 14 days from the date of such abandonment or so soon thereafter as counsel can be heard), the Court of Appeal will be moved by counsel on behalf of the plaintiffs by way of appeal from the order or decree herein of the Honourable Mr. Justice ——, dated the —— day of ——, 19—, and perfected the —— day of ——, 19—, WHEREBY he pronounced that the collision in question in this action was occasioned by the fault or default of the owners, master and crew of the PYTHIAS, or some or one of them, and of the owners, master and crew of the steam tanker DAMON, or some or one of them, and ordered that the damages arising therefrom be borne, as to two-fifths, by the owners of the steam tanker PYTHIAS and, as to three-fifths, by the owners of the steam tanker DAMON, and condemned the above-named plaintiffs in

two-fifths of the defendants' counterclaim, and condemned the defendants in three-fifths of the plaintiffs' claim for damages proceeded for in this action, and made no order as to costs, FOR AN ORDER that the said Judgment may be reversed or varied, and that it be ordered that the damages arising from the collision in question in this action be borne in such proportions more favourable to the plaintiffs and less favourable to the defendants as to this Honourable Court may seem just, and condemning the defendants for such costs of the action and of this appeal as to this Honourable Court may seem just.

AND FURTHER TAKE NOTICE that the grounds of this appeal are:

1. That the learned Judge was wrong on the evidence in finding that the PYTHIAS altered to port. Alternatively, if there was any alteration to port, the learned Judge was wrong in holding that it was causative.

2. That the learned Judge was wrong in holding that, over not more than $4\frac{1}{2}$ miles, the PYTHIAS increased her lateral distance from the ONLOOKER from 3 to 7 cables.

3. That the learned Judge was wrong in criticising the lookout of the PYTHIAS, particularly in finding that extra lookouts, additional to the forecastle head lookout (whom the learned Judge found was posted), were necessary.

4. That the learned Judge was wrong in holding that the speed of the PYTHIAS was somewhat under 7 knots, rather than 4 knots or less.

5. That the learned Judge, on opportioning blame, gave insufficient weight to the most serious error committed by either ship, namely that of the DAMON, in altering to starboard in fog on scanty information, too late to avoid a close quarters situation.

6. That the learned Judge failed to give sufficient weight, in apportioning blame, to the fact that the speed of the DAMON was, on his own findings, very much greater than that of the PYTHIAS.

7. That the learned Judge failed to give any, or any sufficient, weight to the knowledge which those on board the DAMON had, or ought to have had, namely that the PYTHIAS was limited in the actions she could take by the presence of the ONLOOKER.

8. That the learned Judge failed to give sufficient weight in apportioning blame, to the failure of the lookout on board the DAMON, and particularly to the negligent mistaken failure of the officer of the watch of the DAMON to appreciate the situation in sufficient time, whereby he concluded that the echo of the vessel which he had seen on his radar was not that of an unlighted dhow but of the plaintiffs' large steam tanker approaching the DAMON in fog.

9. That the learned Judge was wrong in law, and/or misappre-

hended the facts, in failing to hold the defendants to blame to a greater degree than three-fifths.

Dated this —— day of ——, 19—.

A.B. & Co., of [*address*].

Solicitors for the plaintiffs

To the owners of the steam tanker DAMON and to Messrs. C.D. & Co., of [*address*], their solicitors.

No notice as to the date on which this appeal will be in the list for hearing will be given: it is the duty of solicitors to keep themselves informed as to the state of the lists.

A respondent intending to appear in person should inform the Appeal Clerk, Room 136, Royal Courts of Justice, London, WC2A 2LL, of that fact and give his address; if he does so he will be notified by telegram to the address he has given of the date when the appeal is expected to be heard.

Notice of Appeal in Salvage Action

[*Heading as in* § 480, *supra*]

NOTICE OF APPEAL

483 TAKE NOTICE [*etc.*], whereby he awarded the respondents (plaintiffs) £—— for salvage services rendered by them to the motor vessel DAMON, her cargo and freight, together with costs, and condemned the appellants (defendants) and their bail in the said sum and in costs FOR AN ORDER that the said Judgment may be reversed or varied and that it may be adjudged that the respondents (plaintiffs) are not entitled to salvage in respect of the said services, and the respondents' (plaintiffs') claim may be dismissed, and that Judgment may be entered for the appellants (defendants) with the costs of this appeal and of the Court below OR ALTERNATIVELY FOR AN ORDER that the said Judgment may be varied and that such other and smaller sum may be awarded to the respondents (plaintiffs) in respect of the said services, as to this Honourable Court may seem just, and that the respondents (plaintiffs) may be ordered to pay the costs of this appeal.

AND FURTHER TAKE NOTICE that the grounds of this appeal are:

1. That the learned Judge was wrong in law in holding that the services of the plaintiffs were salvage services.

2. That the learned Judge ought to have found that the plaintiffs were not volunteers and were under a statutory duty to perform the said services.

3. That the learned Judge ought to have found that the services

after DAMON was refloated were all part of the operation of removing the vessel as an obstruction.

4. ALTERNATIVELY, that the learned Judge ought to have found that if the said services were separate, they were in the nature of towage and did not qualify as salvage services.

5. IN THE FURTHER ALTERNATIVE, that an award of £—— is too much in all the circumstances of the case.

Dated [*etc.*].

[*Continue as in* § 480, *supra*]

Petition for Leave to Appeal to House of Lords [2]

484 In the House of Lords

On Appeal from Her Majesty's Court of Appeal (England)

The owners of the motor vessel PYTHIAS Appellants (plaintiffs)

and

The owners of the motor vessel DAMON Respondents (defendants)

To the Right Honourable the House of Lords

THE HUMBLE PETITION OF THE OWNERS OF THE MOTOR VESSEL "PYTHIAS" SHEWETH—

1. That [*set out briefly in numbered paragraphs such facts and arguments as may be necessary to enable the Appeal Committee to report to the House whether leave to appeal should be granted*].

YOUR PETITIONERS HUMBLY SUBMIT that leave to appeal to your Lordships' House should be granted for the following, among other, reasons:

[*Here give reasons, which should be numbered*]

And Your Petitioners will ever pray [*etc.*].

[Signature of petitioners' agents]

Agents for the petitioners

We, Messrs. A.B. & Co., of [*address*], agents for the petitioners within-named, hereby certify that on the —— day of ——, 19—, we served Messrs. C.D. & Co., of [*address*], agents for the owners of the motor vessel DAMON, the within-named respondents, with a correct copy of the aforegoing Petition, and with a notice that on the —— day of ——, 19—, or as soon after as conveniently may be, the Petition for leave to appeal would be presented to the House of Lords on behalf of the petitioners.

[The next paragraph is 490]

[2] See *Admiralty Practice* [B.S.L. 1, §§ 1375, 1376].

CHAPTER 14

ARBITRATION

1. COLLISION

Submission to Arbitration : Collision

490 THIS AGREEMENT, made the —— day of ——, 19—, between Messrs. A.B. & Co., of [*address*], in the City of London, solicitors for and on behalf of the owners of the motor vessel PYTHIAS (hereinafter referred to as " the claimants ") and Messrs. C.D. & Co., of [*address*], in the City of London, solicitors for and on behalf of the owners of the motor vessel DAMON (hereinafter referred to as " the respondents ").

WHEREAS a collision occurred between the said vessels in the Singapore Straits on the —— day of ——, 19—, whereby both the said vessels sustained damage and each party is desirous of having all disputes between them arising out of the said collision determined by arbitration in England;

NOW IT IS HEREBY AGREED as follows:

1. All questions between the parties to this agreement as to liability for the said collision and the assessment of the damage resulting therefrom shall be and are hereby referred to the sole arbitrament of James Counsel of [*address*].

2. The parties may be represented by counsel.

3. The parties shall within 2 months from the date of this agreement, and/or within such further time as the parties may agree or the arbitrator direct, file, with the clerk to the arbitrator, preliminary acts in the form at present in use in the county courts, and each shall give notice to the other when such preliminary act is filed. Such preliminary acts shall have the same force and effect as if they were filed in an Admiralty action in the county court.

4. The claimants shall, within 14 days after the expiration of the time for filing preliminary acts, serve on the respondents' solicitors a Statement of Claim, a copy of which to be filed with the arbitrator's clerk.

5. The respondents shall, within 14 days after the service of the Statement of Claim, serve on the claimants' solicitors a Defence and Counterclaim, a copy of which to be filed with the arbitrator's clerk.

6. The parties shall, within 14 days after the service of the Defence and Counterclaim, exchange lists of documents and, within 7 days

thereafter, give mutual discovery of all such documents as are listed in their lists of documents, as being in their possession custody or power and for which privilege is not claimed.

7. The parties shall, within 7 days after the pleadings are closed, exchange copies of the preliminary acts filed by them, and thereafter consent to the preliminary acts filed being opened and collated.

8. The claimants shall, within 7 days after the completion of mutual inspection of documents, apply to the arbitrator for such directions as to the future course of the arbitration as they may desire, including the hearing of evidence, and shall inform the respondents' solicitors in writing of the directions applied for.

9. The said application for directions shall be dealt with so far as possible as if it were a summons for directions in an Admiralty action in the High Court. The respondents shall inform the claimants' solicitors in writing, not less than 7 days before the hearing of the application for directions, of any directions they intend to apply for, in so far as the same differ from the directions asked for by the claimants.

10. The arbitrator shall make an interim award on the question of liability for the said collision, and shall, if required, later assess the damages and make a final award as to the amount of damage payable by the claimants or respondents.

11. In the event of the arbitrator being required to assess the amount of the damages as aforesaid, the parties shall have the right to place such documents before him and to call such witnesses as they may consider necessary in the proof of damages. In all matters concerning the assessment of damages, the practice and procedure applicable to a reference to the Registrar in an Admiralty action in the High Court shall be followed so far as is possible.

12. Upon publication of his interim award and of his final award, the arbitrator shall inform the parties of the reasons for such interim and final awards, and the said reasons shall form part of the said awards.

13. The costs of, and incidental to, this agreement and of the arbitration and award or awards shall be borne and paid as the arbitrator may direct.

14. Either party may appeal from the interim and/or final award by giving, to the solicitors for the other party, notice in writing specifying the grounds of the appeal. The said notice shall be given within 6 weeks of publication of the award appealed from.

15. In the event of one party appealing, the other, if desiring to cross-appeal, shall give, to the solicitors for the party appealing, notice in writing specifying the grounds of the cross-appeal. The

said notice shall be given within 21 days after receipt of notice of appeal.

16. Any appeal shall be referred to the sole arbitrament of John Lawyer, one of Her Majesty's Counsel.

17. Upon publication of his award, the appeal arbitrator shall inform the parties of the reasons for such award and the said reasons shall form part of the award.

18. In the event of any appeal, the costs of, and incidental to, the appeal and award and the original arbitration and the award appealed from and of this agreement shall be borne and paid as the appeal arbitrator may direct.

19. In the event of the arbitrator or the appeal arbitrator being unwilling or unable to act, the question of liability for the said collision, and/or the assessment of the damages resulting therefrom, and/or any appeal, shall be referred to another arbitrator or appeal arbitrator to be agreed upon by the parties.

20. Save as is hereinbefore otherwise provided, the Arbitration Act 1950, and any statutory modification thereof, shall apply to any arbitration or appeal under this agreement.

IN WITNESS whereof the solicitors to the said parties have hereunto set their hands, the day and year first above written.

A.B. & Co., of [*address*].

Solicitors on behalf of the claimants

B.C. & Co., of [*address*].

Solicitors on behalf of the respondents

[The next paragraph is 492]

Interim Award : Collision

492 WHEREAS by an agreement made the —— day of ——, 19—, between Universal Steam Ship Company Limited, the owners of the motor tanker PYTHIAS and International Steam Ship Company Limited, the owners of the tanker DAMON it was agreed that the question of liability for a collision between the said vessels that took place in the River Thames on the —— day of ——, 19—, and for the damage sustained by the said vessels in consequence, be referred to the sole arbitrament of a barrister-at-law practising in the Admiralty Court of the Queen's Bench Division of the High Court of Justice, who should be nominated by Messrs. A.B. & Co., solicitors, of [*address*], in accordance with the provisions therein contained.

And whereas I, James Counsel, have been duly nominated by Messrs. A.B. & Co. to act as arbitrator in this reference in accordance with the provisions of the said agreement;

And whereas it was further agreed (*inter alia*) that the arbitrator should make an interim award on the question of liability and should direct by and to whom the damages resulting from the collision and the costs of and incidental to the agreement and of the arbitration and award should be borne or paid;

Now I, the said James Counsel, having taken upon myself the burden of the said arbitration and having duly weighed and considered the evidence laid before me do make and publish my interim award on liability as follows:

I award and adjudge that those in charge of pythias were one quarter to blame and those in charge of damon were three quarters to blame for the collision, and that the damages arising therefrom be borne as to one quarter by Universal Steam Ship Company Limited and as to three quarters by International Steam Ship Company Limited and further, that the costs of and incidental to the agreement and the arbitration, including the costs of this my award, be paid, as to one quarter, by Universal Steam Ship Company Limited and, as to three quarters, by International Steam Ship Company Limited.

In witness whereof I have hereunto set my hand this —— day of ——, 19—.

[*Signature*]

In the presence of:

Final Award on Appeal: Collision

493 Whereas by an agreement made the —— day of ——, 19—, between Messrs. A.B. & Co., solicitors for and on behalf of the owners of the motor vessel pythias (hereinafter called " the claimants "), and Messrs. C.D. & Co., solicitors for and on behalf of the owners of the steamship damon (hereinafter called " the respondents "), reciting that a collision had occurred between the said vessels at Milford Haven on the night of January 8/9, 19—, whereby both vessels had sustained damage, it was agreed that the question of liability for the said collision and the assessment of damages resulting therefrom should be referred to the sole arbitrament of ——, one of Her Majesty's Counsel (hereinafter called " the original arbitrator ");

And whereas on the —— day of ——, 19—, the original arbitrator made an interim award finding that the collision was solely caused by the fault or default of those in charge of the damon and that the respondents were liable to pay to the claimants the damages sustained by the claimants by reason of the said collision;

AND WHEREAS, disputes having arisen as to the amount of such damages, the original arbitrator on the —— day of ——, 19—, made a final award whereby he awarded that the amount payable by the respondents to the claimants in respect of the said damages was the sum of £——, with interest thereon at —— per cent. per annum from the —— day of ——, 19—, and directing that the respondents should bear and pay the costs of the reference and final award;

AND WHEREAS, within the terms of the said agreement, the respondents on the —— day of ——, 19—, gave notice to the claimants of appeal against the said final award;

AND WHEREAS the parties by agreement appointed me ——, one of Her Majesty's Counsel, as arbitrator on appeal;

AND WHEREAS the appeal was restricted to and against the findings and allowances of the original arbitrator in respect of items 30 and 34 of the claimants' claim;

NOW I, the said ——, having taken upon myself the burden of this arbitration on appeal, and having duly weighed and considered the documentary evidence adduced before me and the original arbitrator's notes and reasons and final award and the arguments of the parties by their respective counsel who attended before me DO HEREBY MAKE THIS MY AWARD ON APPEAL in writing;

I SET ASIDE THE SAID FINAL AWARD so far as concerns the amount awarded as payable by the respondents to the claimants in respect of the said damages, and, in lieu of such amount I AWARD AND ADJUDGE that the amount payable by the respondents to the claimants in respect of the said damages is the sum of £——, with interest thereon at —— per cent. per annum from the —— day of ——, 19—, and I CONFIRM the original arbitrator's award and directions as to the costs of the reference before him and of his final award, and I AWARD AND DIRECT that the claimants and the respondents shall each bear and pay their own costs of the reference before me and one half of the cost of this my award amounting to £——.

AS WITNESS my hand this —— day of ——, 19—,

[*Signature*]

In the presence of:

2. SALVAGE

Submission to Arbitration

494 THIS AGREEMENT is made the —— day of ——, 19—, between Messrs. A.B. & Co., of [*address*], solicitors for and on behalf of the owners, master and crew of the motor vessel PYTHIAS (hereinafter called " the

claimants ") of the one part, and Messrs. C.D. & Co., of [*address*], solicitors for and on behalf of the owners of the motor tanker DAMON (hereinafter called " the respondents ") of the second part.

WHEREAS:

1. Services which the claimants claim to have been in the nature of salvage were rendered by the claimants to the respondents during the month of ——, 19—.

2. It has been agreed between the parties to refer to arbitration the nature of the services alleged to have been rendered by the claimants to the respondents, and the amount of remuneration if any to be paid by the respondents to the claimants in respect thereof.

NOW IT IS HEREBY AGREED as follows:

1. The question whether the services which the claimants claim to have been rendered to the respondents were in the nature of salvage, and the amount of remuneration, if any, to be paid to the claimants by the respondents in respect thereof shall be, and are hereby, referred to the sole arbitrament of L.M., one of Her Majesty's counsel (hereinafter called " the arbitrator ").

2. Within twenty-one days of the signing of this agreement, the parties shall produce to each other all such documents as would be disclosed by them under an order for discovery in an action in the High Court of Justice.

3. Within twenty-eight days of the signing of this agreement, the respondents shall supply to the claimants details of the value of the DAMON together with documents in support thereof and, if the values are not agreed between the parties, they shall be decided by the arbitrator upon such evidence as the parties may place before him or for which he may call in accordance with clause 7 hereof.

4. At least fourteen days before the date appointed for the hearing of the arbitration, the said solicitors shall meet and agree a bundle of documents to be placed before the arbitrator.

5. It shall be the duty of the claimants to supply the arbitrator with a copy of the agreed bundle.

6. The arbitrator shall determine the matters in dispute on the documents after having heard the arguments submitted by the parties who may be represented before him by counsel.

7. The arbitrator shall have the power to admit any evidence or documents which he may in his discretion think fit, whether the same be admissible in law as evidence or not, and to call for any further evidence as he may require.

8. Any of the parties may, by giving notice of appeal or cross-appeal in the manner hereinafter appearing, appeal to N.O., one of Her Majesty's Counsel (hereinafter called " the appeal arbitrator "),

who shall thereby be appointed arbitrator on appeal and hear the appeal. His award shall be final.

9. Notice of appeal shall be given by either party to the other in writing within twenty-one days of the publication of the award of the arbitrator. Notice of cross-appeal shall be given within seven days of the receipt of the written notice of appeal by the party giving the notice of cross-appeal.

10. The appeal arbitrator shall have the same powers as those hereby vested in the arbitrator.

11. The costs of this agreement of the arbitration and the appeal arbitration, if any, shall be paid in such manner as the arbitrator or the appeal arbitrator shall in his discretion direct.

12. The arbitrator and the appeal arbitrator shall supply to the parties on payment of the proper charges therefor reasons for his award.

13. Save as aforesaid, the provisions of the Arbitration Act 1950, or any statutory modification thereof for the time being in force, shall apply to these arbitrations.

AS WITNESS the hands of the parties hereto the year and day first above written.

A.B. & Co., of [*address*],

for and on behalf of the claimants

C.D. & Co., of [*address*],

for and on behalf of the respondents

Salvage Award

495 WHEREAS by an agreement made on the —— day of ——, 19—, between A.B. & Co., of [*address*], solicitors for Messrs. Universal Salvage Company Limited (hereinafter called " the claimants "), of the one part, and C.D. & Co., of [*address*], solicitors for and on behalf of the owners of the ss. DAMON (hereinafter called " the respondents "), of the other part, RECITING that the claimants claimed to have rendered salvage services to the respondents off Port Muroran, Japan, on or about the —— day of ——, 19—, which the respondents did not admit, AND RECITING that it had been agreed between the parties to refer to arbitration for determination the questions whether the services alleged to have been rendered to the respondents by the claimants were salvage services and the amount of remuneration, if any, to be paid by the respondents to the claimants in respect of the said services, AND FURTHER RECITING that there was an arbitration between the respondents and Messrs. Universal Salvage Company under the terms and conditions of Lloyd's open form of salvage agreement dated —— day of ——, 19—, wherein the Committee of Lloyd's had appointed ——, one of Her Majesty's Counsel, as arbitrator;

IT WAS THEREBY AGREED amongst other things, that the questions whether salvage services were rendered and the amount of remuneration, if any, to be paid to the claimants for services rendered to the respondents should be and were thereby referred to the sole arbitrament of the said —— (thereinafter referred to as "the arbitrator");

AND IT WAS FURTHER AGREED that the costs of the said agreement and the preparation thereof and also of the reference should be paid as the arbitrator or appeal arbitrator may in his discretion direct;

NOW I, the said ——, having taken upon myself the burthen of this arbitration in accordance with the terms of the said agreement, and having duly weighed and considered the evidence and documents laid before me and the arguments of the parties by their respective counsel who attended before me, DO HEREBY MAKE THIS MY AWARD in writing of and concerning the matters in question. I FIND that the claimants rendered salvage services to the respondents AND I AWARD AND ADJUDGE that the respondents do pay to the said claimants, for the services so rendered, the sum of £—— [*amount in words*], AND I FURTHER AWARD AND DIRECT that the respondents do pay their own and the claimants' costs of the said agreement and of its preparation and of the reference before me and the cost of this my award which amounts to £——.

AS WITNESS my hand, this —— day of ——, 19—.

[*Signature*]

In the presence of:

Award under Lloyd's Open Form

496 WHEREAS, by an agreement dated the —— day of ——, 19—, made on the standard form of salvage agreement [1] approved and published by the Committee of Lloyd's and known as "No Cure: No Pay," it was agreed, *inter alia*, between Captain John Smith, for and on behalf of the owners of the DAMON, her cargo and freight (hereinafter called "the respondents"), and James Brown, for and on behalf of Universal Salvage Company Limited (hereinafter called "the contractors"), that the latter should use their best endeavours to salve the said DAMON and her cargo, and take them into Rotterdam,

[1] See *Admiralty Practice* [B.S.L. 1, §§ 1528 *et seq.*].

or other place to be thereafter agreed, and that the remuneration therefor should be decided by arbitration in the manner therein set out and prescribed;

AND WHEREAS the contractors salved the said DAMON and her cargo;

AND WHEREAS, under the provisions of the said agreement, the Committee of Lloyd's appointed me, John Lawyer, one of Her Majesty's Counsel, as sole arbitrator;

AND WHEREAS over fourteen months have elapsed since the said services were rendered;

AND WHEREAS it was agreed that the salved value of the DAMON was £——;

AND I FIND that the salved value of the cargo was £——, making a total salved value of £——;

NOW I, the said John Lawyer, having taken upon myself the burthen of this arbitration in accordance with the terms of the said agreement, and having duly weighed and considered the evidence and documents laid before me and the arguments of the parties by their respective counsel who attended before me DO HEREBY MAKE THIS MY AWARD in writing of and concerning the matters in question. I AWARD AND ADJUDGE that the respondents do pay to the said contractors for the salvage services so rendered the sum of £—— [*amount in words*], which shall be paid by each of the respondents in the same proportions as their respective interests bear to the total salved value, AND I FURTHER AWARD AND DIRECT that the respondents do each bear and pay their own costs of this arbitration and shall pay, in the aforesaid proportions, the said contractors' costs of this arbitration, the fees and/or costs charged by the Committee of Lloyd's for their services in connection therewith, and the cost of this my award which amounts to £——.

AS WITNESS my hand this —— day of ——, 19—,

[*Signature*]

In the presence of:

Authority to Act in Respect of Salvage Claims in Arbitration

497 AUTHORITY to Universal Shipping Company Limited, the owners of the motor vessel PYTHIAS, and to their solicitors, Messrs. A.B. & Co., to act in respect of the salvage claims of the master, officers and crew of PYTHIAS, against the owners of the motor vessel DAMON, her cargo and freight.

WHEREAS:

1. PYTHIAS in the course of her late voyage from Sydney to San

Francisco rendered salvage services in the Pacific Ocean to DAMON, her cargo and freight, during July 12–19, 19—.

2. The said salvage services were performed under the terms and conditions of Lloyd's standard form of salvage agreement.

3. We, the master, officers and crew of PYTHIAS, desire to claim salvage remuneration from DAMON, her cargo and freight, in respect of the said services.

4. We understand that, in accordance with the terms of the said Lloyd's standard form of salvage agreement, the remuneration for the said salvage services will, in the absence of amicable settlement, be determined in arbitration in London by an arbitrator appointed by the Committee of Lloyd's, and, further, in the event of appeal from the decision of such arbitrator, will be finally determined by the appeal arbitrator appointed by the said Committee of Lloyd's.

NOW WE, the master, officers and crew of PYTHIAS, whose names, addresses and ratings are in the document annexed hereto and whose signatures appear at the foot hereof DO HEREBY AUTHORISE the owners of PYTHIAS, Universal Shipping Company Limited, and their solicitors, Messrs. A.B. & Co., for us and each of us and in our names and on our behalf:

1. To protect our interests in all respects concerning the prosecution and arbitration of our said salvage claims, and to conclude the prosecution of the said claims either by amicable settlement or by arbitration as they shall in their sole discretion think fit.

2. To give sign or execute good and sufficient receipts and discharges for all monies which may be payable to us in respect of our claims, and to sign and execute all such deeds and releases or other documents as in their opinion may be necessary or expedient in relation to our said claims.

3. To act do and execute all such acts deeds matters or things as they may think necessary for enforcing payment and satisfaction of our respective claims.

4. To appoint a substitute or substitutes for the above purposes and to revoke such appointments if they shall think fit.

5. For the purposes of arbitration proceedings, to instruct counsel to represent our interests in the said proceedings and, through such counsel, to request the arbitrator and, if appointed, the appeal arbitrator to apportion as between the owners of PYTHIAS and ourselves the amount of the total salvage remuneration awarded and, in the event of amicable settlement, to apportion the total amount of such settlement in accordance with the advice of counsel instructed by Messrs. A.B. & Co.

6. To make collection of the sums due to each of us and to account to each of us or to our personal representatives or to any

party duly authorised by us for the amount of the salvage award recovered on our behalf.

AND WE HEREBY AGREE that we will accept any such apportionment made in accordance with the authority above given, and that we will bear rateably with the owners of PYTHIAS, according to our respective shares of the award, the legal expenses of the prosecution of our claims and of the arbitrations if any, and that we will ratify and confirm, whether by ourselves or our personal representatives, whatsoever shall be done on our behalf in accordance with the authority and the terms of agreement contained herein.

Dated this —— day of ——, 19—.

Notice of Motion to Stay Action Pursuant to Section 4 of the Arbitration Act 1950

[*Heading as in action*]

498 TAKE NOTICE [*etc.*[2]] for an order that all further proceedings in this action be stayed pursuant to section 4 of the Arbitration Act 1950, the plaintiffs and the defendants having, by an agreement in writing on the terms of Lloyd's standard form of salvage agreement (No Cure—No Pay), dated the —— day of ——, 19—, agreed to refer to arbitration the matters in respect of which this action is commenced, and that the plaintiffs do pay to the defendants the costs of and occasioned by this action (including the costs of this application) to be taxed.

To the plaintiffs [*etc.*[2]].

Affidavit in Support

499 I, A.B., of [*residence*], make oath and say as follows:

1. I am the managing director of the defendant company and am duly authorised to make this affidavit on the defendants' behalf. Save as otherwise stated, the matters to which I depose are within my own knowledge and are true.

2. The action is brought to recover salvage remuneration for services rendered by the plaintiffs' motor tug PULLER to the defendants' motor vessel DAMON in the North Sea on the —— day of ——, 19—.

3. By an agreement, in writing on the terms of Lloyd's standard form of salvage agreement, made on the —— day of ——, 19—,

[2] As in § 352, *supra*.

between the master of DAMON, for and on behalf of the defendants, and the master of PULLER, for and on behalf of the plaintiffs, it was agreed, *inter alia*, that the plaintiffs would use their best endeavours to salve DAMON and, by virtue of clause 7 thereof, that the amount of salvage remuneration therefor should be referred to arbitration. The said agreement is now produced and shown to me and is exhibited hereto marked " A.B.1."

4. There is no sufficient reason why the said salvage claim should not be so referred and decided. The defendants are ready and willing to do all things necessary for causing the said claim to be decided by arbitration under the said agreement.

5. The defendants have entered an appearance to the writ of summons in this action, but have taken no further step in the action.

Sworn [*etc.*]

Affidavit in Objection

500 I, R.L., of [*residence*], make oath and say as follows:

1. I am a director of the plaintiff company and am duly authorised to make this affidavit on the defendants' behalf. Save as otherwise stated, the matters to which I depose herein are within my own knowledge and are true.

2. I have read what purports to be a copy of the affidavit of K.L., filed on behalf of the defendants on the —— day of ——, 19—.

3. At the termination of salvage services rendered by the plaintiffs' motor tug PULLER to the defendants' motor vessel DAMON, the plaintiffs notified the Committee of Lloyd's of the amount of security that they required the defendants to give in accordance with clause 4 of the agreement. I have been informed by ——, secretary to the Committee of Lloyd's that the defendants have not furnished any such security.

4. By reason thereof, this claim cannot be referred to arbitration pursuant to the agreement and I am advised and verily believe that the plaintiffs are entitled to proceed with this action.

Sworn [*etc.*]

[The next paragraph is 511]

Chapter 15

COUNTY COURT

1. Commencement of Action

Memorandum to be Printed or Written on every Summons, Notice, Judgment, Order or Process of the Court

511 Address all communications for the Court to: The Registrar, County Court, ——.

The Court office at: [*insert address of office*], is open from 10 a.m. till 4 p.m. on Mondays to Fridays only [*or as the case may be*].

Memorandum of Agreement to Specified County Court having Jurisdiction [1]

512 In the —— County Court.

In the matter of a collision between the ship PYTHIAS and the ship DAMON.

We the solicitors for the owners of the ship PYTHIAS and the owners of the ship DAMON respectively, hereby agree that, pursuant to section 56 (5) of the County Courts Act 1959, the —— County Court shall have jurisdiction to hear and determine all proceedings between the owners of the said ships, arising out of a collision in the River Thames which occurred on the —— day of ——, 19—.

Dated the —— day of ——, 19—.

[*Signature*]

[*Address*]

Solicitors for the owners of the ship PYTHIAS

[*Signature*]

[*Address*]

Solicitors for the owners of the ship DAMON

[1] See the County Courts Act 1959, s. 56 (5).

Praecipe for Commencement of Admiralty Action in Rem

ADMIRALTY JURISDICTION

513 In the —— County Court.

We, A.B. & Co.,[2] of [*address*], solicitors for C.D., of [*address*], desire to commence an action for [*state the nature of the action, e.g.* salvage [3]] against the ship DAMON lying at [Erith Buoys] in the sum of £—— [and we require the summons to be served by the bailiff of the Court].

The facts are such to enable the Court's jurisdiction to be invoked by an action in rem under section 57 (2) or (3) of the County Courts Act 1959.

All instruments and documents in the said action may be left for us at [*address*].

Dated this —— day of ——, 19—.

[*Signature*]

Solicitors for the plaintiff

Praecipe for Commencement of Admiralty Action in Personam

ADMIRALTY JURISDICTION

514 In the —— County Court.

We, A.B. & Co., of [*address*], solicitors for C.D., of [*address and occupation*], desire to commence an action for [*state the nature of the action, e.g.* repairs] against E.F., of [*address and occupation*], owner of the ship DAMON lying at [Erith Buoys] in the sum of £—— [and we require the summons to be served by the bailiff of the Court].

[*If the claim is for damage, loss of life or personal injury arising out of a collision between ships, or out of the carrying out, or omission to carry out, a manoeuvre in the case of one or more of two or more ships, or out of the non-compliance, on the part of one or more of two or more ships, with regulations under section* 418 *of the Merchant Shipping Act* 1894, *or any such rules as are mentioned in section*

[2] If the plaintiff sues in his name, his occupation must be given. Where it is not practicable to give the name of the plaintiff at the time of filing the praecipe, it is sufficient, subject to the right of the defendant to demand the name, to describe the plaintiff as " the owner of the ship —— " or " the owner of the cargo lately laden on board the ship —— " or as may be. See *The Assunta* [1902] P. 150.

[3] If the action is against a foreign ship in respect of wages due, see n. 12 § 294, *ante*.

421 (1) *of that Act or any rules made under section* 421 (2),[4] *add either*:]

The defendant has his habitual residence [*or* a place of business] at the address given,

[*or*]

The cause of action arose at ——,

[*or*]

An action (Plaint No. —) arising out of the same incident or series of incidents is proceeding [*or* has been heard and determined] in this Court,

[*or*]

The defendant has agreed to submit to the jurisdiction of this Court,[5]

[*or*]

The plaintiff has [not] previously brought proceedings in a court outside England and Wales against the same defendant in respect of the same incident or series of incidents [and such proceedings have been discontinued or have otherwise come to an end].

All instruments and documents in the said action may be left for us at [*address*].

[*Signature*]

Solicitors for the plaintiff

Particulars of Claim

[*Heading as in action*]

515 The plaintiffs claim damages in the amount of £——[6] and costs arising out of a collision between the plaintiffs' barge PYTHIAS and the defendants' ship DAMON which occurred in Blackwall Reach of the River Thames on the —— day of ——, 19—, owing to the negligence of the defendants, their servants or agents.

[*Signature*]

Solicitors for the plaintiffs[7] of [*address*], where they will accept service of proceedings on behalf of the plaintiffs.

To the Registrar of the Court and to the defendants.

4 See the County Courts Act 1959, s. 70 (6).

5 See § 512, *ante*.

6 It is usual, unless a liquidated sum is being claimed, to insert the figure of the Court's jurisdiction (see the County Courts Act 1959, s. 56 (2)).

7 Where a plaintiff sues by solicitor, the particulars must be signed by the solicitor in his own name or in the name of his firm. If counsel settles the particulars he should sign them, and his name should appear above the solicitor's.

Summons in Admiralty Action in Rem

ADMIRALTY JURISDICTION

516 In the —— County Court.

The DAMON

Between A.B. [& Co.] of [*address and occupation*]
or The owners of the ship PYTHIAS Plaintiffs
and
The owners of the ship DAMON Defendants

WHEREAS an action for [*state the nature of the action, e.g.* salvage] has been commenced in this Court, on behalf of [the owners of the ship PYTHIAS] against the [*description of ship, e.g.* motorship] called the DAMON [*where the action is against ship and freight, add*: and the freight due for the transportation of the cargo now or lately laden therein], [*or, where the action is against ship, cargo and freight*: and the cargo now or lately laden therein, together with the freight due for the transportation thereof], for the sum of £——[8] according to the particulars of claim hereto annexed;

YOU ARE HEREBY SUMMONED to enter an appearance in the said action within fourteen days of the service hereof.

If you do not enter an appearance as aforesaid [*if the claim is for salvage or towage, and is not of a liquidated nature, and is not for damages*: the Judge of this Court will proceed to hear and determine the said action, or to make such orders therein as he thinks fit], [*or, if the claim is of a liquidated nature*: the plaintiffs will be at liberty to sign final judgment for the amount named in the particulars, with costs to be taxed by the Registrar] [*or, if the claim is for damages*: the plaintiffs will be at liberty to sign interlocutory judgment, with costs to be taxed, in which case the damages will be assessed by the Registrar under the Rules for the assessment of damages].

Dated this —— day of ——, 19—.

[*Signature*]

Registrar

To the owners of and parties interested in the [*description and name of ship or cargo, etc.*]

The solicitors for the plaintiffs are P.Q. & Co., of [*address as given in the praecipe*].

[8] See n. 6, § 515, *ante*.

Summons in Admiralty Action in Personam

ADMIRALTY JURISDICTION

517 In the —— County Court.

Between A.B. [& Co. Ltd.] of [*address and occupation*] Plaintiffs

and

C.D., of [*address and occupation*] Defendant

WHEREAS an action for [*state nature of action*] has been commenced in this Court on behalf of the plaintiffs against you in the sum of £—— according to the particulars of claim hereto annexed:

YOU ARE HEREBY SUMMONED to enter an appearance in the said action within fourteen days of the service hereof.

If you do not enter an appearance as aforesaid [*if the claim is for salvage or towage, and is not of a liquidated nature, and is not for damages*: the Judge of this Court will proceed to hear and determine the said action, or to make such orders therein as he thinks fit], [*or, if the claim is of a liquidated nature*: the plaintiffs will be at liberty to sign final judgment for the amount named in the particulars, with costs to be taxed by the Registrar], [*or, if the claim is for damages*: the plaintiffs will be at liberty to sign interlocutory judgment, with costs to be taxed, in which case the damages will be assessed by the Registrar under the Rules for the assessment of damages].

Dated this —— day of ——, 19—.

[*Signature*]

Registrar

To the defendant.

The solicitors for the plaintiffs are P.Q. & Co., of [*address as given in the praecipe*].

Plaint Note in Admiralty Action in Rem [9]

ADMIRALTY JURISDICTION

518 In the —— County Court.

Between The owners of the ship PYTHIAS Plaintiffs

and

No. of Plaint *or* Matter	Defendant	Fees paid Plaint	Fees paid Warrant
	The owners of the ship DAMON		

[9] This form is prepared by the Court and is, *mutatis mutandis*, the same for both in rem and in personam actions.

The above action [*or* actions] was [*or* were] entered this day.
Dated this —— day of ——, 19—.

[*Signature*]

Registrar

Memorandum by Solicitor Accepting Service and Undertaking to Appear in Admiralty Action in Rem

[*Heading as in action*]

519 We accept service of the summons on behalf of the defendants [the owners of the ship DAMON] and undertake in due course to enter an appearance, and put in bail, or to pay money into Court in lieu of bail [a sum not exceeding £——] [*or, in an action for salvage*: to put in bail or pay money into Court in lieu of bail and to file an affidavit of the value of the property unless such value is agreed].

Our address for service is [*address*].

Dated this —— day of ——, 19—.

[*Signature*]

Solicitors for the defendants

Affidavit of Service of Summons

[*Heading as in action*]

520 I, A.B., of [*residence*], make oath and say as follows:

1. I am over 16 years of age and employed by C.D. & Co., of [*address*], solicitors for the above-named plaintiffs.

2. I did on the —— day of ——, 19—, serve the summons, a true copy of which is annexed hereto and marked "A.B.1," on the defendants by delivering the same to the said defendants personally at [*address*].

[*Or*:
delivering the same at [*address*], to P.Q., who stated he was a partner in the defendant firm [*or* who carried on *or* who stated that he carried on] business in the name of the defendant firm.]

[*Or*:
delivering the same at [*address*], to a person who did not give his

name but stated that he was a partner in [*or* carried on business in the name of] the defendant firm.]

[*Or*:
delivering the same at [*address*], being the principal place of business of the defendant firm within the district of this Court, to P.Q., the person who had, or appeared to have, the control or management of the business there.]

[*Or*:
leaving the same [*or* posting the same] on the previous day in a prepaid envelope by first-class post [*or* on the —— day of ——, 19—, in a prepaid envelope by second-class post] addressed to the defendant company at [*address*], the address stated in the summons to be the registered office of the defendant company.]

[*Or*:
sending the same on the previous day by registered post together with a sealed copy of the order for substituted service of the said summons, addressed to the defendants at [*address*], in accordance with the said order.]

[*Or*:
delivering the same to S.T. the person [*or* a person who did not give his name] who was apparently in charge of the ship DAMON lying at ——.]

[*Or*:
nailing [*or* affixing] the same on the [main] mast [*or* outside of the wheel-house *or as may be*] of the ship DAMON lying at ——.]

[*Or*:
delivering the same at ——, to S.T. [*or* a person who did not give his name] who was apparently in charge of the cargo lately landed from the ship DAMON and who would not permit access to the said cargo.] [10]

Sworn at [*address*],
this —— day of ——, 19—,
before me,

[*Signature of deponent*]

[*Signature*]

A Commissioner for Oaths [*or* officer of the Court appointed to take affidavits].

This affidavit is filed on behalf of the plaintiffs.

[10] A summons in rem may be served on a Sunday, Good Friday or Christmas Day, as well as on any other day.

2. Arrest

Affidavit to Lead Warrant of Arrest in Action Alleging Maritime Lien or other Charge [11]

[*Heading as in action*]

521 I, A.B., of [*residence*], clerk to C.D. & Co., of [*address*], solicitors for the [plaintiffs] in this action make oath and say as follows:

1. I am informed by a report received from the master of the plaintiffs' ship PYTHIAS and verily believe that on the —— day of ——, 19—, a collision occurred in the English Channel between the plaintiffs' ship PYTHIAS and the defendants' ship DAMON of the Port of Monrovia whereby the PYTHIAS suffered damage. In the premises, it is alleged that the plaintiffs have a maritime lien on the defendants' ship DAMON for the damages claimed in this action.

2. The plaintiffs' claim for compensation for the damage occasioned by the collision remains unsatisfied.

3. The ship DAMON is now lying at Nelson Dock, Liverpool, in the course of loading cargo for carriage to Genoa. I am informed by the ship's agents, Messrs. E. F. & Co., and verily believe, that when such loading is completed the ship will sail on the said voyage. The defendants have declined to provide security for the plaintiffs' claim herein, and it is probable that the ship will be removed out of the jurisdiction of this Court before the plaintiffs' claim is satisfied.

4. The aid and process of this Honourable Court are necessary to enforce payment of the damages due to the plaintiffs by the arrest of the ship DAMON.

Sworn [*etc.*].

This affidavit is filed on behalf of the [plaintiffs].

Affidavit to Lead Warrant of Arrest against Ship or Person Liable or Sister Ship [12]

[*Heading as in action*]

522 I, A.B., of [*residence*], clerk to C.D. & Co., of [*address*], solicitors for the [plaintiffs] in this action, make oath and say as follows:

1. The plaintiffs carry on business as ship repairers at North Shields.

[11] See the Countv Courts Act 1959, ss. 57 (2) and 83. In an action for wages, the nationality of the ship must be stated in the affidavit.

[12] See the County Courts Act 1959, ss. 57 (3) and 83. In an action for wages the nationality of the ship must be stated in the affidavit.

2. I am informed by E.F., the plaintiffs' managing director, and verily believe that the plaintiffs effected repairs to the defendants' ship DAMON of the Port of Monrovia at North Shields, between the —— and —— days of ——, 19—, at the defendants' request.

3. The plaintiffs' charges and disbursements for the said repairs amount to the sum of £—— and such sum remains due and owing to the plaintiffs.

4. The said ship DAMON is the ship in connection with which the claim in this action arose.

5. I verily believe that the defendants were, at the time when the cause of action arose, the owners [*or* the charterers *or* in possession or control] of the ship DAMON and are the persons who would, apart from section 70 of the County Courts Act 1959, be liable to the plaintiffs in an action in personam and were also, at the time of the issue of the summons in this action, the beneficial owners of all the shares therein. The grounds for my belief are that it appears from Lloyd's Register of Shipping for 19— to 19—, that the owners of the DAMON are described as X.Y.Z. Ltd., of [*address*], and I am informed by Mr. ——, of Lloyd's Register of Shipping, that no change of ownership has taken place since the cause of action arose.

[*Or, in a sister-ship action*:

4. This action is brought against the ship DEMOS of the Port of Monrovia and is not the ship in connection with which the claim in this action arose.

5. I verily believe that the persons who would apart from section 70 of the County Courts Act 1959 be liable to the plaintiffs, in an action in personam, were, at the time when the cause of action arose, the owners [*or* the charterers *or* in possession or control] of the ship in connection with which this claim arose, and were also, at the time of the issue of the summons in this action, the beneficial owners of the DEMOS as respects all the shares therein. The grounds for my belief are that it appears from Lloyd's Register of Shipping for 19— to 19—, that the owners of the DEMOS are described as X.Y.Z. Ltd., of [*address*], and I am informed by Mr. ——, of Lloyd's Register of Shipping, that no change of ownership has taken place since the cause of action arose.]

6. The ship DEMOS is now lying at Nelson Dock, Liverpool, in the course of loading cargo for carriage to Genoa. I am informed by the ship's agents, Messrs. E.F. & Co., and verily believe, that, when such loading is completed, the ship will sail on the said voyage. The defendants have declined to provide security for the plaintiffs' claim herein and it is probable that the ship will be removed out of the jurisdiction of this Court before the plaintiffs' claim is satisfied.

7. The aid and process of this Honourable Court are necessary to enforce payment of the sum due to the plaintiffs in this action by the arrest of the ship DEMOS.

Sworn [*etc.*]

This affidavit is filed on behalf of the [plaintiffs].

Warrant of Arrest and Detention [13]

[*Heading as in action*]

523 WHEREAS an action has been commenced in this Court on behalf of A.B. & Co., against [*state description and name of ship or property, e.g.* motorship DAMON] for the sum of £——;

These are therefore to require and order you to arrest the said [motorship DAMON] and to keep the same under safe arrest, until you shall receive further orders from this Court.

Dated this —— day of ——, 19—.

[*Signature*]

Registrar

To the Registrar and Bailiffs of the Court.

3. APPEARANCE

Praecipe to Enter Appearance [14]

[*Heading as in action*]

524 Enter an appearance in this action for the defendant A.B., of [*address and occupation*], [*or, in an action in rem, if the defendant's name is not known*: for the owner of the ship DAMON [14] *or*, for P.Q., of [*address and occupation*], who claims to be interested in the property [*or* money paid into Court] in this action].

All instruments and documents in the action may be left for the said [A.B.] at [*address*].

Dated this —— day of ——, 19—.

[*Signature*]

Solicitors for the defendant [*or* said P.Q.]

13 See the County Courts Act 1959, ss. 57 (2), (3) and 83.

14 Where it is not practicable at the time of entering appearance to state the name, address and occupation of the defendant, it shall be sufficient in an action in rem, subject to the right of the plaintiff to demand further particulars, to state that the appearance is entered on behalf of the owners of the property proceeded against, or on behalf of the defendant.

Notice of Appearance

[*Heading as in action*]

525 Take notice that we have today entered an appearance in this action for the defendant A.B., of [*address and occupation*] [*or* name C.D., of [*address and occupation*] who claims to be interested in the property [*or* money paid into Court] in this action].

[*Signature*]

Solicitors for the defendant [*or* said A.B.]

Notice of Hearing [15]

[*Heading as in action*]

526 Take notice, that this action will be heard at a Court to be held at [*address*], on [Monday] the —— day of ——, 19—, at o'clock.

[*Signature*]

Registrar

To Messrs. A.B. & Co., solicitors for the plaintiff.

[To Messrs. C.D. & Co., solicitors for the defendant.]

4. Bail

Notice Dispensing with Affidavits of Justification

[*Heading as in action*]

527 Take notice that the proposed sureties to bail on behalf of the plaintiff [*or* defendant] are satisfactory to the defendant [*or* plaintiff] and that affidavits of justification may be dispensed with.

Dated this —— day of ——, 19—.

[*Signature*]

Solicitors for the defendant [*or* plaintiff]

To C.D. & Co.,
solicitors for the plaintiff [*or* defendant].

[15] See C.C.R., Ord. 35, rr. 20 (*a*) and 26.

Notice to Party Requiring Bail of Time Appointed for Taking Bail

[*Heading as in action*]

528 Take notice that P.Q., the defendant [*or* S.T., the intervener] in this action, has proposed as his sureties C.D., of [*address and occupation*], and E.F., of [*address and occupation*], and that, if you have any valid objection to make to the proposed sureties, or either of them, you must attend at the Court office at the address given below [16] on [Monday], the —— day of ——, 19—, at —— o'clock, when bail will be taken in this action.

[*Signature*]

Registrar

To [A.B., the plaintiff].

Notice to Party giving Bail of Time Appointed for Taking Bail

[*Heading as in action*]

529 Take notice that you and your proposed sureties must attend at the Court Office at the address given below on [Monday], the —— day of ——, 19—, at —— o'clock when bail will be taken in this action.

[*Signature*]

Registrar

To [P.Q., the defendant].

Notice requiring Sureties to Attend for Cross-Examination

[*Heading as in action*]

530 Take notice that we require the proposed sureties to bail to be given on behalf of the plaintiff [*or* defendant] in this action to attend before you, for the purpose of being cross-examined as to their means, and we request you to appoint a date and time for such cross-examination.

[*Signature*]

Solicitors for the defendant [*or* plaintiff]

To the Registrar of the Court
and to C.D. & Co., solicitors for
the plaintiff [*or* defendant].

[16] See § 511, *ante*.

Notice of Time Appointed for Cross-Examination of Sureties

[*Heading as in action*]

531 Take notice that I have appointed [Monday], the —— day of ——, 19—, at —— o'clock for the cross-examination of the sureties in this action, when the said sureties are to attend at [*address*], for the purpose of such cross-examination.

[*Signature*]

Registrar

To A.B. & Co., solicitors for the plaintiff, and
E.F. & Co., solicitors for the defendant.

Affidavit of Justification

[*Heading as in action*]

532 I, C.D., of [*residence and occupation*], one of the proposed sureties for [the defendant P.Q.], make oath and say that I am worth more than the sum of —— pounds [17] after the payment of all my debts.

Sworn [*etc.*].

This affidavit is filed on behalf of the [defendant].

Notice of Bail taken before Commissioner for Oaths

[*Heading as in action*]

533 Take notice that bail has been given in the sum of £—— on behalf of the above-named [defendant] to answer judgment in this action by the [plaintiff] and that such bail has been taken before ——, a Commissioner to administer oaths in the Supreme Court of Judicature.

[*Signature*]

Solicitors for the [defendant]

To Messrs. G.H. & Co., solicitors for the [plaintiff].

[17] In words, for the same amount for which bail is given.

Affidavit of Service of Notice of Bail taken before a Commissioner for Oaths

[*Heading as in action*]

534 I, E.F., of [*residence*], clerk to A.B. & Co., of [*address*], solicitors for the [defendant] in this action, make oath and say as follows:

That I did on [Monday], the —— day of ——, 19—, at the hour of —— in the [fore] noon, serve on P.Q. & Co., the solicitors for the [plaintiff], a notice of bail in the words and figures following, *viz.*,

" Take notice that bail has been given in the sum of £—— on behalf of the above-named [defendant] to answer judgment in this action by the [plaintiff] and that such bail has been taken before ——, a Commissioner to administer oaths in the Supreme Court of Judicature."

Sworn [*etc.*].

This affidavit is filed on behalf of the [defendant].

Bail Bond

[*Heading as in action*]

535 Whereas an action for [salvage] has been commenced in this Court on behalf of A.B., of [*address*], against P.Q., of [*address*], [R.S., of [*address*], intervening].

Now, therefore, we, C.D., of [*address and occupation*], and E.F., of [*address and occupation*], jointly and severally submit ourselves to the jurisdiction of the said Court, and consent that, if the said P.Q. shall not pay what may be adjudged against him in the said action with costs, execution may issue against us, our heirs, executors, and administrators, our goods and chattels, for a sum not exceeding —— pounds.[18]

And we hereby consent and agree that this bond shall apply to any compromise or settlement between the parties of the subject matter of the action or to an admission of liability therein, and to any amount of salvage, damages, interest and costs agreed by the [parties] to be paid in the said action or assessed by the Registrar [and assessors] after admission of liability or compromise, so that, if the said P.Q. shall not pay such amounts we shall be liable for the

[18] The amount must be set out in words.

same in the same manner as if they had been adjudged by the Court, not exceeding the above mentioned sum.

[*Signatures of sureties*]

This bond was signed by the
said C.D. and E.F., the sureties,
the —— day of ——, 19—,
before me,

[*Signature*]

Registrar [or officer of the Court appointed to take affidavits].

5. Pleadings and Preliminary Act

Notice Requiring Filing of Statement of Claim

[*Heading as in action*]

536 Take notice that the defendant requires you, within ten days of the receipt of this notice, to deliver a Statement of Claim in this action.

Dated this —— day of ——, 19—.

[*Signature*]

Solicitors for the defendant

To the plaintiff and C.D. & Co., his solicitors.

Preliminary Act

[*Heading as in action*]

PRELIMINARY ACT ON BEHALF OF THE OWNER OF THE "PYTHIAS"

I

537 The names of the ships which came into collision and of their masters.	PYTHIAS: Henry Morgan DAMON: William Brock

II

The time of the collision.	At about 13.45 hours on March 26, 19—.

III

The place of the collision.	In the River Thames; in Blackwall Reach off Folly House Roads.

IV

The direction and force of the wind.	There was little or no wind.

V

The state of the weather.	Fine and clear.

VI

The state and force of the tide.	The tide was flooding up-river at a rate of about 3 knots.

VII

The course and speed of the ship when the other was first seen or immediately before any measures were taken with reference to her presence, whichever was the earlier, and all subsequent alterations to the course or speed of the ship up to the time of the collision.	The tug PULLER was proceeding on a normal up-river course towing PYTHIAS and was making about 4 to 5 knots through the water. When abeam of Sussex Wharf, the speed of the tow was reduced to about 2 to 3 knots. Shortly thereafter, the wheel of PULLER was put hard-a-starboard. Shortly before the collision, the wheel of PULLER was put hard-a-port and her engines were put full ahead.

VIII

The lights (if any) carried by her.	None.

IX

The distance, bearing and approximate heading of the other ship when first seen.	DAMON was first observed ahead of PULLER, distant about half a mile, and proceeding down-river on her starboard side.

X

The lights (if any) of the other ship which were first seen.	None.

	XI
Whether any lights of the other ship, other than those first seen, came into view before the collision.	None.
	XII
What measures were taken, and when, to avoid the collision.	Shortly before the collision, the wheel of PULLER was put hard-a-port and her engines were put full ahead.
	XIII
The parts of each ship which first came into contact and the approximate angle between the two ships at the moment of contact.	The stem and port bow of DAMON struck PYTHIAS amidships at an angle of about 40° leading aft on PYTHIAS.
	XIV
What sound signals (if any) were given and when.	A signal of four long and one short blast was sounded by PULLER when speed was reduced to 2 to 3 knots and again when PULLER went hard-a-starboard.
	XV
What sound signals (if any) were heard from the other ship and when.	None.
	XVI
What act of negligence, or what breach of any navigation rule, by-law or regulation, was committed by those in charge of the other ship.	(a) They failed to keep a proper look-out; (b) They proceeded at an improper speed; (c) They failed to take any or any appropriate helm and/or engine action in order to avoid a collision; (d) They attempted to overtake the vessel GEORGE at an improper time; (e) They improperly altered course to port; (f) They failed to keep to that side of mid-channel which lay on their starboard side;

(g) They failed to alter course to starboard in due time or at all;
(h) They failed to indicate alterations in their course with the appropriate sound signals;
(i) They failed to comply with Rules 25, 27, 28 and 29 of the Collision Regulations 1965, or Rules 8 and 42 of the Port of London River By-laws 1967.

XVII

[*In the case of a defendant add the following*]

The name of any ship, other than the plaintiff's ship, which the defendant alleges to have caused the collision or damage, or with reference to which those in charge of the defendants ship had to act.	None.

Filed this —— day of —— 19—, by
A.B. & Co.

Solicitors for the plaintiff

Notice that the Defendant does not intend to File any Defence or Counterclaim

[*Heading as in action*]

538 Take notice that the defendant does not intend to file any [Defence *or* Counterclaim] in this action.

Dated this —— day of ——, 19—.

[*Signature*]

Solicitors for the defendant

To the Registrar of the Court
and to C.D. & Co., solicitors for the plaintiff.

6. Appraisement

Praecipe for Appraisement

[*Heading as in action*]

539 Take notice that the plaintiff hereby requires to have the value of the property the subject of this action ascertained by appraisement.

Dated this —— day of ——, 19—.

[*Signature*]

Solicitors for the plaintiff

To the Registrar,
—— County Court.

Request for Appraisement to Registrar of another Court

[*Heading as in action*]

540 The plaintiff having required the value of the property the subject of this action to be ascertained by appraisement.

You are hereby requested to choose an experienced person to make an inventory of and to appraise the [ship DAMON], being the property the subject of this action, and to return this request, with the inventory and appraisement to me, with an account of the fees and expenses of the appraiser.

Dated this —— day of ——, 19—.

[*Signature*]

Registrar

To the Registrar of the —— County Court.

Certificate of Appraisement

[*Heading as in action*]

541 I, S.T., Registrar of the —— County Court, hereby certify that, in pursuance of a request dated the — day of ——, 19—, and issued in this action, I have chosen Y.Z., of [*address*], an experienced person, to make an inventory of and to appraise, at the true value thereof, the [ship DAMON] being the property the subject of this action.

Dated this —— day of ——, 19—.

[*Signature*]
Registrar

And I, the said Y.Z., do certify that I have made the inventory hereto annexed of the said property and that I have appraised the true value thereof at the sum of £——.

Dated this —— day of ——, 19—.

[*Signature*]

Appraiser

To the Registrar —— County Court.

7. Judgment and Execution

Interlocutory Judgment in Action for Damages

[*Heading as in action*]

542 It is adjudged that the plaintiff is entitled to recover [*if the judgment is in personam, add*: against the defendant] damages for damage caused to the [cargo carried in the] ship PYTHIAS, by the defendant's ship DAMON together with the costs of this action, to be taxed by the Registrar.

And it is ordered that it be referred to the Registrar [and two assessors] to assess the said damages under the rules for the assessment of damages.

[*Signature*]

Registrar

Final Judgment in Action in Rem

[*Heading as in action*]

543 It is adjudged that the plaintiff do recover the sum of £—— for damage caused by the defendant's ship DAMON [*or as the case may be*], together with the costs of this action, to be taxed by the Registrar.

And it is ordered that [*insert such directions as may be given by the Judge*].

[*Signature*]

Registrar

To the parties.

Final Judgment in Action in Personam

[*Heading as in action*]

544 It is adjudged that the plaintiff do recover against the defendant the sum of £—— for damage caused by the defendant's ship DAMON [*or as the case may be*], together with the costs of this action, to be taxed by the Registrar.

And it is ordered that the defendant do pay the said sum and costs to the Registrar of this Court forthwith [*or* within —— days] after taxation [*or* the said sum of £—— to the Registrar of this Court forthwith [*or* on the —— day of ——, 19—,] and do pay the amount of the said costs when taxed forthwith [*or* within —— days after taxation]].

[*Signature*]

Registrar

To the parties.

Praecipe for Issue of Notice of Judgment or Order in Rem, for Service on Persons not before the Court Appearing by the Ship's Register to have an Interest in the Ship

[*Heading as in action*]

545 I, [A.B., of [*address*], solicitor for] C.D., of [*address and occupation*], the above-named plaintiff, have annexed hereto a certified copy of the register of the ship DAMON to which this action relates.

I request that a notice in Form 301 of the judgment [*or* order] obtained in this action on the —— day of ——, 19—, may be issued for service on P.Q., of [*address and occupation*], and R.S., of [*address and occupation*], whose names appear on the register as having an interest in the said ship, but who are not before the Court.

Dated this —— day of ——, 19—.

[*Signature*]

[Solicitor for the] plaintiff

Notice of Judgment or Order in Rem to Persons not before the Court Appearing by the Ship's Register to have an Interest in the Ship

[*Heading as in action*]

546 To P.Q., of [*address and occupation*].

Take notice, that on the —— day of ——, 19—, the above-named action for [salvage] was commenced in this Court on behalf of A.B., of [*address*], against the [ship DAMON].

And that on the —— day of ——, 19—, it was adjudged that [*recite the judgment*].

And that the plaintiff has filed a praecipe in this Court, and has annexed thereto a certified copy of the register of the said ship on which your name appears as having an interest in the said ship.

And further take notice, that, if you do not, within seven days from the day of the service of this notice on you, deliver to me at the Court office at the address stated below, a praecipe applying for a re-hearing of this action, the ship to which this action relates will be taken and sold in execution.

Dated this —— day of ——, 19—.

[*Signature*]

Registrar

Praecipe for Issue of Notice of Judgment or Order in Rem for Service on Ascertained Owners of and Persons Interested in Property

[*Heading as in action*]

547 I, [A.B., of [*address*], solicitor for] C.D., of [*address and occupation*], the above-named plaintiff, have ascertained that the names, addresses and occupations of the owners of [the ship DAMON] to which this action relates are as follows:

P.Q., of [*address and occupation*]

R.S., of [*address and occupation*]

[*If the ship is British owned, add*: A certified copy of the register of the said ship is hereto annexed.]

I request that a notice in Form 303 of the [judgment or order] obtained in this action on the —— day of ——, 19—, may be issued for service on the said P.Q. and R.S. [*if the ship is British owned, add*: and on the other persons whose names appear on the register as having an interest in the said ship].

Dated this —— day of ——, 19—.

[*Signature*]

[Solicitor for the] plaintiff

Notice of Judgment or Order in Rem to Ascertained Owner of and Person Interested in Property

[*Heading as in action*]

548 To P.Q., of [*address and occupation*]

Take notice that on the —— day of ——, 19—, the above-named action for [salvage] was commenced in this Court on behalf of C.D., of [*address*], against [the ship DAMON].

And that on the —— day of ——, 19—, it was adjudged that [*recite the judgment*].

And that the plaintiff has filed a praecipe in this Court stating that you, the above-named P.Q., are the owner of the property to which this action relates.

[*If the ship is British, add*: And has annexed hereto a certified copy of the register of the said ship on which your name appears as having an interest in the said ship.]

And further take notice, that, if you do not, within seven days from the day of the service of this notice on you, deliver to me at the Court office at the address stated below, a praecipe applying for a re-hearing of this action, the property to which this action relates will be taken and sold in execution.

[*Signature*]

Registrar

Affidavit to Lead Notice of Judgment or Order in Rem to Unascertained Owners and to Persons Claiming to have an Interest in Property

[*Heading as in action*]

549 I, E.F., of [*residence*], clerk to A.B. & Co., of [*address*], solicitors for the plaintiffs in this action make oath and say as follows:

1. The plaintiffs, as owners of the ship PYTHIAS, claim in this action in respect of damage occasioned to the PYTHIAS by the defendants' ship DAMON, on the —— day of ——, 19—. This action was commenced by summons on the —— day of ——, 19—. No appearance has been entered thereto on behalf of the defendants the owners of the ship DAMON and on the —— day of ——, 19—, the ship DAMON was arrested by this Court and remains under arrest.

2. The action was heard before His Honour Judge ——, who

pronounced for the plaintiffs' claim and referred the assessment thereof to the Registrar. The Registrar in his report dated the —— day of ——, 19—, assessed the plaintiffs' damages herein at the sum of £——.

3. The plaintiffs have been unable to ascertain who are the owners of the DAMON and have therefore no means of enforcing their judgment without the assistance of this Court.

4. I therefore request that the necessary order may be made directing notice of the said judgment to be given by advertisement or otherwise to the owners of, and all persons claiming to have an interest in, the ship DAMON, together with notice informing them that, if they do not apply for a re-hearing of this action, the said ship will be taken and sold in execution.

Sworn at [*etc.*].

This affidavit is filed on behalf of the plaintiffs.

Order Directing Notice by Advertisement or Otherwise of Judgment or Order in Rem to be given to Unascertained Owners of and Persons Claiming an Interest in Property

[*Heading as in action*]

550 Upon the application of [the plaintiff] and upon reading the affidavit of E.F. sworn the —— day of ——, 19—,

It is ordered that notice in Form 305 of the [judgment or order] obtained in this action on the —— day of ——, 19—, be given to the owners of and all persons claiming to have an interest in the property to which this action relates, by the publication of such notice in —— [*as the Court may direct*].

Dated this —— day of ——, 19—.

[*Signature*]

Registrar

Notice of Judgment or Order in Rem to Unascertained Owners and Persons Claiming an Interest in Property

[*Heading as in action*]

551 To the owners of and all persons claiming to have an interest in the property to which the above-mentioned action relates.

Pursuant to an order made by the Court in the above-mentioned action on the —— day of ——, 19—.

Notice is hereby given that on the —— day of ——, 19—, the above-named action for [salvage] was commenced in this Court on behalf of C.D., of [*address*], against the [ship DAMON].

And that on the —— day of ——, 19—, it was adjudged that [*recite the judgment*].

And notice is hereby further given that, unless the owners of and other persons claiming to have an interest in the said property shall, within —— days from the date of the publication of this notice, file in the Court office at the address stated below a praecipe applying for a re-hearing of this action, the property to which this action relates will be taken and sold in execution.

A.B. & Co.

Solicitors for the plaintiff

Praecipe for Re-hearing

[*Heading as in action*]

552 Enter an appearance for P.Q., of [*address and occupation*] who claims to be the owner of [*or* have an interest in] the property to which this action relates, and applies for a re-hearing of this action, pursuant to the notice in this action dated the —— day of ——, 19—.

All instruments and documents in this action may be left for the said P.Q. at [*address*].

Dated this —— day of ——, 19—.

[*Signature*]

[Solicitors for the said P.Q.]

Praecipe for Execution in Action in Rem

[*Heading as in action*]

553 Issue a warrant of execution against [the ship DAMON], the Judge [*or* Registrar] having ordered the same to be taken and sold in execution.

Dated this —— day of ——, 19—.

[*Signature*]

[Solicitors for the] plaintiff

Warrant of Execution in Action in Rem

[*Heading as in action*]

554 WHEREAS on the —— day of ——, 19—, it was adjudged that the plaintiff in this action should recover the sum of £—— for [*recite the judgment as in* § 543] together with the costs of this action, which have been taxed and allowed at the sum of £—— and it was ordered that [*insert any directions given by the Judge, as in* § 543].

AND WHEREAS default has been made in payment according to the said order, and the Court has ordered the property to which this action relates to be taken and sold in execution, and has allowed to the plaintiff the costs of obtaining such order and suing out execution, which have been taxed and allowed at the sum of £——.

These are therefore to require you forthwith to seize and take in execution the [ship DAMON] wheresoever the same may be found within the district of this Court, and to reduce into writing an inventory of the said [ship].

And having chosen one or more experienced person or persons to cause him or them to appraise the same according to the true value thereof, and upon a certificate of such value having been reduced into writing, to cause the said [ship] to be sold by public auction for the highest price, not under the appraised value, that can be obtained for the same.

And you are further required, immediately on the sale being completed, to bring the proceeds arising therefrom into Court and to return this warrant with an account of the sale and the fees thereon, and of the costs of the appraisement, signed by you, together with the certificate of appraisement signed by the appraiser.

Dated this —— day of ——, 19—.

[*Signature*]

Registrar

To the Registrar and Bailiffs of the Court.

	£	p
Amount for which judgment was obtained:		
Costs taxed at:		
Subsequent costs, allowed and taxed at:		
Fee for issuing this warrant:		
Solicitor's costs of issue:		
Total amount to be levied:		

Application was made to the Registrar for this warrant at —— minutes past the hour of ——, in the —— noon, on the day last above-mentioned.

Order for Transfer of Sale to High Court

[*Heading as in action*]

555 WHEREAS in an action commenced in this Court on behalf of A.B. of [*address*], against C.D., the Judge of this Court has ordered [*recite the terms of the order*];

AND WHEREAS the plaintiff [*or* defendant] in the said action is desirous that the sale of the property should be conducted in the Admiralty Court of the Queen's Bench Division of the High Court of Justice, and has given security for the sum of ten pounds;

NOW I, A.B. the plaintiff [*or* C.D. the Defendant *or* E.F. the solicitor for the plaintiff *or* defendant] apply for an order to transfer the proceedings for sale to the said Admiralty Court of the Queen's Bench Division of the High Court of Justice.

Dated this —— day of ——, 19—.

[*Signature*]

[Solicitor for the] plaintiff
[*or* defendant]

I hereby certify that the security above mentioned has been duly completed.

[*Signature*]

Registrar

I hereby order the transfer to be made.

[*Signature*]

Judge

Praecipe for Execution against the Sureties to a Bail Bond

[*Heading as in action*]

556 Issue a warrant of execution against the goods of S.T., of [*address and occupation*], and V.W., of [*address and occupation*],[19] who on the —— day of ——, 19—, jointly and severally submitted themselves to the jurisdiction of this Court, and consented that, if C.D. should not pay what might be adjudged or assessed against, or agreed to be paid by him in this action with costs, execution might

[19] *i.e.* the parties to the bail bond.

issue against them, the said S.T. and V.W., their heirs, executors and administrators, their goods and chattels, for a sum not exceeding £——, the said C.D. having been ordered by the Court on the —— day of ——, 19—, to pay to the plaintiff the sum of £—— [*insert for what the sum was ordered to be paid*] and not having paid the said sum so ordered.

Dated this —— day of ——, 19—.

[*Signature*]

Solicitors for the plaintiff

Warrant of Execution against the Sureties to a Bail Bond [20]

[*Heading as in action*]

557 WHEREAS on the —— day of ——, 19—, S.T., of [*address and occupation*], and V.W., of [*address and occupation*],[20] jointly and severally submitted themselves to the jurisdiction of the Court, and consented that, if C.D. should not pay what might be adjudged or assessed against, or agreed to be paid by him in this action, with costs, execution might issue against them, the said S.T. and V.W., their heirs, executors and administrators, their goods and chattels, for a sum not exceeding £——.

AND WHEREAS on the —— day of ——, 19—, the plaintiff obtained a judgment in this Court in this action against the said C.D. for the sum of £—— for damages [*or as the case may be*] and costs to be taxed, and it was thereupon ordered by the Court that the said C.D. should pay the said sum and costs to the Registrar of the Court forthwith [*or* within —— days after taxation].

AND WHEREAS the said costs were on the —— day of ——, 19—, taxed and allowed at the sum of £——.

AND WHEREAS default has been made in payment according to the said order:

These are therefore to require you forthwith to make and levy the sum stated at the foot of this warrant, being the amount due to the plaintiff under the said order [*or, if the amount remaining due exceeds the sum specified in the bail bond*: the sum for which, in default of payment of the amount adjudged or assessed against, or agreed to be paid by, the said C.D., the said S.T. and V.W. con-

[20] *i.e.* the parties to the bail bond.

sented that execution might issue against them] [21] together with the costs of this warrant and the costs of executing the same, by distress and sale of the goods and chattels of the said S.T. and V.W., wheresoever they may be found within the district of this Court (except the wearing apparel and bedding of them or their families, and the tools and implements of their trades to the value, as regards each such party, of —— pounds), and also by seizing and taking any money, bank notes, bills of exchange, promissory notes, bonds, specialties, or securities for money of the said S.T. and V.W. which may be there found, or such part or so much thereof as may be sufficient to satisfy this execution, and to bring what you have so levied into Court, and to make return of what you have done under this warrant immediately upon the execution thereof.

Dated this —— day of ——, 19—.

[*Signature*]

Registrar

To the Registrar and Bailiffs of the Court.

	£ p
Amount for which judgment was obtained:	
Costs:	————
Total:	
Amount paid:	————
Amount remaining due:	————
[*If this amount exceeds the sum specified in the bail bond, add*:]	
Amount for which bail bond given:	
Fee for issuing this warrant:	
Solicitor's costs of issue:	————
Total amount to be levied:	====

Application was made to the Registrar for this warrant at —— minutes past the hour of ——, in the —— noon of the day last above mentioned.

Notice: The goods and chattels are not to be sold until after the expiration of five days next following the day on which they were seized, unless they are of a perishable nature, or at the request of the sureties to the bail bond.

21 Execution may not issue for a sum greater than that specified in the bail bond. See n. 17, § 532, *supra*. If the amount due under the judgment order does not exceed the sum specified in the bail bond, execution may issue for that amount; if it exceeds that sum, it must issue only for the sum specified in the bail bond.

8. Reference to Registrar

Agreement to Assessment of Damages by Registrar

[*Heading as in action*]

558 WHEREAS the plaintiff [*or* defendant] has admitted liability for the claim [*or* counterclaim] in this action, we, the undersigned solicitors for the plaintiff and defendant respectively, hereby agree that the assessment of the plaintiff's [*or* defendant's] claim [*or* counterclaim] be referred to the Registrar assisted if necessary by an assessor.

Dated this —— day of ——, 19—.

[*Signature*]

Solicitors for the plaintiff

[*Signature*]

Solicitors for the defendant

Admission of Liability and Consent to Reference to County Court Registrar

[*Heading as in action*]

559 We, the solicitors for the [defendant], hereby admit liability for the collision [*or* damage *or as may be*], the subject of this action, and we the solicitors for the said [defendant] and the [plaintiff] hereby consent to a reference to the Registrar [assisted by two assessors] to ascertain the amount of damages and interest due to the plaintiff [*or* defendant].

Dated this —— day of ——, 19—.

[*Signature*]

Solicitors for the plaintiff

[*Signature*]

Solicitors for the defendant

Registrar's Report on Assessment of Damages

[*Heading as in action*]

560 WHEREAS, by the judgment [*or* order] in this action dated the —— day of ——, 19— [*or* by consent of the parties upon an admission of liability *or as the case may be*] the damages recoverable by the

plaintiff [*or* defendant upon his counterclaim] have been referred to me [and two assessors] to assess the amount thereof.

Now I hereby report that I have [, with the assistance of Messrs. S.T., and V.W., the assessors appointed,] carefully examined the claim and vouchers filed in this action, and, having heard evidence on affidavit and counsel [*or* the solicitors] on behalf of the plaintiff and defendant, I find that the defendant [*or* plaintiff] is indebted to the plaintiff [*or* defendant] in the sum of £——, as shown by the schedule hereto annexed, which sets forth in separate columns the several amounts claimed and the amounts which I [in conjunction with the said assessors] consider justly due to him in respect of each item.

I am of opinion that interest at the rate of —— per cent. per annum from the —— day of ——, 19—, should be allowed on the said sum of £—— until the date of payment.

I am further of opinion that the costs of the reference should be paid by the defendant [*or* plaintiff] [*if for any special reasons, add reasons*].

Dated this —— day of ——, 19—.

[*Signature*]

Registrar

SCHEDULE TO REPORT

	Claimed		Allowed	
	£	p	£	p
Together with interest				

[*Signature*]

Registrar

Notice of Filing of Registrar's Report on Assessment of Damages

[*Heading as in action*]

561 Take notice that I have filed my report on the reference ordered by the judgment [*or* order] in this action, dated the —— day of ——, 19—, and the report can be inspected by the parties at the Court office.

And further take notice that unless within seven days from the day of service of this notice on him either party lodges an objection to the report the same will become final and binding on all parties, and judgment may be entered accordingly.

[*Signature*]

Registrar

To the parties.

Notice of Objection to Registrar's Report

[*Heading as in action*]

562 Take notice that we intend to apply on behalf of the [plaintiff] to the Judge at [*address*] on [Monday], the —— day of ——, 19—, at — o'clock in the [fore] noon, to vary the report of the Registrar dated the —— day of ——, 19—, in so far as [*state the parts of the report objected to*].

The grounds of the [plaintiff's] application are [*state the grounds and particularise the variation or remission sought*].

[*Signature*]

Solicitors for the [plaintiff]

To the Registrar of the Court
and to C.D. & Co., solicitors
for the [defendant].

Order for Transfer of Proceedings to the High Court or another County Court

[*Heading as in action*]

563 Whereas [on the application of the defendant] it appears that the above action can be more conveniently or fairly tried in the High Court [*or* —— County Court] [*or* that it would be a hardship on the defendant for the above action to proceed in this Court *or as the case may be*].

It is ordered that the above action be transferred to the High Court [*or* —— County Court].

[*Signature*]

Judge [*or* Registrar]

INDEX

[References in **bold** type are to paragraphs where the subject receives detailed treatment]

[*All references are to paragraph numbers*]

[*All references are to paragraph numbers*]

[*All references are to paragraph numbers*]

[*All references are to paragraph numbers*]